THE POLITICAL ECONOMY OF POST-ADJUSTMENT

The Making of Modern Africa

Series Editors: Abebe Zegeye and John Higginson

Ecology, Civil Society and the Informal Economy in North West Tanzania
Charles David Smith

Ghana in Search of Development
The challenge of governance, economic management and institution building
Dan-Bright S. Dzorgbo

From Dictatorship to Democracy
Economic Policy in Malawi 1964-2000
Jane Harrigan

Manoeuvring in an Environment of Uncertainty
Structural change and social action in sub-Saharan Africa
Edited by Boel Berner and Per Trulsson

Gender, Family and Work in Tanzania
Edited by Colin Creighton and C.K. Omari

Contesting Forestry in West Africa
Edited by Reginald Cline-Cole and Clare Madge

Electoral Territoriality in Southern Africa
Stephen Rule

Community Health Needs in South Africa
Ntombenhle Protasia Khoti Torkington

Consolidation of Democracy in Africa
A view from the South
Edited by Hussein Solomon and Ian Liebenberg

Regional and Local Economic Development in South Africa
The experience of the Eastern Cape
Etienne Louis Nel

The Political Economy of Post-Adjustment

Towards New Theories and Strategies of Development

HAKIM BEN HAMMOUDA

Routledge
Taylor & Francis Group
LONDON AND NEW YORK

First published 2003 by Ashgate Publishing

Reissued 2018 by Routledge
2 Park Square, Milton Park, Abingdon, Oxon OX14 4RN
711 Third Avenue, New York, NY 10017, USA

Routledge is an imprint of the Taylor & Francis Group, an informa business

A Library of Congress record exists under LC control number: 2002190887

ISBN 13: 978-1-138-71399-4 (hbk)
ISBN 13: 978-1-315-19797-5 (ebk)

Contents

Introduction

From the mid-1980s, the South started to experience profound changes and transformations. In fact, the Southeast Asian economies pursued sustained growth dynamics and improved their integration into the international economy. On the other hand, the Latin-American economies were experiencing a deep depression in their economic activity and runaway inflation. And yet, even though the inflation had been controlled by stabilisation policies, these economies were not able to initiate new growth dynamics and reconstruct their competitiveness in order to regain an active integration into the international economy. At the same time, the African and Arab economies underwent deep economic and social crises and were marginalised in the international economy.

These changes were confirmed and exacerbated during the 1990s when, more than ever, the break-up of the unity of the Third World was a noticeable reality at the end of the twentieth century. In fact, even though the Southeast Asian economies pursued their strong growth, the other Third World economies, particularly Africa and the Arab world did not succeed in either resuming growth or ending the marginalisation, despite the implementation of Structural Adjustment Programmes (SAPs), recommended by the World Bank and the International Monetary Fund.

The SAPs sought to establish a stabilisation component in order to reduce the deficits and promote a series of structural reforms, to ensure a greater private regulation of the economy, and to increase the integration of national economies into a globalisation that is considered as essential and irreversible. These two aspects of adjustment policies are crystallised in the strong state disengagement trend. First, the state relinquishes its prerogatives to regulate a coherent functioning of the economy. Thus, planning activities are abandoned and the transfer of high profit activities towards low profit activities are called to question in the name of efficiency. The state then disengages itself from its social functions by reducing its expenditure on health, education and social transfers.

And yet, if it is true that the SAPs enabled some economies to improve and restore their macroeconomic equilibria, they failed to initiate new dynamics of sustained growth in these economies following the loss of impetus in the import-substitution strategy of the 1960s and 1970s.

But we have already started measuring the social impact of adjustment policies in the South. Indeed, the hindrance of dynamics has led to a decrease in job creation. This economic slowdown, associated with a relatively strong demographic growth, gave rise to a rapid increase in unemployment. However, more than this general increase, it is youth unemployment in particular, especially in the urban areas, which developed more rapidly. At the same time as the rapid increase in unemployment, reforms related to adjustment policies led to a decline in real salaries. In addition, the expansion of poverty and exclusion was the immediate effect of the increasing casualisation of the social situation.

Thus, the SAPs did not promote the construction of new economic and social norms to replace the norms in crisis. On the contrary, they accelerated the decomposition of those in crisis and thus exacerbated economic and social regression. At the economic level, the deflationary trends have become stronger. At the social level, more than a deterioration in living conditions of communities, we are faced with two ambivalent societies: on the one hand, a modern society, that is shrinking every day and one that is integrated into the modes of production and consumption that are increasingly globalised; and on the other hand, a field of ruins spreading from the Cairo suburbs to those of Algiers, from rural Burundi and Rwanda to Chiapas and Colombia, where the world of marginality and exclusion unfolds and where violence, disease and drugs are the order of the day.

This economic and social crisis has had important political consequences in the form of protests against the legitimacy of the state. In the Third World, the overtaking of traditional forms of political organisation and the construction of the modern nation-state in the post-colonial period took place on the basis of the commitment of the nationalist elite to ensuring the construction of a consistent economy likely to meet the social needs of the population. Thus, economic development and social promotion form the basis of social compromise in all the countries and constitute the bases for legitimising the nation-state.

And yet, today, alienation and urban misery are the main characteristics of the planet after the passage of the adjustment-storm. This situation is the cause of the radicalisation of the protests against the state which gradually leads to its delegitimisation. The destructuring of the state legitimisation universe is exacerbated by the stripping of its prerogatives in terms of economic decision, development option and social regulation by supranational authorities (IMF, World Bank) within the framework of globalisation. Thus, technocrats turn into politicians in the management of city matters and politics becomes restricted to a minimalist conception which confines itself to the art of managing the possible. Thus, more than a delegitimisation of the state, competitiveness, excellence, expertise and advice, and new values of a dominant techno-bureaucracy, lead to a depreciation of the political, in favour of entertainment politics. And yet, these new values cannot fill the gap left by the debasement of the 'grand narratives' which gave meaning to history. In this way, the peripheral spaces increasingly give rise to political discourses and practices which we thought had ceased with the Shoah and other Nazi crimes. Thus, in the name of the refusal of the separation of the temporal and the spiritual, embodied by the modern state under the influence of Islam, of the return to ethnicity, or of fear or exclusion of the other immigrant or foreigner, the 'foul beast' invades our daily existence and threatens our humanity.

Moreover, state disengagement and economic liberalisation advocated by the SAPs found expression in the emergence, in most countries, of politico-financial maffias which sought to control the economy. The weakening of the state and its demise in some Third World regions resulted in the emergence of private interests with armed militias. In this context, violence, chaos and insecurity characterised the major Third World regions.

These results gave rise to the challenging of the theoretical basis and neo-liberal development choices of the Washington Consensus. In fact, a new era has opened in the field of development economy since the 1990s, which can be referred to as the *post-adjustment period*, and the Third World entered into the post-liberalism of the early 1980s. This period is characterised by a decline in SAPs, even though institutions like the World Bank and the IMF are desperately attached to them in their practices in developing countries, and through a dynamic and plural research to establish new development strategies and new theoretical practices to catch up with the Washington Consensus and the SAPs.

Gone is the time of adjustment and neo-liberal consensus, which dominated reflection on development throughout the 1980s. The last World Bank Development Report is indicative of this shift.[1] In fact, this report lays emphasis on the place of the state and the role that it should play in development (World Bank, 1997).

From the point of view of strategies, the questioning of SAPs goes hand-in-hand with the emergence of new practices. In fact, since the mid-1980s, UNICEF has called for an 'adjustment with a human face' concept to emphasise the harmful social consequences of adjustment programmes (see UNICEF, 1987). Moreover, in the face of the ecological and social crisis confronting the planet, reflection on development practices distanced itself from the imperatives of stabilisation to include concerns for the protection of nature, focusing on humankind. Thus, the United Nations Conference on Development and Environment, held in Rio de Janeiro in 1992, laid emphasis on the ecological hazards that weigh on humanity (the depletion of the ozone layer, the greenhouse effect, nuclear and chemical waste, deforestation, uncontrolled growth, etc.) and showed the need to define a lasting development to face these disasters.

The sustainable development concept originates from the deliberations of the Brundtland Commission, named after the Norwegian Prime Minister who, in 1983, was entrusted by the United Nations General Assembly with the mission of preparing a report on development. This report, entitled 'A Future for All of Us', submitted in 1987, defined sustainable development as 'the development that meets the needs of the present without jeopardizing the capacity of future generations to meet theirs'.[2] The Rio Conference popularised the sustainable development concept and adopted a plan of action or agenda for the twenty-first century with a view to reducing ecological hazards.

Moreover, as from the end of the 1980s, the United Nations Development Programme (UNDP) initiated a reflection on development practices and the need to refocus them on humankind so as to free humanity from the constraints of adjustment. The reflection was intended to result in the development of the Human Development Index and the preparation, from 1990, of an Annual Human Development Report.

For the UNDP, the main objective of development is to 'create an environment that offers the population the possibility to live for a long time and in good health'. The UNDP recalls that this aim has often been overshadowed by the race for growth in order to present the best economic indicators. In this context, traditional indicators such as the gross national product (GNP) were used to appraise development performance. Such indicators, despite their usefulness, show neither the composition of economic growth nor the real beneficiaries.

Sustainable human development is defined, according to UNDP, as 'a process that leads to the expansion of possibilities opened to all'. Living for a long time and in good health, being educated and having access to the resources necessary to enjoy an adequate standard of living are the most important of these. Then come political freedom, the enjoyment of human rights and self respect. To measure human development, the UNDP makes use of three elements: lifespan, knowledge and standard of living. For the lifespan component, the authors of this report retained life expectancy at birth as an indicator. With regard to knowledge, the authors chose the literacy rate. Finally, for the standard of living, the per capita income was adopted as an indicator.

A few years after it was prepared, the Human Development Report has become a key factor in debates on development aimed at appreciating contrasting developments among countries. The emergence of sustainable human development concepts is indicative of the decline in the neoliberal orthodoxy which dominated the debate on development in the early 1980s. In fact, these concepts made it possible to highlight the ecological and social damages caused by the stabilisation programmes. But, despite their success and increasing media coverage, the reflections inspired by the human development problematic did not succeed in influencing the development practices and strategies that continue to be informed by SAPs.

At the theoretical level, we also witness the questioning of the theoretical basis of the Washington Consensus and the emergence of new reflections. In fact, the failure of the Structural Adjustment Programmes, defined at the beginning of decade by the Bretton Woods institutions, the World Bank and the International Monetary Fund, as an alternative to the failure of modernisation experiences centred around the nation-state in most Third World countries, encouraged the expression of different opinions to contest the ultra-liberal options of the Washington Consensus. Thus, at the theoretical level, the pure Walrassian model, on which this consensus is based and which reduces the process of socialisation to a confrontation between the economic projects of various agents on the market, has come under sharp criticism. To some of them, the introduction of the auctioneer in the Walrassian model excludes, by hypothesis, the case of decentralised economy. For others, the neoclassical conception of the market reduces the whole complexity of the social regulation to trade mechanisms.[3] All the critiques agreed to acknowledge the plurality of the forms of social regulation and, in particular, the role of institutions and social conventions in the coherence of individual choices.

The neoclassical theory was not left out of this movement and has gradually abandoned the basic Walrassian model to develop a methodological neo-classicism which admits the place and role of contractual procedures in the regulation of societies, by seeking to integrate them in its analysis. At the same time as the rejection of the prescriptive nature of the basic model and the increasingly displayed determination to test its relevance, the neoclassical concept of development theory asserts, from the methodological point of view, its preference for macroeconomy, and the pre-eminence of the analysis of interindividual relations among agents.[4] Thus, while favouring individualism from the methodological point of view, the 'new' neoclassical economics of development seeks to study and highlight the role of institutions and all forms of non-trade coordination in the regulation of underdeveloped economies.

The heterodox approaches have also re-emerged – having undergone a rapid renewal at the end of the 1980s, following their decline and marginalisation in the beginning of the century – in response to the Washington Consensus offensive. Thus, Taylor's work provided a theoretical framework for the criticism of orthodox stabilisation programmes and made it possible to outline the contours of a heterodox stabilisation programme.[5] Moreover, other heterodox concepts, in response to the profound disintegration of under-developed economies under the weight of the crisis and the difficulty of producing global analysis, have opted for institutionalism as a way of renewing heterodox development thought. These approaches took over the point of departure of the conventionalist research programme and its criticism of the traditional Walrassian model. This criticism is based on the fact that coordination between economic agents cannot be reduced to private rationality. Hence, it is important to take into consideration other rules and institutions which determine individual behaviour as the community rule in Africa.[6]

Furthermore, gone are the days when there was no way out except through adjustment and laws of the market in the South. The new era being ushered in, which we referred to as the post-adjustment era, is one in which there is a proliferation of theories and research on development strategies to get out of the constraints of the Washington Consensus and structural adjustment.

The aim of this work is to give an account of this development and initiate a reflection on the limitations of the liberal model and the Washington Consensus and the attempts to overcome these theoretical and political practices. However, despite the interest in the reflection on trends of post-adjustment development economics, in this work we contend that they did not make it possible to overcome the crisis of the development theory.

In fact, despite this renewal, one cannot but note that the crisis of the development theory persists. Its pervasiveness can be observed from a dual point of view: first, development theory as a 'normative' framework, i.e. aiming to formulate projects and development strategies, is today incapable of proposing solutions to the actual Third World crisis. Indeed, since the crisis of the strategies of modernisation focused around the nation-state, societies of the South have become more and more torn between:

- *the choice of globalisation and international integration* with the preponderant role played by the World Bank and IMF. And yet, the experience of the 1980s showed that even though some Third World countries have successfully implemented the stabilisation component and reduced deficits, structural adjustment has failed to prevent greater

marginalisation of the South in the international economy, and the deepening of world polarisation between the North, which has become increasingly rich, and the South, which has been crippled by the crisis;
- *the temptation of identity retreat*, with ideologies based on identity that are increasingly appealing to the populations who are desperately in search of survival strategies (see Haubert and Rey, 1995).

In this respect, development theories, despite their renewal, could not formulate new strategies capable of 'reconciling the globalisation induced inter-dependence and the unequal power which characterises the various social "partners" as commonly called: workers from various sectors of the economy that are, unequally "competitive" (in terms of capital) like the various "national partners" (the dominant centres, intermediate powers, the industrialised peripheries, the marginalised Fourth World' (Amin, 1995, p. 37). Such a recognition of the globalisation and economic space-regionalisation trends of the day must be combined with a thorough understanding of internal regulation norms. This means the completion of national construction efforts in Third World countries. In fact, 'the efficient functioning of the desirable regional solidarity and an adequate pluricentric world system, requires that the units that constitute them acquire real consistency themselves' (ibid., p. 39).

Today, the issue of the future of development in a context of globalisation is a crucial one. SAPs have tried to impose on Southern economies a greater opening-up to the movements of goods and capital at the international level. This, together with an increased submission of the economies of the South to international norms, brought progress and development and made it possible, according to adjustment advocates, to eliminate all rentier situations that have been created by states and some social groups in the South, and to reduce their competitiveness. And yet this opening, carried out by some economies the South, immediately exposed the fragility of these economies in relation to those in the North, as well as their inability to resist international competition. From this angle, the Asian crisis is a case in point regarding the limitations of the economies of the South in terms of competitiveness. In fact, these economies which have, however, been the most successful in building dynamic economies and in integrating themselves into the international economy, were not able to resist the pressures of globalisation.

At this juncture, reflection on economic development should give priority to two central issues. The first is linked to the nature of the *creative distortions* to be established for rapid and competitive growth dynamics. Of course, it is difficult to envisage today a 'closure' and compartmentalisation of national economies. But, it seems that a full-scale and uncontrolled opening of national economies to the globalisation movement is not more appropriate either. In this context, it is necessary to undertake a reflection for each economy, and taking into account its level of development and its recent economic history, on the mechanisms and procedures, which we referred to as *creative distortions*, capable of helping them construct their competitiveness. These ideas – which were rejected and resisted a few years ago by advocates of the Washington Consensus, including the World Bank and the International Monetary Fund – are increasingly being accepted. Thus, after the Asian crisis, the Bretton Woods institutions today avoid recommending that developing countries open up their borders to capital movements. On the contrary, they even recommend strengthened control of capital movements in those economies with fragile structures. Finally, over the past months, these institutions have been considering the G7's request regarding the means of reducing speculative capital movements. As we have pointed out, *the triumphant liberalism of the early 1990s has lost ground.*

The second issue which, in our view, needs to be thoroughly reflected on, relates to the space in which these new development strategies should operate. At this point, there is need to stress that globalisation has been manifested in a large movement of fragmentation of spaces for political and economic functioning. The nation-state, considered as the space for economic and political coherence, is increasingly being traversed by overwhelming contradictory movements which tend to challenge its legitimacy. It is also necessary to reflect here on the spaces which will constitute the new framework for the deployment of the economic and the political.

The continuous crisis in development theory, despite its recent renewal, can also be analytically observed through its inability to offer a framework or interpretation grid capable of analysing the recent developments of the realities in most countries of the South. In fact, in the 1970s Third World countries experienced strong fluctuations and great instability. These fluctuations can be explained by internal causes as well as by the weight and shock of the international economy that Third World countries could not easily absorb.

And yet these fluctuations were contained within tolerable limits during the 1960s and 1970s. The contradictory articulation of the system's forces of attraction and repulsion was maintained in a dynamic equilibrium, thus preventing any chaotic development. However, this configuration changed profoundly during the 1980s with the break-up of regulation and reproduction norms established in the 1970s. Thus, a variety of *transitions* in the systems was noted during this period. These transitions ranged from deviation in a chaotic universe in the case of some economies, to more controlled transitions towards other dynamic equilibria. *Thus, dynamic instability and plurality of transitions have been the two main characteristics of the evolution of economic systems in the South during the last decades.*

Yet, with a linear and determinist conceptual framework, the various development theory concepts could not offer theoretical frameworks capable of capturing these developments. In this respect, the analyses are limited to an accumulation of empirical facts, and to the monitoring of trends that could not serve as a theory. Moreover, it is to avoid these pitfalls that new development theories have found refuge in individualistic methodological positions.

This crisis is not peculiar to development theory or to social sciences, but concerns the whole Newtonian paradigm of the classical sciences. In fact, in their reading of the real, classical sciences have, according to Wallerstein (1995, p. 228):

> clearly chosen the determinist aspect, the face of linearity and simplification. Thus, scientists consider still larger areas of the universe and, in conclusion, the human world, as being under their aegis. It is in this tradition that the nomothetic social sciences were established.

And yet, these epistemological choices of linearity and determinism are not peculiar to the liberally-inspired social sciences: they have even marked the critical theories in the social sciences. Thus:

> Marxism which had gradually developed following the 2nd International, according to Samir Amin the 3rd International, reclaimed the economism of middle class thought, gave in to the call of its determinist vision that made 'the laws of history' equivalent to those that are ruthlessly imposed by nature, proposing – under the term of socialism – the utopia of a rational management through the knowledge of these 'laws' abolishing, at the same time, the dialectics of human liberty (Amin, 1994, p. 2).

The influence of the Newtonian ideal of the classical sciences was not limited to the social sciences in Europe. In fact, this determinist ideal dominated the intellectual and political life in Europe and marked a generation of Third World intellectuals, either through the teachings of the colonial administration, or through the travelling of these intellectuals to the colonial cities. The Arab world rediscovered Europe and the progress of these societies at the end of the eighteenth century with the campaign of Napoleon who, surrounded by physicians, scientists and mathematicians, greatly influenced the intelligentsia and political power in Egypt at that time. From then on, Arab intellectuals sought to understand the origins of this progress and, at the same time, the reasons for the backwardness of the Arab world. Such questioning reopened ways of thinking that had been closed since the twelfth century with the marginalisation of reasoning and the domination of tradition in Arab thought. The obstruction of this thought was encouraged by dictatorial political regimes. For the Nahda Arab intellectuals, the reasons for Europe's progress reside in political systems based on freedom and equality, which ensure the conditions necessary for development, for the blossoming of free thought and for the construction of modern societies based on reason and science.

As from the early nineteenth century all the underdeveloped countries were to discover Western modernity through colonial penetration. On the one hand, this discovery and its attendant euphoria were combined with feelings of uneasiness and concern, since the rationality which allowed the development of European societies also served the colonial masters in the exploitation and domination of their colonies. On the other hand, the local population, excluded from this development drive, could not accede to this way of life and thinking that the colonial authorities kept building up into a myth and an objective of its enterprise of 'civilisation'.

Connected with oppression and colonial domination, classical reason continued to exert its influence and maintain its grip over the elite of colonised countries. In fact, this classical ideal – through its emancipation in relation to divine forces, its capacity to translate theoretical results into usable techniques, and its command and domination of nature – offered to the local elite an alternative to a traditional society in crisis. In the twentieth century, the classical, modernist ideal was at the centre of the nationalistic movement and later became the ideological basis of national liberation movements. In this respect, the fight for independence became a fight by the country's elite to adopt a scientific ideal, a mode of organisation of society and, finally, to claim the right to establish them in the country.

After independence, the modernist classical ideal dominated the elite in power and the process of construction of the post-colonial state. As pointed out by Mafeje (1994, p. 223) during the 1960s 'the modernisation ideology, taken in the historical sense, i.e. the linear progression towards a given universal end, capitalism, was all encompassing'. At the economic level, the modernising action of the state, within the framework of natural resources rehabilitation strategy or import-substitution strategies, should allow the construction of coherent economies, structured and capable of meeting the basic needs of the population. Moreover, the rational action of the state should also ensure a gradual modernisation of structures for the exercise of politics in these societies. Thus, rationalising economic structures and modernising the political structures were the objectives of the nationalist and modernist ideology in all Third World countries.

This ideology reappropriated, in its discourse and praxis, the characteristics of the ideal of the classical Newtonian science, which has dominated European thought since the nineteenth century. In fact, the determinism of classical science is found in this ideology. Nationalism considered that the benevolent action of the state at the political and economic levels should ensure the take-off of the South and guarantee economic development. This conception of history conveys a vision of monotony and linearity, considered as the site for the smooth deployment of laws of history and economies. Besides, society and nature are considered as actionless bodies whose transformations in favour of mankind are ensured by the rational action of the state.

And yet, less than three decades later, the nationalist ideology was in crisis and the South is far from having reached the economic and political objectives that the post-colonial powers had forecast. In fact, economic crisis and identity retreat today constitute the main characteristics of societies of the South. The post-colonial nation-state project and its action are being increasingly contested, with the rise of political and social forces that claim to be representative of the tradition or the community, at a time when they were thought to have disappeared for good. This challenge to the nation-state has been reinforced by the globalisation movement that objects to the national framework being a locus for organising economic activities, and increasingly subjects the states to a forced opening of their economies, through structural adjustment programmes.

The crisis of the nation-state, the 'burned-out' nationalist ideology and its modernising determinism paved the way for the unexpected and chance in the study and understanding of underdeveloped societies. In fact, post-colonial era is not a linear time allowing regular unfolding of economic laws. It is a plural time in which different trajectories, dissimilar and sometimes contradictory logics and rationalities, are intertwined. Moreover, the traditional vision of a passive society subjected to the modernising action of the state, is yielding to new problematics with the rise of the civil society. In a nutshell, the classical nineteenth-century Newtonian ideal which dominated the theory and praxis in underdeveloped countries is succumbing to new theories in which indecision, uncertainty and, consequently, freedom, are central concerns.

The aim of this work is to reflect on the new historical period that has been opened in the South since the beginning of the 1990s. It involves questioning all theoretical practices and strategies with a view to understanding better and grasping the development of societies of the South. Basically, we believe that these societies have entered into a new era which we identify as post-adjustment, marked by the rejection of the Washington Consensus and the theoretical basis of SAPs, particularly in institutions like the World Bank which have, for a long time, defended these concerns in the reflection on development. Moreover, authors and economists today acknowledge the limitations of SAPs, which failed to bring about profound social transformation in the South. All these reflections resulted in new theoretical practices, which we refer to as post-adjustment theories, considering the role of institutions and contractual procedures in the regulation and coordination of the activities of economic agents. However, we argue that these new theoretical practices have not succeeded in constructing new theoretical grids capable of understanding the social changes in the South. Besides, these theories were not able to establish new practices as far as development is concerned. Hence the persisting crisis in development theory. In this work, we attempt to present a few elements with a view to contributing to the debate on how to overcome this crisis, particularly through the study of the contributions of regulation theories and a comparative analysis of historical development experiences.

This work will revolve around six chapters. The first chapter will attempt to examine the limitations of the Washington Consensus. The second chapter will deal with the debate on the 'Asian success stories' as a strong challenge to the SAPs. The third chapter tries to make a critical presentation of post-liberalism development theories on the post-adjustment currents of thought, close to the traditional microeconomic. The fourth chapter is devoted to currents close to heterodoxy. Finally, the two last chapters will be devoted to the introduction of new theoretical practices and development strategies with a view to contributing to the critical debate on how to overcome the Washington Consensus and SAPs.

Notes

1 The evolution of the World Bank and its alienation from the neoliberal model began as far back as the end of the 1980s with the publication of the 1989 Development Report, devoted to problems of development funding. These positions were dealt with in greater depth in the 1991 Development Report and the study of the Southeast Asian economies with the formulation of the 'market-friendly' hypothesis which develops a complementary conception of the state-market relations. This ideological and theoretical refocusing was reaffirmed with the appointment, in early 1997, of Stiglitz, a neo-Keynesian, as Chief

Economist at the World Bank. However, despite these theoretical developments, World Bank practice in developing countries continues to be characterised by structural adjustment and fails to keep up with its analytical discourses.

2 See 'Sustainable Development', the Special Issue of the *Alternatives Sud Review*, Vol. II, no. 4, 195, CETRI and Harmattan.

3 See, in this regard, the Special Issue of *Actuel Marx* on the criticism of the orthodox conception of the market, no. 9, 1991. In this issue, see particularly the contributions of Amin, 'Le système mondial peut-il être réduit à un marché mondial'; Barrère, 'Penser le marché'; Di Ruzza, 'Le marché, quelques observations théoriques'.

4 For reviews on the literature with regard to the evolution of the neoclassical concept of development theory, see Bardhan, 1993; Guillaumont, 1995; Romo, 1994; Stern, 1989.

5 Taylor wrote many critical contributions on orthodox stabilisation. Moreover, this author did not restrict himself to a factual criticism of experiences of stabilisation in the Third World, but he developed an original theoretical modelisation drawing inspiration from the IS-LM model. See, in this regard Taylor, 1991.

6 See, in this regard, Favereau, 1995; Mahieu, 1990.

Chapter 1

The Failure of the Washington Consensus

Introduction

Development economics, which appeared at the end of World War II, was concerned with the study of 'backward' economies that had, according to these pioneers, certain specific characteristics that distinguished them from the economies of developed countries and that justified the creation of a new discipline. These economists sought – as a substitute for the mono-economics of neoclassical economic theory, which assumed that the explanatory power of its basic hypotheses could be extended to underdeveloped countries – new theoretical frameworks capable of constructing the intelligibility of these specific situations (Stern, 1989).

The theory of development played a fundamental role without rupturing the unity of the neoclassical economics and without questioning its ability to explain phenomena specific to underdeveloped countries. The pioneers in this field rapidly succeeded in identifying a specific object of study that justified the creation of a new scholarly discipline and that broke with the neoclassicists' desire to extend their basic hypotheses to this new field of study. This break was quickly acknowledged in various scholarly circles, and toward the end of the 1950s the theory of development underwent a clear expansion and was the object of genuine fascination on the part of economists. Thus, from that time on we have seen a proliferation of research centres and university programmes concerned with problems of development.

Starting in the 1950s, and especially in the 1960s, the theory of development renewed studies on underdeveloped countries and opened up new avenues for research. First, the theory of development demonstrated that under-development was not a simple phenomenon occurring at a specific time in history that corresponded to a stagnation of accumulation and the processes of growth in underdeveloped countries. From this point of view, underdevelopment is characterised by the domination exercised by developed countries over underdeveloped countries, the discontinuity of productive structures in these countries and the failure to cover labour costs.

In addition, the theory of development was concerned with studying the relationships of dependency between North and South. Thus, in 1969

Emmanuel developed the theory of unequal trade, basing himself on the theory of production costs. According to this thesis, international trade is not, as the theory of comparative advantages suggests, profitable to all participants, but on the contrary, works to the detriment of underdeveloped countries.

Thought on development during this period was characterised by a series of postulates accepted by every author. First, external factors were seen as hostile to development. It was considered necessary to convert them into positive factors through international cooperation. In addition, the state, through its intervention, was considered an important agent of development. Finally, industrialisation was seen as the motor of development.

Parallel with the increasing interest in problems of development shown by writers on economics, the Third World increasingly appeared as a force to be reckoned with in international economic relations. Thus the Afro-Asian Conference held in Bandung in 1955 led to the formation of a group of non-aligned countries. In this framework, all the Third World countries sought to escape the bipolarity that characterised the world during the Cold War. This group established itself as a genuine interlocutor of the great powers on the international scene and forced the creation of international organisations such as UNCTAD (the United Nations Conference on Trade and Development), which took an interest in the problem of stabilising the prices of basic products. On the other hand, in the 1970s the nonaligned countries were the source of the rise of protests against the new international order.

The theory of development was radicalised in the 1960s and was essentially dominated by theories of dependency. In a climate of political agitation, accentuated by the Cuban Revolution and urban guerrilla movements in addition to the crisis in strategies of import-substitution and the marginalisation of the lower social strata, the theory of development was influenced by this political and ideological effervescence.[1] The development of the theory of dependency in Latin America led to the popularisation of Frank's famous thesis (1967) concerning development and underdevelopment. This theory called for strategies breaking with capitalism and envisaged an autonomous mode of development centred on the country's own interests.[2]

During the 1960s, the theory of dependency exercised a broad influence on thinking about development and made a significant contribution to the study of mechanisms of dependency between home countries and satellite countries. However, despite its diversity, this theory was very quickly associated with the single notion of the development of underdevelopment and with theses of the stagnation of peripheral economies following the 'inevitable crisis of dependent capitalism' and the impossibility of autonomous capitalist development on the periphery. Thus the resumption of growth and the performance of underdeveloped economies in the early 1970s resulted in a questioning of this theoretical framework. The dynamism of accumulation in the Third World, and in particular in the countries of Southeast Asia, led radical development economists to a rethink of the theory of dependency and to question its investigations and results.[3]

In the 1970s the theory of development was strengthened by Third World countries' successes in modernising their economic structures and accelerating the processes of accumulation. These processes of growth benefited from the increased resources of Third World countries following rises in the prices of raw materials. On the other hand, this industrial growth was fed by the investment of international liquidities in the form of loans to Third World countries.

However, this context favourable to development changed towards the end of the 1970s. The change in priorities in matters of economic policy that accompanied the appointment of Paul Volcker as head of the Federal Reserve in 1979 and the imperatives of the battle against inflation were reflected in a rise in interest rates and the explosion of the debt crisis in the 1980s. In addition, the fall in the prices of raw materials accentuated internal and external imbalances in underdeveloped countries and aggravated the debt crisis. In this context, and in order to keep the debt crisis from turning into a generalised financial crisis, the international financial community established the World Bank (WB) and the International Monetary Fund (IMF) as the sole interlocutors in managing the debt crisis.

The forceful entry of the Bretton Woods institutions into the debate on development was accompanied by deep transformations in both practice and thinking about the Third World. A new era in development began, which specialists associated with the Washington Consensus. This Consensus questioned the theory of development and the specificity of underdeveloped societies. It amounted to the revenge of neoclassical theories. On the basis of the failure of strategies of development and the crisis in the theory of development that they implied, neoclassical theorists extended the field of application of their analytical framework to include underdeveloped societies.

From the theoretical point of view, the Washington Consensus questioned any form of state intervention and proclaimed the supremacy of the market in allocating resources. This discourse is connected with the problematics of the general equilibrium that conceives the possibility of a decentralised economy following the emergence of balanced prices resulting from the interaction of supply and demand within the market. On the other hand, the Washington

Consensus revived theories of comparative advantage in order to criticise the choice of strategies of import-substitution or industrialisation connected with the internal market, and to justify participation in the international market based on the factors with which underdeveloped countries are endowed. *Thus the disengagement of the state, regulation by the market and comparative advantage were the buzzwords of the 1980s Washington Consensus.*[4]

The theses of the 1960s and 1970s regarding development were replaced by a new orthodoxy characterised by three basic postulates. The first postulate stipulates that the growth of nations is connected with their greater openness to the outside. The second postulate explains that the increase of overall supply depends on the allocation of resources. The optimal allocation can take place only in a competitive market subject to the pressures of the world market. Finally, the rapidity of development depends, according to the new orthodoxy, on incentives offered to economic actors and their social compatibility.

The decline of theories of dependency (see Frank, 1991) and the challenge to theories of development were the chief characteristics of the intellectual context of the 1980s. The Chilean 'Chicago boys' presented themselves as mentors for development in Latin America and other regions of the Third World (Romo, 1994). The age of protest was over and Third World countries concerned themselves with managing the effects of the debt crisis (Hugon, 1989). Resigned, the pioneers of development economics watched helplessly the rise of a neo-liberalism that rejected their theoretical frameworks and broke with developmentalist practices.[5]

In effect, the market logic of structural adjustment was substituted for planned development and state intervention. In addition, the logics of participation in international markets and specialisation in accord with comparative advantages were substituted for the earlier logics of the development of the internal market and the coherence of the structures of production in the Third World.

In this contribution, we are concerned with the rise of the Washington Consensus in the 1980s, both in thinking about development and in the practices adopted by Third World countries and international organisms. However, toward the end of the 1980s and especially in the 1990s, this Consensus was subjected to a profound rethinking. We hypothesise that this criticism had its origins in the limited achievements of Structural Adjustment Programmes (SAPs) in the South and the 'successes' of Southeast Asian countries in the process of accumulation during the 1980s and into the 1990s. The SAPs, alongside their relatively high social costs, did not succeed in defining new processes of growth in Third World countries. Moreover, the studies made on the origins of the dynamics of accumulation in Southeast Asian countries demonstrated the crucial role played by the state at various levels, such as that of industrial policy, the financing of development and the acquisition of new technologies. These results put in question the paradigm of the pure theory at the basis of the Washington Consensus. These historical experiences are the source of a deep reconsideration of the basic neoclassical paradigm and the emergence of new theoretical frameworks in the analysis of the phenomena of underdevelopment.

In the first section of this chapter we will be concerned with the evolution of economic theory in the 1980s, which clearly influenced neoclassical analyses of underdevelopment. The second section will be devoted to a presentation of the Washington Consensus,which dominated the analysis of development in the 1980s. The third section will focus on the results of the SAPs, which provided the basis for a challenge to this consensus.

The Evolution of Economic Thought in the 1980s

In the 1950s and 1960s the field of economics was dominated by the Keynesian school, both from the theoretical point of view and from that of the conduct of economic policies. During this period of stability in capitalist economics, the Phillips curve offered economists a way of acting on the economic environment. Thus one could choose, depending on the mix of budgetary and monetary policies, between reducing unemployment and high inflation on one hand, and ensuring monetary stability at the cost of higher unemployment on the other.

The dominance of this school proceeded from a broad consensus regarding the Keynesian hypothesis of the *fixity of prices* which prevented markets from spontaneously balancing themselves and which consequently created a situation in which factors are underemployed (see Maillard, 1990). If demand for goods and services is lower than the level of production with full employment, actual production is corrected to lower it in order to adjust to the level of actual demand projected by the entrepreneurs, which leads to an underemployment of factors of production and especially to the development of unemployment. On the other hand, if demand for goods and services is greater than production with full employment, inflationary tensions will develop that indicate that the economy is overheating.

In both scenarios, state intervention, particularly through budgetary policy, seems legitimate and necessary in order to regulate economic activity and to compensate for the differences in demand with respect to the normal situation. Thus the fixity of prices and state regulatory intervention appear as the buzzwords of theoretical reflection and practical policy in the 1950s and 1960s.

In the United States, Keynesian economics was influential at the end of World War II and was particularly evident in the adoption of the Employment Act of 1946, but it was only with the arrival of President Kennedy in 1960 that Keynesian ideas became actually dominant (see Klamer, 1988). In a speech given at Yale University in 1962, Kennedy adopted the point of view of his committee of Keynesian advisers, presided over by W. Heller, by rejecting the option of a 'sane' fiscal policy and insisting instead on the importance of drastically reducing taxes in order to relaunch growth. These ideas were adopted by Lyndon Johnson after Kennedy's assassination. The fascination with Keynesian ideas was not limited to the president's advisers, but also affected the whole economic field. Thus in 1967 the Federal Reserve's Council of Governors defined the FRB-MIT model, which was inspired by Keynesian economics and was intended to improve monetary policy (see Willes, 1986). In addition, firms and universities elaborated models with several equations for developing and analysing economic predictions. This predominance was promoted by American expansionism in the 1960s. Thus Heller stated that:

> the expansion has, over the past five years [since 1961], created more than seven million jobs, doubled production, increased the Gross National Product by one third, and reduced the deficit of fifty billion dollars that was undermining the American economy in 1961 (Heller, 1966, quoted in Klamer, 1988, p. 17).

However, while the strong economic growth in the 1950s and 1960s was associated with Keynesianism, the explosion of the crisis in the early 1970s and the coexistence of unemployment and inflation ended up discrediting this school and its ability to formulate policies that would make it possible to emerge from the crisis.

In addition to this disconfirmation by the facts, the end of the 1960s and the early 1970s experienced a new resurgence of neoclassical theory. But we must add that despite the predominance of the Keynesian school, orthodox economists were still active and they continued to resist the main Keynesian themes, such as the fixity of prices or state intervention. This kernel of 'resisters', constituted as early as 1947 at the initiative of F. Hayek, was known as the Plymouth Rock Society, and they sought to defend classical economics against the Keynesian offensive (see Beaud and Dostaler, 1993). Some of these economists taught at the University of Chicago, and they gave rise to the Chicago School, of which Milton Friedman became the chief spokesman. This school reasserted, despite the predominance of the synthetic school, the necessity of returning to the neoclassical theory of prices and the ability of the market to reduce imbalances and thus ensure perfect regulation of the economy.

Thus the economic crisis and the persistence of neoclassical traditions, which are better known as 'monetarism', provided the basis for a criticism of Keynesian economics and opened the way to a renewal of economic theory marked by a strong comeback of microeconomic theory. However, while the monetarists played an important role in maintaining the orthodox tradition, the revival of the neoclassical programme of research resulted in the emergence of new conceptions such as the theories of rational expectations and the marginalisation of the Chicago School This turnabout involved the abandonment of the normative procedure characteristic of neoclassical theory and an attempt to elaborate explanatory analyses of certain economic phenomena. This return to an explanatory procedure led, as we shall see, to the abandonment or relaxing of certain hypotheses in the basic model, such as the hypothesis of complete information.

In the next section we will focus on the theory of rational expectations that was central to the renewal of neoclassical theory. We will also discuss the main thesis of the new classicists concerning the ineffectiveness of economic policies, which was to exercise a major influence on theories of development, and which was at the foundation of the Washington Consensus.

The Theory of Rational Expectations at the Heart of the Neoclassical Paradigm

The school of rational expectations became dominant in the field of political economics in the early 1970s. Its dominance was not unrelated to the economic context of the period, and particularly with the explosion of the crisis of the mode of regulation in capitalist economies. This school justified at the level of propositions the work of destruction carried out in the first phase of the crisis of the former procedures of regulation.

However, while this school was new within the field of political economy, the idea of expectations is much older. According to Beaud and Dostaler (1993), it was first introduced in an explicit way by Myrdal in 1927. Later on, other economists, such as Ohlin, Lindhal, and Lundberg, introduced expectations into their macroeconomic analyses. This concept was adopted by Keynes and played a central role in his *General Theory of Employment, Interest and Money*. In Keynesian analysis, expectations are the result of uncertainty concerning the future.

In 1956, in a collective work edited by Friedman on the quantitative theory of money, Cagan introduced the concept of adaptive expectation, which stipulates that agents make their predictions about the future on the basis of the difference between their past expectations and the current values of these expectations (Beaud and Dostaler, 1993). This conception was to be fundamental for the works of the monetarists. It was criticised by Muth, who maintained that it suggests that economic agents learn only from their past errors and do not make use of the information available to them. In this perspective, and in order to increase the rationality of economic agents, Muth put forward a hypothesis of rational expectations in which agents have an unlimited ability to process the information available to them, in order to define a rational mode of behaviour that excludes any uncertainty about the future.

These expectations differ from adaptive expectations insofar as they hypothesise that agents take into account not only past errors in prediction, but all the available information. This amounts to applying to the hypothesis of the *homo oeconomicus* to the agent dealing with information in an uncertain world. An expectation is thus defined as rational if it coincides with the mathematical likelihood of the conditional probability of the aleatory variable to be anticipated.

Thus the new theory of rational expectations assumes that agents collect information and process it in an effective way before determining their behaviour. These theories also see economic agents as taking into consideration the various changes in the rules of the game or in the functioning of economies. Thus we have here a strong hypothesis of an economic agent capable of foreseeing and building into his project any modification in his environment.

The works of the new classicists had important consequences in the field of political economy, and especially in the theoretical domain. From a theoretical point of view, rational expectations led to a profound questioning of traditional econometrics, both monetarist and Keynesian, by assuming that the behaviour of agents does not change following a change in the rules of the game or of economic policy. The results of the policies of stimulation carried out on the basis of conventional econometric models were challenged. From this point of view, classical macroeconomics sought to construct a new economic modelling by defining and developing sophisticated models and exploring chronological series with advanced econometric techniques. The goal of this 'new econometrics' was to demonstrate that the only effective components of an economic policy are those that are unexpected by agents. This brings us back to the second important result of the new classical macroeconomics, regarding the ineffectiveness of economic policies due to the fact that they are completely anticipated by economic agents.

The New Classicists and the Challenge to State Intervention

During the 1950s and 1960s, the field of political economy was dominated, as we have emphasised, by the Keynesian school, which maintained that the fixity of prices prevented the markets from being balanced. Thus the demand for goods and services did not automatically adjust to the supply, which also led to imbalances on the market for factors. On that basis, Keynesian economics recommended action through budgetary policy in order to compensate for deviations in the market for goods. Thus, if private demand is insufficient and might lead to unemployment, public demand, by means of direct purchases by administrations or by the stimulation of household revenues, should relaunch the economic process and reduce unemployment. On the other hand, if supply is insufficient, budgetary policy should contain public demand by reducing expenditures or increasing taxes, in order to slow inflation.

The according to the theoreticians of Keynesianism, economic policies were supposed to play an important role in regulating the economic situation. Moreover, this role was recognised by the monetarists as well. However, the two schools disagreed regarding the most effective means of intervention. While for the Keynesians budgetary policy made it possible to regulate the economic situation, the monetarists emphasise monetary policy, and especially interest rates, which have a major influence on investment and the private consumption of economic agents and ultimately on overall demand.

However, this consensus concerning the effectiveness of state intervention came under attack in the mid-1970s with the explosion of the crisis and the inability of the various economic policies to reduce the growing imbalances in all the markets. In this context of a profound questioning of state regulatory action, the new classical macroeconomics developed the hypothesis of the ineffectiveness of economic policies.

In 1974, R. Barro (1974) published an article in which he showed the inefficacy of budgetary policies. The demonstration of this proposition, based on the state's inter-temporal constraint, is relatively simple. To relaunch economic processes in a recessionary situation, the state increases its deficit by increasing its expenditures or reducing its revenues, and consequently increases its indebtedness. However, in the long run the state will be forced to repay its debt by increasing future taxes or reducing expenditures. In this context, economic agents, provided with this information and the tool of rational expectation, will very quickly realise that the additional income made available to them today will be tapped as soon as the state tries to reduce its deficit. Thus these rational agents will not modify their behaviour in any way and the budgetary policy intended to relaunch economic activity will be totally ineffective. This ineffectiveness is explained by the fact that 'public debt is not true wealth for private agents, as is well indicated by the title of Barro's article. It is not true wealth because it is, in fact, a debt that private agents are holding on themselves' (Maillard, 1990, p. 27) Sargent and Wallace (1975, 1976) extend this analysis to monetary policy and generalise it to economic policy as a whole.

Thus the field of political economy has been characterised by a strong comeback of analyses inspired by neoclassical economics. In this context, the theory of rational expectations has been the most powerful expression of this comeback. In the wake of the new classical macroeconomics, and when it ran out of steam in the early 1980s, the theory of real cycles emerged. This theoretical trajectory must be analysed in relation to the explosion of the crisis in the mode of regulation in capitalist economies. The neoclassical revival not only justified the crisis theoretically, but also created an intellectual context that was favourable to it, and particularly to the destruction of capitalist economies' former norms of reproduction (see, for example, the assertion of the ineffectiveness of economic policies in the context of the neo-liberal wave of the 1970s and 1980s).

Microeconomic schools inspired by neoclassical economics developed considerably during this period and invaded various other domains. Thus microeconomics was concerned with problems of uncertainty and chance and was used by bankers, insurers and stock analysts (Maillard, 1991). In addition, microeconomic studies developed in industrial economics, in finance and public options, in management and even in political strategies.

But despite this development, neoclassical theory, and more particularly the model of rational expectations, was subjected to a series of criticisms. The first criticism is connected with the relatively strong nature of the hypothesis of rational expectations. If economic agents do not limit themselves to extending their past information and seek to anticipate future developments, they still cannot foresee all the information and uncertainty at the centre of the economic process. In other words, economic agents do not have economic models and therefore cannot raise themselves to the level of the theoretician.

The second criticism relates to the ability of agents to collect the information necessary to form their expectations. Several elements explain the difficulties agents experience in gaining access to information, including its scarcity and its cost, which make expectations clearly aleatory.

But beyond these limits, the theory of rational expectations, and more generally the comeback of neoclassical theories, influenced theories of development and was at the foundation of the emergence and rise of the Washington Consensus.

The Washington Consensus

The beginning of the 1980s represented an important turning point for Southern countries. There was a decrease in the price of the raw materials that constituted most of the exports of many of these countries. In addition, the slowing of growth in the developed countries led to a decrease in their demand for the products of the Third World and weighed heavily on the latter's growth. Finally, rising interest rates and the rapid increase in the value of the dollar resulted in the debt crisis in the Third World. The explosion of this crisis in August 1982 led moneylenders to determine the means and the institutions which were to prevent this crisis from turning into a genuine financial crisis that could cause the collapse of the international financial system, and which were also intended to elaborate an international strategy for dealing with debt. From that point on, the IMF became, at the institutional level, the main organ for managing the Third World's debt. Thus, before negotiating its debt with the Club of Paris for public debts, every underdeveloped country had to have signed a confirmation agreement with the IMF. The signature of this agreement required a commitment on the part of the country concerned in a letter of intention approved by the IMF, to apply a programme of structural adjustment (SAP) defined in close collaboration with the IMF's experts. The goal of the SAPs was to reduce internal and external imbalances and to slow inflation while at the same time preserving a stable level of growth. But more than an adjustment of large macroeconomic balances, this involved a true reorganisation of the productive structures of underdeveloped countries in order to align them with prices on the world market and the needs of the world economy.

However, the turnabout of the 1980s was not limited to changes in policy and development strategies. These strategies were increasingly justified by profound transformations in theory. The crisis of the attempts to modernise economic structures in most underdeveloped countries resulted in the development of a discourse on the crisis of development economics. A context unfavourable to development economics was quickly established in economic circles. The initial enthusiasm yielded to a certain scepticism and sense of powerlessness when confronted by the crisis of development and the rising power of the World Bank and the IMF. In this context, neoclassical theory began once again to dominate the field of development economics and to question theories of development. Neoclassical theory ended up acknowledging that underdeveloped economies had certain specific characteristics (Berthélemy, Devezeuax de Lavergne and Gagy, 1991). The latter consisted of:

- a functioning of markets less harmonious than in underdeveloped countries;
- a dualistic character of the economy, with an advanced segmentation of the labour market;
- a situation of extreme poverty, which gives rise to behaviours on the part of agents less in conformity with the postulates of standard theory. Communitarian bonds, for example, play a determining role in establishing networks of solidarity among agents: 'Under the influence of factors unusual in wealthy countries, supporters of the standard approach explain, rationality can lead to reactions that appear paradoxical with regard to the evolutions of the system of prices' (ibid., p. 1);
- the consumption-savings distribution not guided by the same factors as in developed countries.

But according to the supporters of the standard analysis, these differences do not justify the creation of a new discipline, development economics, in order to analyse the problems of underdeveloped economies. On the contrary, standard economics is capable of analysing and understanding questions of development. All that is required is to make a few adjustments, in particular to take into consideration the unusual behaviours in underdeveloped countries, and to develop local statistical systems in order to improve the quality of the information collected.

Thus, from the early 1980s on, neoclassical theory made a comeback on the basis of the questions raised regarding the theory of development. Neoclassical theory hypothesised the superiority of the market and competition in allocating productive resources. From this point of view, the basic Walrassian model that dominated studies of development under the influence of theories of rational expectation criticised any state intervention in regulating underdeveloped economies. The World Bank and in particular the Reports on Development were the voice of this new religion in the debate on development.

The World Bank explained that effective state intervention was not easy, 'for when trying to improve the conditions in which the private sector functions, it doesn't take much to make them worse' (World Bank, 1987, p. 89).

This new, dominant theoretical corpus elaborated a new interpretation of the crisis in underdeveloped economies. The crisis was analysed as resulting from a strategy of development and industrial growth which was directed toward the internal market and which had not succeeded in developing a sector that was competitive at the international level. Krueger (1974) resumed the analyses she had made in the 1970s regarding the revenues created by protecting the internal sector and its consequences in terms of the relative ineffectiveness of industrial investments. According to Krueger, the competitiveness of Asian economies demonstrates that there is a strong correlation between liberalisation of imports, the promotion of exports and economic growth (Krueger, 1990). Moreover, the imbalances that appear in the markets in underdeveloped countries are connected, according to neoclassical studies, with strong state intervention that produces major distortions, thus preventing an equalisation of supply and demand.

Thus the crisis in the economies of underdeveloped countries is explained, according to the new prophets of the economics of development, by strategies of growth oriented toward internal markets, the obstacles put in the way of free trade and competition, the excess of demand and the state's regulatory intervention.

Drawing on the Walrassian theoretical framework and basing itself on the crisis in the attempts at modernisation in the Third World, the neoclassical school constructed a new orthodoxy in the field of development economics. This new orthodoxy is generally referred to as the Washington Consensus. This consists of the whole of the economic practices and discourses inspired by the theory of equilibrium that were to dominate debate on development and which were erected by the Bretton Woods institutions (located in Washington), the IMF and the World Bank, into a norm determining what was licit and illicit in matters of development. But, more than the Washington Consensus, it was above all its tools that became the best known: the Structural Adjustment Programmes and the calculable models of general equilibrium.

The Structural Adjustment Programmes (SAPs)

In the 1980s, SAPs replaced strategies of development. The goal of these programmes is to reduce internal and external imbalances and guarantee underdeveloped countries better participation in the international economy. SAPs can be defined as 'a process of reorganising the productive structures of the countries concerned in order to ensure, within the framework of international economic relationships freed from any restrictive policy, the equilibrium of the balance of payments' (de Bernis, 1989, p. 2).

In SAPs, we can distinguish two components:

- *stabilisation*, which seeks to reduce short-term imbalances between supply and demand and to re-establish a positive balance in the balance of payments. Stabilisation gives priority to action to control demand in order to diminish macroeconomic imbalances;
- *adjustment*, whose goal is to reduce sectorial imbalances in order to relaunch production, and in particular production of exportable goods in order to re-establish on a long-term basis an equilibrium in the balance of payments. From this point of view, structural reforms give priority to action to control supply in underdeveloped countries and to redirect it in relation to the needs of the international market. These reforms are essentially of a microeconomic nature and seek to influence arbitrages and choices made by firms regarding investment and production.

The IMF and Stabilising Action in the Third World

The stabilisation component of SAPs is the concern of the IMF. As we have said, this institution played an increasingly important role in the 1980s, with the explosion of the debt crisis. In addition, the abandonment of fixed rates of exchange and the development of financial markets in the 1980s diminished developed countries' recourse to the resources of the IMF in dealing with difficulties in their balances of payments (Polak, 1991). Thus this institution concentrated more and more on interventions in underdeveloped countries. In order to augment its resources and to respond to the increasing needs expressed by these countries, the IMF sought to develop its resources by raising the contributions to be made by member countries and by borrowing on the financial markets.

From a theoretical point of view, while the World Bank generally refers to the basic Walrassian model, the IMF has a more precise theoretical framework that makes use of the monetary theory of the balance of payments that tried to control the supply of credits in particular.[6] This conception evolved at the end of the 1980s, taking into consideration the whole of the monetary supply. In addition, the IMF revised its position regarding rates of exchange and increasingly recommended that underdeveloped countries opt for flexible rates of exchange, and also began to introduce a fiscal element into its suggestions (see Polak, 1991).

The IMF's basic model considers the case of a small, open economy with a financial market that is not very developed. In this context, the excess of money supply leads to additional demand. In this economy, the macroeconomics targeted by the model depends on three equations:[7]

- the first equation expresses monetary demand,

  $M_d = l\,PY$ (1),

  where

  P = the general level of prices,
  Y = real income,
  l = the proportion of monetary demand;

- the second equation expresses the money supply M_s in relation to the credits allocated by the banking system to enterprises and the state C and the variation of trade reserves with other countries B that can influence internal monetary creation:

  $M_s = C + B$ (2);

- the third equation expresses the general level of internal prices P as a function of the level of external prices P_m with the exchange rate:

  $P= e\,P_m$ (3).

  In this model, equilibrium depends on the balancing of the money supply and demand for money:

  $M_s = M_d$ (4)
  $C + B = l\,e\,P_m\,Y.$

  Thus the external balance is written:

  $B = l\,e\,P_m\,Y - C.$

Hence the balance of external payments depends on credits granted by the banks, on prices, and on incomes. In this framework, an external imbalance has its source in an excess of demand (consumption and investment) connected with a relatively large issue of money.

The IMF does not limit itself to this monetary approach to external imbalances, but extends it through an approach in terms of reduction that connects the growth of demand with excesses in the distribution of revenues. In this perspective, inflation is the immediate consequence of an excess in overall demand in relationship to supply.

On the basis of this analysis, the IMF proposed a series of recommendations intended to lead Third World states to manage internal demand more restrictively. In this perspective, the reduction of the external deficit involves decreasing credit, devaluation, or an increase in the supply of goods. According to the IMF, most of the monetary creation in underdeveloped countries comes from the political power's requirement that the banks finance the budget deficit. At this level, control of the growth of monetary aggregates and credit involves the reduction of budget deficits. In this framework, Jedlicki and de Bernis (1989, p. 37) write:

> by privileging the budget deficit to contain monetary expansion, the IMF clearly shows its distrust with regard to the public sector's ability to distribute national resources among the different sectors in a rational way.

In studying the budget deficit, the IMF does not make any pronouncement concerning its size, which remains in the domain of the states' choice of economic policy, but is concerned primarily with the means of financing it. In order to battle the deficit and clean up public finances, the IMF proposes putting a ceiling on bank credits extended to the state, a limitation on the recourse to new external indebtedness, and a reduction of public expenditures. In this framework, it suggests a series of measures, including:

- a moderation of salary hikes;
- a moderation of job creation;
- a decrease of investment expenditures;
- a decrease of transfer expenditures (consumption subsidies).

For the IMF, devaluation also plays an important role in reducing external debt. It allows Third World economies to recover their competitiveness by achieving parity in purchasing power between the national economy and the international economy (see equation (3) in the model). Devaluation is to have as its objective the reduction of the differential of inflation, and should be guided by the actual real rate of exchange, which measures the evolution of the rate of exchange with the currencies of the country's chief external trading partners (actual), weighted by the relation between internal and external prices (real).[8]

According to the IMF, devaluation should play an important role in the reduction of the external deficit. The effects of devaluation are twofold: there is an effect on incomes and an effect on prices. By increasing the price of imported products and consequently the general level of internal prices, devaluation has a deflationary effect on real internal incomes, which leads to a decrease in internal demand. On the other hand, so far as prices are concerned, devaluation is supposed to have positive effects on foreign demand for national goods exported, as well as on the demand addressed to the sector producing imported goods. The re-equilibration of the trade balance following action on these two requirements depends, according to the theorem of critical elasticities, on the size of the initial deficit and the fact that the sum of the elasticities of demand must be superior to 1.

Thus control over the progression of monetary aggregates, devaluation and the growth of supply will be the main tools used by the IMF's programmes of stabilisation to battle deficits and re-establish the macroeconomic balance.

The World Bank and Reforms of Structure

In addition to the component of stabilisation, SAPs include a component of structural reforms supported and initiated by the World Bank. These reforms do not refer to a precise economic model, as is the case for the policies of stabilisation (see Mosley, 1992). They rely much more on a general reference to the basic Walrassian model that hypothesises the superiority of competition and market allocation of the factors of production. In addition, the prescribed reforms are inspired by a certain interpretation of experiments with economic development in the Third World (see Nash, 1992).

The World Bank completed the IMF's diagnosis of the causes of external imbalances by introducing analyses in terms of the fixity of supply. These rigidities proceed from excessive state intervention (the maintenance of unprofitable public enterprises, subsidies for products considered essential, price controls, relatively low interest rates, the overvaluation of rates of exchange) that is reflected in distortions of relative prices and a poor allocation of resources in underdeveloped countries (see Balassa, 1982). This state intervention results in rigid productive structures and leads to a mode of participation unfavourable to underdeveloped economies.

This twofold reference to the basic Walrassian model and to the limits of the experiments with industrial development in underdeveloped countries allowed the World Bank to structure the new orthodoxy in matters of development.[9] According to the World Bank, underdeveloped countries should implement a set of structural reforms guided by the primacy of private rationality, for only the free play of market forces allows the prices of goods and the costs of factors to express the rationality and the preferences of the actors in an environment characterised by a scarcity of resources. These reforms are supposed to be inspired by a series of principles on which the Bank never ceases to reinforce. The first principle concerns state intervention, which the Bank tries to limit to the setting of rules and the improvement of the functioning of infrastructures and the market. But the Bank questions any form of state intervention in the functioning of economies. More particularly, the Bank asks Third World countries to privatise public enterprises whose performance it considers to be 'in general poor, especially in developing countries. Everything indicates that these enterprises have not succeeded in playing the strategic role in industrialisation that the governments hoped they would' (World Bank, 1987, p. 77).

In addition, at the industrial level the Bank deems it better to avoid sectors whose profitability is deferred, such as heavy industries, and to give priority instead to sectors providing immediate profitability. The 1987 Report on Development cites an observation that appeared in the memorandum submitted by the United Nations Commission on Economic and Employment Issues in 1949, which emphasises that:

> giving excessive priority to industry as an end in itself, and especially to heavy industry, threatens to give an undeveloped country the symbols of development, but not its substance. Of course, heavy industry can be justified in a certain number of cases ... But in general capital should be allocated where profitability is highest (ibid., p. 5).

Another important element of the new orthodoxy concerning development defined by the World Bank concerns the redirection of options and strategies of development toward the external market and no longer toward the satisfaction of the needs of the internal market. This choice is reaffirmed by the Bank in all its publications, which explain that:

> countries should orient themselves toward the adoption of a trade strategy directed outward, that is, they should eliminate biases with regard to exports, replace quantitative restrictions by tariffs, and adopt rates of exchange more in conformity with realities (ibid.).

At the macroeconomic level, the Bank recommends, in line with the IMF's stabilisation programmes, the reduction of public deficits and an increase in saving by means of an increase in real positive interest rates.

Finally, the Bank encourages the growth of competition on internal markets in order to ensure a better allocation of resources. To this end, it suggests eliminating administrative controls on prices. Interest rates a special target of the Bank's recommendations. It explains that 'although control over interest rates and selective credit policies make it possible to achieve certain specific objectives, on the whole they have unfavorable effects on the behaviour of savers, lenders, and borrowers' (ibid., p. 136).

This new orthodoxy underlies the structural reforms proposed by the World Bank in most underdeveloped countries. The Bank's reforms have essentially attacked prices and have tried to align them with those of the international economy with a view to reducing overall demand and ensuring a better distribution of resources among the various sectors in order to encourage activities promoting equilibrium in the balance of payments. In this perspective, the Bank recommends the devaluation of national currencies. The second price targeted is the interest rate. At this level, the Bank envisages a rise in interest rates so that the real rates become positive. According to the Bank, this should halt monetary expansion in countries with deficits and ensure a distribution of resources that favours the most profitable sectors. In addition, the Bank advises that managed prices be raised by raising public rates and suppressing subventions. These measures have as their goal the re-establishment of the profitability of the public sector, an increase in public saving and the reduction of demand. The final price targeted by the Bank is that of the labour force. At this level, modifications of exchange rates, interest rates, and managed prices are supposed to lead to a decrease in real salaries that is reflected in a decrease in overall demand. In order to sustain this development, the Bank recommends stopping nominal salary increases in order to prevent them from compensating for the decrease in real salaries. On the other hand the Bank advises greater flexibility in labour legislation in order to encourage foreign internal and external investment.

This new orthodoxy dominated reflection on development in the 1980s, and SAPs represented most of the practices of development. Few researchers and countries resisted the overwhelming advance of the Bretton Woods institutions and adjustment. But despite this domination of the orthodoxy, we must emphasise certain heterodox efforts to escape from this suffocating consensus, particularly in Africa and in Latin America.

Confronted by imbalances in external payments and the debt crisis, most African countries found themselves obliged to adopt Programmes of Structural Adjustment under pressure from the World Bank and the International Monetary Fund. But faced with the limits of these programmes, the African intelligentsia mobilised in order to define new strategies of development better adapted to the realities and specificities of African economies. This effort took place under the aegis of the United Nations Economic Commission for Africa (ECA), and culminated on 10 April 1989 in Addis Ababa with the adoption by African ministers for economic planning and development and ministers of finance of the African Frame of Reference for Programmes of Structural Adjustment (CARPAS), which sought to work toward socio-economic recovery and transformation. CARPAS explains clearly that:

> the classical approaches to stabilisation and structural adjustment are not suitable to ensure socio-economic recovery and transformation in Africa. This is because the basic model of classical programmes of stabilisation and structural adjustment puts the emphasis almost exclusively on the use of market forces with unlimited competition – internal and external. This kind of model is certainly not adapted to the African situation, which is characterised by weak structures of production and markets with limited competition. Moreover, because the programmes seek essentially to ensure internal and external financial balances, they ignore fundamental structural factors that are important both for economic growth and for socio-economic transformation (ECA, 1990).

From this point of view CARPAS, based on a better understanding of the realities of African economies, seeks to define an overall framework of orientation in order to relaunch economic development in Africa. This development will focus on human beings and will try to reduce poverty and improve the well-being of African peoples. According to CARPAS, these new strategies of development should not be limited to the level of nation-states, but require that aspects connected with regional integration and economic cooperation among African countries be taken into account. According to ECA, regional integration in Africa should be founded not only on economic considerations but also on 'the African sense of uniqueness and solidarity' (ibid.). However, this intellectual framework has never given rise to attempted applications. Bogged down in a deep crisis in payments, African countries, despite their commitments to CARPAS, have sought to negotiate SAPs with the IMF and the World Bank in order to gain easier terms for the payment of their debts and for contributions of new capital.

In addition, some countries in Latin America, faced with the limits of the SAPs in the first years of their application and the strong local resistance, have sought to apply heterodox programmes of stabilisation. These policies were initiated in the context of hyperinflation these economies experienced in the 1980s. Classical policies of stabilisation did not succeed in slowing this inflation. These policies sought essentially to control prices administratively and to do away with the indexing of salaries. Price controls are in conflict with the recommendations of the IMF and the World Bank, which believe that once controls are lifted inflation will take off even more strongly. Nonetheless, Argentina's Austral plan and Brazil's Cruzado plan have continued to exercise administrative price controls with the goal of diminishing the boomerang effects of the inflationary spiral and inflationary expectations on the part of agents. In addition, the governments that have applied these heterodox programmes have also sought to eliminate salary indexing in relation to prices, because this is considered a basic element in sustaining the inflationary cycle.

However, these heterodox experiments have failed.[10] In some cases, administrative price fixing did not prevent inflationary spikes just before or just after. In others, the relatively short periods over which these heterodox policies were applied were too brief to provide satisfactory results.

The failure of these attempts sounded the death knell for alternatives to SAPs in underdeveloped countries. Starting in the second half of the 1980s, the domination of SAPs in thinking about development was definitive. Even Latin American countries such as Argentina and Brazil adopted the classical and orthodox versions of these programmes. The domination of the SAPs was aided by the rise of models of the calculable general equilibrium that gave the Washington Consensus the calculating tool required to justify and legitimate these options in matters of development.

Models of Calculable General Equilibrium

These models were developed in the 1970s and reached their apogee in the 1980s, and were elaborated chiefly within the World Bank in studies by de Melo, Dervis, Robinson and Adelman.[11] They enjoyed broad success in underdeveloped countries to the extent that they made it possible to resolve the problem of the absence of reliable statistical series by resorting to a limited numerical base. These were simulation models that made it possible to represent transactions in a market economy.

The construction of a model of equilibrium includes two steps. The first is the construction of the empirical base, the matrix of social accountancy of the model that sums up all the flows of exchange among agents over a given period. In this matrix each category of goods or services and economic agents corresponds to an entry on a line and in a column. This makes it possible, as in the framework of an input-output matrix, to sum up all the resources of a national economy and their uses. These matrices are constructed on the basis of information provided by the national accounts and inquiries into incomes, household expenditures, etc.

The matrix of social accountancy gave rise to the construction of a large number of models that were inspired by neoclassical economics, to judge by the hypotheses used by their authors (Zatman, 1995). The accounting equations of the matrix have to be supplemented by functions of behaviour derived from the Walrassian model. In this framework the choice to be produced proceeds from a decision to maximise profit. The supply of products and the demand for factors are a homogeneous function of prices.[12]

Production

(1) Q^s_i (p, w, r) : the output of the sector i
p : price,
w : salary,
r : interest rate.
F^d_i (p, w, r) : sector i's demand for a factor

Demand

(2) Q_i, k^d (p, w, r, F_k)
k being the index of the class,

Equilibrium

(3) $Q_i = \sum Q_i,k$
$\sum F^d_i = \sum F_i,k$

The encounter of supply and agents' demand on the market makes it possible to attain a price vector (p^*, w^*, r^*) that allows the market to be audited and the needs of different agents to be maximised.

The resolution of the model adopts Walrassian tentative procedures. Initial prices and salaries are assumed and the demand for labour is then calculated. If the encounter of supply and demand allows a disequilibrium to appear, then the variation of the initial salary makes it possible to achieve a situation of equilibrium on the labour market and thus to cancel the supplementary supply or demand. One proceeds in the same way for the market for goods. The calculated supply is compared with the demand expressed and the adjustment is carried out by manipulating prices. This tentative approach makes it possible to achieve situations of equilibrium on the various markets and to do away with all imbalances.

These basic models played an important role in justifying economic choices and setting up SAPs. Models of calculable general equilibrium allowed the World Bank to carry out simulations of the results of different strategies of development. In particular, through these models it was able to compare its proposed SAPs with other political alternatives. These comparisons permitted the World Bank to demonstrate the superiority of the SAPs and to show that the countries that had applied them the most vigorously had had better performance than those that had not applied them.

However, these models were subjected to broad critiques in the theory of development, particularly because the basic hypotheses of Walrassian equilibrium adopted by these models are far from being proven in underdeveloped countries. These criticisms gave rise to the development by new generations of economists of models less concerned with proximity to the basic model than with the pertinence of the research hypotheses. In this perspective, Robinson (1989) distinguishes two categories of studies:

- those whose authors remain attached to the neoclassical tradition in their modellings, but which introduce new hypotheses concerning the fixity of prices or imperfections in the functioning of markets (Adelman and Robinson, 1978);
- those whose authors deviate from the Walrassian model and adopt a more structuralist approach, taking into consideration questions related to the distribution, coherence, and articulation of productive structures.[13]

This proliferation of studies has made it possible to envisage other kinds of macroeconomic connections than those favoured by the neoclassical school, which give priority to saving and see ex post facto equality as guaranteed by the variation in investment. Thus Taylor and other authors have proposed Keynesian or Kaldorian connections. Keynesian connections assume that savings adjust to outside investment. The Kaldorian point of view differs from Keynesian approaches insofar as it emphasises the problems of distribution that influence savings.

But despite these heterodox attempts, models of calculable general equilibrium remain determined by the basic neoclassical model, and from this point of view they are an integral part of the Washington Consensus that dominated development economics in the 1980s. A sort of division of labour has been made between the tools used by this consensus: the SAPs define the options for development, and the models of calculable general equilibrium justify and legitimate them.

In the early 1980s, however, this consensus encountered strong resistance on the part of populations confronted with the hard social consequences of adjustment. Moreover, economists, after being resigned and sceptical in the early 1980s, started criticising the theoretical foundations and results of SAPs again.

The Decline of the Washington Consensus

The Washington Consensus marked thinking and practice concerning development in the 1980s. Starting in the mid-1980s, and especially at the beginning of the 1990s, this consensus was challenged, first of all because of the weak or mixed results produced by SAPs. While some countries recorded some successes in efforts at stabilisation, on the whole SAPs failed to initiate a new process of growth based on encouraging exports and dynamic participation in the flows of the international economy. However, in addition to these weak results from an economic point of view, SAPs had major social consequences, including increased unemployment, rising inflation and the state's disengagement from the economic sphere and in particular from subsidies for the most necessary products (Sinha, 1995).

The limits of the reforms strongly recommended by the World Bank and the IMF allowed economists to recover their voices and to show greater daring in criticising SAPs. Thus there was a strong challenge to the theoretical foundations of the Washington Consensus. This criticism of the Walrassian ideal and the market's ability to ensure the coordination of various actor's projects and the socialisation of individual agents was the source of the emergence of what has been called *post-adjustment development economics*. This involves a set of ideas and theoretical propositions that take into account pure Walrassian models' inability to constitute a framework for thought and action in underdeveloped countries, and that set out to formulate new representations and theoretical hypotheses that can take into consideration the influence and the role of institutions in the regulation and functioning of economies in underdeveloped societies.

In the following section we will attempt to account for this questioning of the Washington Consensus by examining the results of the reforms and reviewing the theoretical criticisms that have been made of SAPs.

The Results of Adjustment

The assessment of the economic results of SAPs has been the subject of debates and controversies between the defenders of these programmes and their critics. According to the latter, SAPs produce few positive results at an enormous social cost and have not led to a substantial improvement in the situation of countries showing a deficit. It was in this perspective that a controversy opposed the World Bank to the Economic Commission for Africa (ECA). In a study of the economic results of SAPs in Africa, the World Bank tried to demonstrate that the countries that had applied these SAPs had registered better performances than those that had not. Thus, according to the World Bank's study, between 1985 and 1987 the countries which undertook reforms within the framework of SAPs recorded real growth in the GDP and an increase in agricultural production significantly greater than that in countries which remained outside this reform movement. The Economic Commission for Africa, in a counter-study, contested the World Bank's conclusions from methodological and statistical points of view. According to the ECA, the choice of the years to be studied, the periods of reference and the methods of measurement strongly influenced the World Bank's conclusions.[14]

The analysis of SAPs' record of achievement in underdeveloped countries raises certain methodological problems.[15] First of all, the implementation of SAPs is accompanied by a major inflow of foreign capital that allowed an improvement in the balance of payments. However, in this context it is difficult to attribute this recovery in external accounts to the reforms prescribed within the framework of SAPs. It is also difficult to tell whether in a given country the improvement in economic conditions is the result of reforms applied within the framework of SAPs, or proceeds instead from an improvement in the international context. Finally, the World Bank often suggests that the weakness of the results is attributable to Third World governments' lack of enthusiasm in implementing reforms.

Despite these methodological difficulties, it is now possible, after almost 20 years of experience with the application of SAPs, to draw up an initial balance sheet. The first question to examine has to do with the processes of growth that the Bretton Woods institutions promised to restore after the application of SAPs. At this level, we have to emphasise the inability of SAPs to relaunch processes of growth. During the 1980s, only Southeast Asian countries registered high levels of growth averaging about 7 per cent. However, these countries did not participate in SAPs and in fact adopted policies of boosting credit-favouring enterprises in order to diversify the structures of production and exports. In the rest of the countries of the Third World which have vigorously applied SAPs, the 1980s were marked by a rapid contraction of growth, with annual average rates of 1.7 per cent in Sub-Saharan Africa, 0.2 per cent in North Africa and the Middle East, and 1.7 per cent in Latin America.[16]

To be sure, growth resumed in the 1990s. But it remained very weak and fragile in most of the regions under adjustment. The annual rates of growth between 1990 and 1994 were 2.3 per cent in North Africa and 3.6 per cent in Latin America. In Sub-Saharan Africa, growth continued to decrease, running around 0.9 per cent throughout this period.

The slowing of processes of growth is explained by a decrease in productive investments in most Southern countries. In Sub-Saharan Africa, the rate of investment declined from 23 per cent in 1980 to 17 per cent in 1994 and in Latin America it declined from 36 per cent to 29 per cent. Despite a slight recovery of investment in the 1990s, the rate of investment did not reach 1970s levels. Only the countries of Southeast Asia recorded a rise in their rates of investment, which moved from 29 per cent to 36 per cent over the same period.

This information regarding growth and investment makes it possible to emphasise the inability of reform movements to give new impetus to the process of development in Third World countries. The blockage of investment and the development of financialisation in Third World economies is explained in part by the financial reforms undertaken in the framework of structural adjustment. These countries undertook financial reforms inspired by Gurley and Shaw's theories of financial repression. According to these theories, underdeveloped countries must take into account the exhaustion of external sources of financing and mobilise their internal resources in order to ensure that their economies will be financed. These resources are not lacking, as the various 1960s and 1970s models of debt with growth claimed, but they are repressed because of the low levels of remuneration and failure of financial systems to adapt.

On that basis, the financial reforms conceived within the framework of SAPs had to provide the conditions required to mobilise internal financial resources and thereby to make possible a profound change in the structure of the financing of development, at the expense of external resources. These new conceptions extend traditional theories of the financing of development insofar as they make savings a necessary precondition for financing investment. From this point of view, the encouragement of internal savings involves liberalising capital markets and moving to positive real interest rates.

Most Southern countries have adopted a series of financial reforms aimed at liberalising the formation of interest rates for debtors and creditors, the granting of bank credits, the creation of an inter-bank market and the revitalisation of the financial market. However, the abolition of controls on credit resulted in a rapid increase in its cost, thus discouraging productive investment to the benefit of financial activities. As a result, there was a rapid increase in interest rates in the main African countries. Between 1980 and 1994, interest rates moved from 8.3 per cent to 11.8 per cent and from 5.5 per cent to 11.1 per cent in Nigeria and in South Africa, respectively. In Tunisia, real interest rates rose from an average of -3 per cent during the period 1981–84 to an average of 4.71 per cent in 1991. This rise in interest rates was estimated at 27 per cent for the year 1991 alone. In Egypt, interest rates moved from 10 per cent for the decade of the 1980s to 19 per cent in 1991. This increase in the cost of credit represents a heavy burden for enterprises and discourages any new investment.

However, SAPs have allowed a reduction of budgetary deficits in most Third World countries. This reduction was made possible by an increase in revenues, and especially by a reduction of expenditures following the disengagement of the state from certain public enterprises by privatising them and by decreasing subsidies for basic products. This avenue of gaining control over expenditures, in addition to the tensions it may generate, puts additional pressures on the dynamics of growth, and especially on the priority granted to the export sector, insofar as it results in increased costs of reproducing the labour force and gradually cancels out the comparative advantages of underdeveloped countries. In Africa, it is estimated that of the 24 countries that have applied SAPs, 16 have succeeded in reducing their budget deficits. In Tunisia, the budget deficit significantly improved, dropping from 3.6 per cent to 2.9 per cent of the GDP between 1988 and 1992, before worsening again in 1993, when it reached 3.3 per cent of the GDP. This development, which was, of course, lower than predicted, was achieved through a significant increase in revenues and a reduction of expenditures. In 1992, revenues rose to 14.8 per cent of the GDP following the growth of tax revenues (14 per cent), non-tax revenues resulting from the increase in oil revenues (+24.4 per cent in 1993) and treasury revenues (+7 per cent in 1993). Expenditures increased moderately and this made it possible to reduce their percentage of the GDP from 39.2 per cent to 35.9 per cent in 1991.

In addition, Algeria had a budget surplus in 1990 and this allowed the treasury to pay 16 billion dinars back to the central bank (Yachir, 1993). This surplus was explained in large measure by the increase in revenues resulting from devaluation and the lifting of price controls. Devaluation led to an increase in the national currency held by Sonatrach, which specialises in exporting hydrocarbons, and an increase in export taxes. In Morocco, the budget deficit was only 2 per cent of the GDP in 1993. But the most spectacular results were achieved in Egypt, where the deficit decreased from 17 per cent of the GDP in 1990–91 to 4.5 per cent in 1992–93. This reduction was obtained thanks to an upturn in fiscal revenues and especially a major reduction in public expenditures on subsidies and investments. Only Sudan did not reduce its deficit, which rose from £0.7 billion in 1988–89 to 8.6 billion in 1992–93. This deepening of the deficit was explained by the military expenses arising from the war and the junta's desire to arrive at a military solution to the secession movement in the southern part of the country.

These elements allow us to bring out the logic of SAPs. These reforms sought to reduce internal deficits by increasing control over internal demand and reducing economic activity. This was control from below that had recessionary consequences leading to a rapid increase in unemployment and poverty. The slow-down in job creation associated with a relatively high rate of population growth also resulted in increased unemployment. But more than its overall volume, it was especially unemployment among urban youth that grew fastest.

Alongside the rapid growth of unemployment, the whole of the reforms connected with adjustment led to a decrease in real salaries. The growing insecurity of the social situation following the application of programmes of structural adjustment had as its immediate consequence an increase in poverty throughout the world. The 1997 UNDP Report on Development emphasises that despite the progress achieved in reducing poverty in the twentieth century, over the past few years there has been a deterioration of living conditions (UNPD, 1997). The UNDP notes that more than a quarter of the inhabitants of developing countries live in total deprivation and that 1.3 billion individuals have to get along on an income of less than US$1 a day. In its report, the UNDP stresses the rapid increase of world poverty. Between 1987 and 1993 the number of people having an income less than one dollar a day increased by nearly 100 million.

These results were confirmed by the trade and development report for 1997 published by UNCTAD (United Nations Conference on Trade and Development) in September 1997 (UNCTAD, 1997). According to UNCTAD, in recent years there had been a twofold growth of inequalities. First of all between developed and underdeveloped countries, where the difference in revenues rose from 20 times as great in 1965 to 39 times as great in 1995. Moreover, inequalities were accentuated within underdeveloped countries where, according to UNCTAD's estimates, in more than half of the countries the richest 20 per cent of the population receives more than 50 per cent of the national income, and the poorest 20 per cent receives less than 10 per cent of the wealth.

The rise in inequalities explains, according to UNCTAD, the fall in consumption in underdeveloped countries and the tendency of investment to be oriented toward the export sectors. However, these growth strategies are increasingly faced with the gloomy outlook of the external markets and decreasing demand on the part of the developed countries.

The reduction of the deficit in balances of payments is one of the primary goals of SAPs. There has been an improvement in this regard in some countries, in differing ways. These advances have been achieved in certain countries by going increasingly into debt and they therefore remain heavily dependent on foreign moneylenders. In other countries, there has been an improvement in the foreign balances thanks to a large reduction in imports or to a rise in the prices of exported raw materials.

Over the past few years, debt has significantly increased in most Third World countries, despite the World Bank's and the IMF's efforts to reduce it. The debt of Sub-Saharan African countries rose from US$84 billion to US$212 billion, and debt service increased from 9.7 per cent to 14 per cent between 1980 and 1994. Over the same period, debt in the Middle East and North Africa rapidly increased, rising from US$84 billion to US$207 billion, and debt service rose from 5 per cent to 15.4 per cent. In Latin America, despite a decrease in debt service, which fell from 36.9 per cent to 27.5 per cent, debt increased, rising from US$258 billion to US$562 billion between 1980 and 1994.

This record allows us to conclude that SAPs have not succeeded in relaunching economic growth and represent no more than strategies for managing the crisis. In fact, deflation, with its perverse effects in the social and political domains, seems to characterise the processes of economic growth brought about by structural adjustment in Third World countries. This view prevailed among public authorities in re-establishing the internal balance that had been achieved through a drastic reduction in state intervention in matters of development and social regulation. The same logic guided the re-establishment of the external balance, with a major reduction in imports, which aggravated tendencies toward depression in underdeveloped economies. In some economies, such as the Egyptian, the improvement of the external balance was facilitated by rescheduling external debt. The reduction in external imbalances made it possible to re-establish the import capacities of certain economies. However, this capacity is increasingly used for final consumption, and at much higher costs than in the past.

On the other hand, SAPs failed in setting up a new dynamics of growth based on encouraging exports. Despite voluntarist policies, export activities were limited, outside Southeast Asian countries, to labour-intensive activities and to an increase in service activities (essentially tourism).

Let us recall that SAPs were envisaged by official authorities, with the support of the World Bank and the IMF, as a response to the crisis in Third World economies. In addition to re-establishing large balances, the goal of SAPs was to implement structural reforms in order to promote these countries' participation in the international market by encouraging export sectors at the expense of sectors connected with the internal market.

However, on examining the recent tendencies of FDIs (foreign direct investments), we see that underdeveloped countries have been increasingly marginalised in these flows. A new polarisation on the global scale has transformed some Third World countries into Fourth World countries. Direct foreign investments in underdeveloped economies have declined in various sectors and they have been refocused on developed countries. Thus the annual share of flows of FDIs toward underdeveloped countries declined from 26 per cent of the total in 1981–85 to 17 per cent of the total between 1986 and 1990. In addition, the underdeveloped countries' share of the total stock of FDIs declined from 21.2 per cent in 1987 to 19.2 per cent in 1990. Alongside this marginalisation of the Third World, from a geographical point of view these FDIs were concentrated in Latin America and Southeast Asia, which received almost 80 per cent of these flows, and there was a net regression in other areas, such as the Arab world and Africa.

These new tendencies indicate changes in the logic of the process of transnationalising production. The redirection of FDIs toward highly technological sectors and their relocalisation in developed countries shows that the search for low labour costs is no longer the multinational firms' chief concern. These changes in attitude are explained by the emergence of new technologies, and more precisely by technologies based on electronics and computers. The latter have diminished the labour component of traditional industrial activities and have thereby reduced the comparative advantage of underdeveloped countries. Henceforth, the competition among multinational firms will take place on the basis of the development of new technologies and access to markets. This explains the changes in the structure as well as the geographical destination of FDIs.

Critical Theories

The poor concrete results produced by SAPs have led to questionings and critical reinterpretations of their theoretical foundations. The inability of reforms to initiate new processes of growth and to improve underdeveloped countries' participation in the international economy encouraged the emergence of voices critical of the neo-liberal consensus that dominated thinking about development. Several theoretical aspects of the liberal consensus were subjected to criticism and challenge.

These authors criticised the financial reforms imposed by the IMF and the World Bank. Both institutions encouraged underdeveloped countries to liberalise the structures of financing for the economy and to do away with restrictions on the inflow and outflow of capital in order to ensure a more effective and rational distribution of capital. However, instead of increasing savings and investment, financial liberalisation has increased financial instability (Akyüz, 1994). Underdeveloped countries' experience has shown that saving does not automatically respond to an increase in interest rates, as theories of financial repression suggested. Saving depends on structures of the distribution of revenues in underdeveloped countries. Moreover, the increase in interest rates discouraged productive investment.

These observations were the source of a challenge to the view conveyed by theories of financial repression regarding savings as a precondition for investment. In this context, some authors went back to the Keynesian tradition, emphasising the role of credit and banks in monetary creation and financing investments. From this point of view, Asian experiments played an important role in challenging the theses of the financial repression school and in the rehabilitation of credit. This context of higher interest rates discouraged productive investments, and was the source of a major movement of financialisation in underdeveloped economies. On the other hand, the liberalisation of financial markets and the lifting of restrictions on inflows and outflows of foreign capital were the source of underdeveloped countries participation in international movements of capital. However, flows of capital toward Third World countries were essentially portfolio investments characterised by high mobility, and this increased instability and uncertainty in underdeveloped economies (Felix, 1994).

SAPs were also criticised because of their inability to re-establish external balances. The reduction of the external deficit required an increase in exports and a decrease in imports in the short term, and in the long term it required a thorough diversification of the structures of exports and imports (see Fontaine, 1994). However, short-term re-equilibration is hindered by the weakness in the elasticities of exports and the fixity of the demand for imports. In this context, the liberalisation of foreign trade and successive devaluations result in the deepening of external deficits. In addition, opening to the outside does not promote long-term investments in order to encourage greater diversification of the structures of the economy. From this point of view, public authorities and private enterprises limit themselves to acting on the existing sectors, seeking to improve efficiency and the allocation of resources. These options do not encourage new strategies of industrial investment with a view to constructing new comparative advantages.

The question of the state's disengagement and the relations between public authorities and the private sector have also been central to criticisms of the Washington Consensus (see Colclough and Manor, 1993). The Bretton Woods institutions' recommendations regarding the liberalisation of economic structures do not take into consideration the weakness of the private bourgeoisies in many Third World countries. In the Third World, the state has played an important role in the emergence and development of the private sector and of middle-class entrepreneurs. This new social stratum has always enjoyed the state's protection and has sought to make the most of the privileges the state has made available to it (Boratav, 1994). A study of the trajectories of the formation of the dominant social strata in the post-colonial period shows that they occurred in parallel with the constitution of states. Hibou (1996) notes:

> In fact, the appropriation of wealth, of the means of production, and especially of resources thus constituted not only an act of asserting a newly-acquired power but also an instrument allowing these various political factions to attempt, by making alliances and compromises, to constitute themselves as a true dominant class.

From this point of view, programmes of liberalising the economy, far from increasing entrepreneurial behaviour, actually strengthened the material bases of these social strata.

The economic recession in Southern countries that followed the application of SAPs led to a revival of the structuralist school. This school questions the privileged role accorded to supply, which led to an adjustment from below, and sought to rehabilitate demand in order to relaunch economic activity in underdeveloped countries (see Fontaine, 1994). The recessionary monetary policy recommended by the Washington Consensus resulted, according to the structuralists, in a major increase in production costs, and could bring about a decrease in supply leading to a greater imbalance between supply and demand. According to the structuralists, the reconstruction of competitiveness and the improvement of participation in the international economy require a relaunching of investment in Third World countries and a true strategy for rehabilitating demand.

Other theoretical aspects of the Washington Consensus have also been the target of criticisms. The central hypothesis of SAPs regarding the ability of markets to ensure an effective allocation of resources has been questioned. Brohman (1995) emphasises the role of institutions in regulating the political and economic order, while Lall (1995) stresses the fact that enterprises in underdeveloped countries do not have a complete knowledge of their environment, contrary to the claims of neoclassical theories. With regard to new technologies in particular, Lall notes that state intervention is necessary in order to ensure better access and to help develop local technological ability.

The results of SAPs and the theoretical criticisms led to a breakdown of the consensus that the Bretton Woods institutions had succeeded in constructing during the 1980s. The new options for development imposed by this consensus did not allow underdeveloped countries to initiate new processes of growth or to improve their participation in the international economy. Referring to the failures of the SAPs, Singer (Singer and Roy, 1993) has even described the 1980s as a lost decade for the Third World.

Notes

1 On this period of political turmoil, see Malley, 1996.
2 For a presentation of theories of dependency, see Blomström and Hettne, 1984.
3 For a critique of theories of dependency, see de Janvry, 1981; Seers, 1983.
4 On the development of these issues, see Stern, 1989.

5 See the testimony of a dozen of the pioneers in this field in Meir and Seers, 1988.
6 The IMF's basic model is founded on the work of Polak, 1957.
7 For a presentation of the IMF's models, see also L'Hériteau, 1986.
8 For a presentation of the IMF's model, see also Assidon, 1992.
9 On the various orthodoxies in matters of development, see Grellet, 1994.
10 On heterodox experiments in development, and in particular on the Austral and Cruzado plans, see Grellet, 1994.
11 We now have a relatively large literature on these models. See Adelman and Robinson, 1978; Bourguignon and Morrisson, 1992; Dervis, de Melo and Robinson, 1989; Ginsburg and Robinson, 1984; Robinson, 1989.
12 This presentation is based on Suwa, 1991.
13 See especially Taylor, 1980, 1990.
14 On the debate between the World Bank and the ECA, see Mosley and Weeks, 1993.
15 On these questions, see especially Fontaine, 1992, 1993; Mosley, 1992.
16 For the records of SAPs in various parts of the world, see Mosley, 1992; Hugon, 1995; Salama, 1995; Cornia, von der Hoeven and Mkandawire, 1992; Lall, 1995; Trotignon, 1993.

Chapter 2

Structural Adjustment and the Asian Model

Introduction

Alongside the inadequate results of structural adjustment programmes (SAPs) and the theoretical criticisms of the model underlying these experiments with stabilisation, the Washington Consensus was put in question by experiments with development in Southeast Asia. In the 1980s and early 1990s, when most Third World countries were experiencing a major slow-down in the processes of growth and were being heavily marginalised in the world economy, despite the application of several SAPs, Asian economies were achieving record rates of growth and improving their participation in the international economy by becoming active exporters of products involving new technologies.

These Asian experiments were all the more important because their strategies seemed to challenge the recommendations of the Washington Consensus and the prescriptions of the programmes of structural adjustment. In fact, at the time when the SAPs were recommending that the state disengage itself, Asian countries were building their success on strong state regulatory intervention. Moreover, whereas the SAPs called for international specialisation on the basis of the principle of comparative advantages and therefore the exporting of labour-intensive products, Asian economies were constructing their competitiveness on the basis of dynamic participation in new technologies. Finally, at the time when the Bretton Woods institutions were advising under-developed economies to redirect their growth processes towards external markets, Asian economies maintained close, dynamic relationships between activities connected with the internal market and export activities. Thus all these characteristics made the Asian experiments genuinely antinomic with regard to the practices and strategies for development suggested by supporters of the Washington Consensus.

The Asian experiments gave rise to an important debate about the causes of these successes in a context of a deep crisis in underdeveloped economies. The supporters of the Washington Consensus tried to make use of this debate in order to renew their analyses and demonstrate that the gap between Asian experiments and their prescriptions was not as deep as it seemed. The World Bank even suggested that African countries follow the model of Asian countries – revisited, of course, by liberal theories (Harrold, Jaywickrama, and Bhattasali, 1996). Other observers set out from these experiments to show that, on the contrary, the strategies for development proposed by supporters of the Washington Consensus were ineffective, and to challenge the latter's theoretical foundations.

These differing analyses gave rise to a plurality of representations of models of development in Asia. In this chapter, we will offer a critical presentation of the various ways of interpreting experiments with development in Asia. Despite the diversity and the plurality of the analyses devoted to these experiments, it is possible to distinguish four main types of interpretation:

- the first seeks to renew the analyses of the model of general equilibrium by taking into consideration the lessons to be drawn from these experiments in development;
- the second situates itself in the institutionalist tradition and tries to grasp the role of institutions in these experiments;
- the third belongs to the school of late industrialisation established by Gershenkron, who sought to analyse the strategies adopted by 'late comers' in order to find substitutes for the missing links in their development;
- the fourth is interested in the international conditions that made the emergence of new industrialised countries (NICs) possible.

Despite their diversity, these different schools constitute a radical critique of the pure model of general equilibrium that was at the base of the Washington Consensus. It must be emphasised that from the late 1980s to the mid-1990s, these experiments in development exercised strong pressure on programmes of structural adjustment and on the Bretton Woods institutions. In fact, economists increasingly referred to a 'new model of development' that presented itself as an alternative to adjustment. However, the Asian crisis lessened the attraction of these experiments in development for other Southern economies.

The Asian Experiments Revisited by the Market.

The Traditional Neoclassical Analyses and the Asian Experiments

In the mid-1970s, experiments with development in Southeast Asia constituted an important stake for the neoclassical school in the field of development economics. From that time on, the various neoclassical schools tried to bring these experiments within their analytical frameworks. At first, orthodox economists presented the successes of Asian countries as resulting from their respect for the principles of liberal economics and the laws of the market. In fact, the first neoclassical theses claimed that the dynamics of strong growth in Asia were the result of the state's neutrality within the framework of strategies of development oriented towards encouraging exports (Lanzarotti, 1992).

These tried to challenge state intervention in most Third World countries within the framework of strategies of import substitution. The state sought to aid industries directed towards the external market by means of a policy of protecting these industries against foreign competition and the adoption of a policy of relaunching internal demand in order to create the necessary outlets for these economic activities. However, according the supporters of state neutrality, the policies of import substitution did not make it possible for Southern countries to set up strong and durable processes of growth. In this context, it was imperative to carry out major changes in the strategies for development in underdeveloped countries by redirecting growth processes towards external markets. The implementation of a strategy of promoting exports and international participation in accord with the principle of comparative advantage required a decrease in state support for import-substitution activities, or at least a certain neutrality with regard to these different dynamics of growth.

Bhagwati (1978) was one of the first to defend the state neutrality necessary for the development of export activities and a dynamic mode of participation for underdeveloped countries in the international economy. Neutrality presupposes, according to Bhagwati, the equality of actual rates of exchange for exports and imports. For Krueger (1983), state neutrality presupposes an equality between the gap separating internal prices of products made for the internal market and that between the gap separating the internal prices of exportable products and their prices on the international market. This neutrality is necessary, according to these two authors, for the development of export processes that are capable of accelerating growth and promoting better participation for underdeveloped countries in the international market. According to Krueger (1980), it is this neutrality, and even a slightly more favourable bias in favour of exports, that explain the success and the performance of Asian economies.

In this first generation of neoclassical studies on the experiments in Asian countries, we must single out the research of Balassa (1981, 1982), which was highly influential in the early 1980s. In his studies, Balassa proposed the hypothesis that at the first stages of development Third World countries adopted strategies of import substitution of labour-intensive products. However, these strategies very soon came under a large number of constraints, such as the availability of new technologies and deficits in external balances. These difficulties led underdeveloped countries to redirect their development strategies towards external markets in order to re-establish external balances, lift the financial restrictions and gain access to new technologies. From this point of view, the path of development and progress for underdeveloped countries was the path of exports and participation in the international economy. In this perspective, the success of Asian economies in the 1950s and 1960s is explained by the reorientation of their dynamics of development towards encouraging exports in the 1970s and especially in the 1980s.

Balassa's studies were at the origin of the development of strategies of promoting exports in the Third World. On this view, state intervention should be limited to:

- the maintenance of the stability of the macroeconomic environment;
- the construction of physical infrastructures;
- making public goods – defence, basic education, the functioning of the judicial system and the protection of the environment – available to the various economic agents;
- the improvement of the functioning of the markets for labour, technology and financing;
- the elimination of the price distortions that lead to imperfections in the markets; and
- redistributing certain resources in order to help the poorest segments of the population.

Other studies in the liberal tradition continued to elaborate the hypothesis of the supremacy of dynamics of growth connected with the external market in relation to those connected with the internal market, and recommended that underdeveloped countries implement strategies to encourage exports (Berger, 1979; Bhagwati, 1988). All these studies constituted the schema used by the neoclassical school to interpret the strong processes of growth in Southeast Asia. For this school, state neutrality or temporary incentives to encourage exports and its disengagement from economic activity were at the origin of the growth processes drawn from the international market in Southeast Asia. These experiments demonstrate the ability of the free play of supply and demand on the market to provide an optimal allocation of resources in underdeveloped countries and to initiate balanced processes of growth.

However, these studies were very quickly challenged. A series of studies has shown that the rates of actual exchange for exports were superior to those of imports, and 'as a result, in South Korea, a bias in favour of exports existed, was important, and persisted' (Lanzarotti, 1992, p. 158). In addition, various studies have also shown that Asian countries set up strong protections (Lanzarotti, 1992). More and more economists emphasised the fundamental role played by states in regulating and setting up these dynamics of growth in most Asian countries (Johnson, 1981, 1982, 1984; Rosovsky, 1972). Other authors have proposed the hypothesis that there was a form of state capitalism in Asian countries, in order to bring out the pre-eminence of the state in economic development and the strong interpenetration linking the state and private companies (White, 1988).

Thus, far from verifying the pertinence of the claims made by the neoclassical school, Asian experiments with development demonstrated the necessity of state regulatory intervention and a strong bias in favour of exports. In addition, while actively committing themselves to exports, Asian countries continued to develop and protect their internal markets. All these results represent a challenge to the development strategies and theoretical foundations of the Washington Consensus. These criticisms led neoclassical authors to renew their perceptions and analyses of Asian realities with the development of the thesis of the *friendly market*.

A Small History of a Great Turnaround

The neoclassical attitude to the success of Asian experiments became increasingly untenable. Moreover, from the beginning of the 1980s on, Japan grew increasingly influential in international authorities and demanded to play a more important role in these authorities. The rise of Japan met with growing resistance on the part of the Americans, who had commercial conflicts with the Japanese and criticised the interventionist positions defended by Japanese leaders in the international authorities. From a theoretical point of view, Japan deviated from Anglo-Saxon doctrines of free trade and defended the necessity of state regulatory intervention in order to ensure the coherent functioning of decentralised economies.

In this perspective, from the end of the 1980s the World Bank was the site of a conflict between Japanese interventionist positions and American doctrines of free trade (Wade, 1996). Japan's influence increased as a contributor to the

World Bank and as a provider of aid for development on the international level. Japan encouraged the governments it aided to break with the liberal rhetoric of the World Bank and to promote a more dynamic and interventionist role for the state. From this point of view, Japan pointed to the Japanese and Korean 'successes' as proof of the interest and pertinence of its conceptions of development. Japan considered two series of interventions as fundamental. First, sectorial actions in order to promote the strategic sectors in economic development. Second, action in the financial domain with a view to favouring these strategic sectors through financing on concessional terms on the part of credit institutions.

Starting at the end of the 1980s, the divergences of opinion separating the World Bank and Japan became more marked, particularly after the publication of the 1987 Report on Development. The free-trade credo of this report is asserted in the analysis of the trade strategies, regarding which the Bank explains that:

> countries should move toward the adoption of a trade strategy directed toward the outside, that is, they should eliminate the bias with regard to exports, replace quantitative restrictions with tariffs, and adopt rates of exchange more in conformity with realities (World Bank, 1987, p. 3).

In addition, in this report the World Bank confirms its opposition to any form of state intervention in the functioning of economies, 'for when trying to improve the conditions in which the private sector functions, it doesn't take much to make them worse' (ibid., p. 89). It was in this context that the World Bank took up the issue of controls on interest rates, which were defended by Japan, and reasserted its opposition to this kind of state intervention and the capacity of the mark to ensure a rational allocation of the resources available for financing. Thus the report explains that:

> although control of interest rates and policies of selective credit make it possible to achieve certain specific objectives, on the whole they have unfavourable effects on the behaviour of savers, lenders, and borrowers (ibid., p. 136).

Japan criticised the new orthodoxy of this report and argued that the World Bank, despite the growing role played by Japan in its authorities and in its financing, had paid little attention to the specific characteristics of Asian experiments with industrialisation. According to Japan, the World Bank should draw its inspiration from these experiments in making its recommendations for Southern countries.

When L. Preston became the head of the World Bank, Japan undertook to finance a study on development in Asia in order to put into perspective its most important characteristics, particularly with regard to state intervention. This study was entrusted to a group of economists directed by J. Page and supervised by L. Summers, the Bank's vice-president in charge of research. Work on this study led to strong conflicts between Japan, who had commissioned the study, the team asked to prepare it, and the leadership of the World Bank. The final document resulted from a compromise among the different parties.

But work on this study and the World Bank's obligation to rethink its analyses led to the emergence of a new way of explaining the Asian experiments. This new hypothesis, couched in 'market-friendly' terms, was developed by Summers, and was to be central to the analyses of the 1991 Report on Development. This new approach develops a complementary view of the relationship between the state and the market and turns away from the neo-liberal and overtly anti-state approaches of the early 1980s. It is clearly formulated by Barber B. Conable, the former president of the World Bank, in the preface to the 1991 Report on Development, which emphasises that:

> one of the great lessons to be learned is that interaction between the state and the market promotes development. Experience shows that the chance of promoting economic growth and reducing poverty will increase to the extent that the action of the state and that of the market complete each other and inversely, and that conflict between them leads to dismal failures. The report describes a strategy for establishing cooperation between the state and the market, in which the latter has an opportunity to do what it does well and in which the former seeks essentially to make up for the inadequacies of the market (World Bank, 1991, p. iii).

Thus, the success of Southeast Asian countries is explained, according the World Bank, not by an excess of liberalism, but by convergent action on the part of the state and the market. Away with the radical and orthodox recommendations made by the Bank at the beginning of the 1980s, and hurray for synergy between state and market!

However, these analyses favouring a certain interventionism were already present in the Bank in 1989. In the Report on Development devoted to financial reforms, the Bank explains that 'public authorities have been forced to regulate and supervise the system' (World Bank, 1989, p. 45). Insofar as the impact of programmes of directed credit is concerned, even if the report emphasises the ineffectiveness of these programmes for certain countries, it recognises that:

> in other countries, on the contrary, these programs have had important effects. In Korea, the directives orienting credit toward industry increased the share allocated to industry from 44 per cent to 69 per cent between 1965 and 1967 (World Bank, 1989, p. 69).

This report uses the case of Korea to show the interest of a policy of directed credit. In fact, according to this report:

> the Korean government has exercised a significant control over the distribution of credit by combining moral persuasion and explicit programs. This policy has succeeded: the economy has rapidly developed (ibid., p. 70).

This view, which seeks to free itself from the normative character of the Walrassian model and to construct an approach capable of analysing current developments in Asian countries, was reaffirmed in the 1991 Report on Development. The latter asserts that:

> if markets are capable of playing their role, and they are allowed to do so, the economy will profit from it, and its gains will be substantial. When they fail and public authorities intervene prudently and knowledgeably to supplement them, the economy will gain still more. But when these two elements are combined, the facts tend to show that the whole is greater than the sum of the parts (World Bank, 1991, p. 2).

Later, the same report asserts that 'state intervention is not bad in itself. On the contrary, it is essential in numerous respects if one wants to exploit to the fullest an economy's potential' (ibid., p. 150).

Thus, this analytical schema breaks with the dogmatism and normativism of traditional neoclassical approaches and recognises the dynamic role that can be played by state intervention on behalf of development. The World Bank tried to use this new approach to understand the dynamics of growth in Asian countries.

The 'Market-friendly' Approach and Asian Experiments

The World Bank's report on development in Asia (World Bank, 1993) concerned eight countries: Japan, the NICs (new industrial countries) of the first generation (Hong Kong, Taiwan, Singapore, and South Korea) and the NICs of the second generation (Indonesia, Thailand, and Malaysia). All of these countries, with the exception of Hong Kong, began their process of development by adopting strategies of import-substitution, setting up activities whose production was intended for the internal market. Then, at different moments in their economic histories, they redirected their development towards the promotion of exports (at the end of the 1950s and the beginning of the 1960s for Japan, at the end of the 1960s for the first generation of NICs and the end of the 1980s for the second generation of NICs).

All of these countries experienced strong processes of growth during the period 1960–90, with a rate of investment exceeding 20 per cent of the GDP. A large part of this investment was made by private enterprises. In addition, most of these countries made large investments in human resources and in the acquisition of new technologies, which led to a strong increase in productivity.

Alongside these macroeconomic characteristics, the Asian countries studied were distinguished by different types of state intervention, the most important of which are:

- the subvention of credits for certain strategic sectors;
- the maintenance of low interest rates;
- protection for import-substitution industries;
- subventions for industrial activities in decline;
- support for public banks;
- public investments in research;
- support for export activities;
- making available to private enterprises the information necessary for their activities.

Once these interventions are identified, the World Bank had to analyse and explain them. This interpretation is all the more important because the Bank recommended totally different policies in underdeveloped countries in the framework of programmes of structural adjustment. How can these state interventions constitute the origin of the 'Asian success' when the Bank continued to prescribe the contrary to underdeveloped economies?

In the analysis of Asian experiments the Bank distinguishes two analytical schemas. The neoclassical schema sees free trade as leading to the success of Southeast Asian countries (Balassa, Bhagwati, Krueger), while heterodox schemas (Amsden, Wade) hypothesise that state intervention is the source of growth processes in Asia and recommend that other underdeveloped countries follow the Asian path in their efforts to restart development. The Bank's analysis differs from that of either of these schools, elaborating a new approach in 'market-friendly' terms that emphasises the coexistence of the state and the market in these experiments. In fact, according to the report, in underdeveloped countries the market cannot play its role of coordinating individual agents' projects, because of the imperfect character of the information and of competition. In such conditions, regulatory intervention on the part of the state becomes necessary in order to correct the market's imperfections.

In the World Bank's approach, it is possible to distinguish between two kinds of state intervention (World Bank, 1993). First, there are *fundamental interventions*, which seek to guarantee macroeconomic stability, to encourage investments in human capital, to set up a stable financial system, to diminish distortions in the system of prices and to allow access to new technologies. Alongside these interventions, the bank describes a second set that it calls *selective*. Among these selective interventions on the part of the state, it emphasises:

- a relative financial repression through the maintenance of positive but low interest rates;
- an orientation of credits towards certain sectors considered as strategic;
- a selective intervention in industrial matters, in favour of certain kinds of activities;
- an intervention in commercial matters in order to promote non-traditional exports.

After having established this distinction between the different types of state intervention, the World Bank's study tries to identify those which have played a fundamental role in the dynamics of growth set up in Asian countries. In this perspective, the Bank regards the first series of interventions, the *fundamental interventions*, as having played a basic role in the 'Asian successes'. In most of these countries, in fact, the state has tried to maintain macroeconomic stability and to preserve the major balances, and it has supported the development of a stable financial system capable of responding to the needs of the different activities. In addition, the states have played an important role in the development of human capital and in providing access to new technologies. Finally, the states have also sought to reduce distortions in the various systems of prices.

However, according to the World Bank, the achievements of selective interventions have varied (World Bank, 1993). Thus, according to this report, subvention for credit and its direction towards strategic sectors have played a significant role in the processes of growth in Asia. But these interventions were costly and this led Asian countries to reduce these interventions.

Nevertheless, these experiments are not easy to export, and cannot constitute a model to be followed by other underdeveloped countries. In addition, financial globalisation and the liberalisation of financial markets in many underdeveloped countries no longer allows states to repress their financial markets.

Intervention in matters of industrial policy is also difficult to implement. It requires a great deal of information about trade as well as a major prospective analysis in order to determine the sectors that should be privileged in matters of industrial development. In addition, some interventions are no longer compatible with the WTO's new regulations. According to the report, only interventions favouring exports have played an important role in experiments with development in Southeast Asia.

Ultimately, for the World Bank only interventions seeking to guarantee a stable macroeconomic environment and the absence of distortions in the price system have proven necessary and fundamental in the Asian experiments. Selective policies, apart from support for export activities, are expensive and difficult to implement. In addition, the success of some state interventions in Asia should not encourage underdeveloped countries to imitate them and to reject liberal economic reforms.

Thus, despite its critique of the basic neoclassical model, the approach in market-friendly terms nonetheless adopts that model's chief recommendations regarding development strategy by making the market central to the regulation of economic activity in underdeveloped countries and by directing their development strategies towards the external market. Everything has to change in order for everything to remain the same, says the hero of Lampedusa's novel *The Leopard*.

The Limits of the Market-friendly Approach

As soon as the Bank's report was published, the market-friendly approach was the subject of a series of commentaries and criticisms. Most economists recognised, however, that this report made it possible to elaborate the approach sketched out in the 1991 Report on Development (Yanagihara, 1994). In fact, the Bank sought to give a more precise content to its approach by distinguishing fundamental state interventions from selective interventions, and the role played by each of these in the Asian successes. In addition, the Bank acknowledged for one of the first times the positive role played by the state in the dynamics of growth in Asia (Lall, 1994). Such intervention is justified, according to the report, by the inability of the market to ensure the regulation of economies because of the imperfect nature of the information and of competition, particularly in underdeveloped countries. From this point of view, the Bank considers any intervention whose goal is to correct an imperfection of the market as market friendly.

However, this approach has attracted much criticism on the part of a large number of economists who emphasise the World Bank's desire to replicate Asian successes and build them into its analytical framework. This ideological concern put its stamp on the whole of the study and weakened the scientific work that had been done. The first series of criticisms has to do with the statistical studies that provided the basis for the econometric calculations in this document. In fact, a large number of authors emphasised the vague and often incomplete and selective character of the statistical information in this report, which casts doubt on the conclusions drawn by the Bank (Amsden, 1994; Lall, 1994; Wade, 1996).

In addition, the Bank's distinction between fundamental and selective interventions has no analytical basis (Lall, 1994). Why should investment in human capital be considered as fundamental, whereas interventions in the industrial sector are described as selective? Insofar as fundamental interventions are concerned, several authors contest the Bank's conclusion that the state played an important role in limiting distortions in the system of prices. A number of studies have shown that these distortions were relatively large in Southeast Asian countries (Hong, 1990; Kim and Roemer, 1979). Other authors tested the positive impact on economic growth produced by the distortion of prices created and maintained by the state (Kwon, 1994). Finally, Lall has demonstrated that price distortions in Southeast Asia were greater than in other underdeveloped countries (Lall, 1994). Thus, the Bank's report, for ideological reasons, seeks to minimise one of the strong points of the models of Southeast Asian countries, namely their lack of respect for the laws of the market in setting prices on the various markets. In fact, Amsden has drawn attention to a conscious strategy on the part of Korean governments aimed at structuring the system of prices in contradiction to the rules of commercial rationality. However, the 'wrong prices' respond to the needs of the productive apparatus and the necessity of maintaining and developing certain strategic sectors (Amsden, 1989).

But generally, many authors think that, because of the ideological limits imposed by the leadership of the Bank, this report did not make it possible to account for the complexity and richness of Asian experiments with development. In fact, many aspects that played a role in the 'Asian successes' were not mentioned in the report or were mentioned only in a peripheral manner. Thus, for example, the role of the state in acquiring and adapting new technologies was not sufficiently examined by the World Bank. And alongside these expenditures in the domain of research and development, states set up dynamic strategies for acquiring new technologies and making them available to business enterprises. Foreign direct investment (FDI) was one of the components of this strategy. From this point of view, Asian countries, contrary to the Bank's claims, did not open their borders to FDIs in an unlimited way. On the contrary, they opted for a controlled opening that was oriented first of all towards sectors having a strong content in new technologies.

In addition, the Bank's report did not sufficiently emphasise state intervention in the organisation and planning of competition among various groups in Asian countries. States were able to set up structures of cooperation and competition among the different groups. Thus groups engaged in strategies giving priority to growth in productivity rather than to immediate financial profitability in exchange for the protection that was provided by the state, and that allowed the various groups to realise substantial gains. Asian firms chose to increase their productivity rather than to reduce salaries in order to improve their competitiveness. States played an important role in organising competition and in arbitrating among the different groups. Thus control over the financial system allowed states to favour the groups that turned in good performances and to punish those that produced mediocre economic results.

State intervention also played a crucial role in determining the transition of Asian economies from labour-intensive activities to activities which were intensive in capital and new technologies. At this level, state support for these new strategic sectors allowed them to achieve a growth in productivity more rapid than that in labour-intensive sectors that had only minimal support, contrary to the claims made in the World Bank's report. In addition, support for these export sectors allowed them to enjoy very elevated benefits of scale.

Ultimately, the Bank's report and the new approach in market-friendly terms reduced the complexity and richness of Asian experiments to respect for the great macroeconomic equilibria and a series of state interventions in the financial domain, in the industrial domain and in order to promote exports – interventions that it hastened to forbid other underdeveloped countries to imitate (World Bank, 1993; Page, 1994). For the World Bank, the Asian experiments are time-bound and cannot be imitated by underdeveloped countries. The WTO's new regulations prohibit any state intervention in industrial matters. Moreover, the liberalisation of financial markets in the Third World and their opening to the outside reduced the various states' room for manoeuvre and action with regard to subsidies or the allocation of credit. What remained, then, of the Asian model in the 1990s, and how could the

Southern countries reproduce these experiments? For the World Bank, the only lesson the Third World should learn from these experiments was that they should respect the great macroeconomic balances and promote exports. In short, the Washington Consensus, so decried and criticised, was all that remained of the 'Asian success story' for the Third World, and its basic content revolved around the re-establishment of macroeconomic balances and the redirection of the processes of growth towards external markets.

Thus the market-friendly approach was only the World Bank's attempt to rehabilitate the Washington Consensus after the criticisms of the SAPs, based on their inability to reduce imbalances and restart growth in underdeveloped countries. This rehabilitation required the recuperation of the Asian experiments, which were beginning to be seen as alternatives to SAPs. However, this interpretation reduced and impoverished the content of these experiments in order to empty them of their subversive impact with regard to the model of general equilibrium in the field of development economics and SAPs. This interpretation was gradually abandoned by the Bretton Woods institutions and replaced by other interpretive schemas inspired by the institutionalist school.

The Asian Experiments Revised by Institutionalism

The neo-institutionalist school emerged in the field of development economics in the late 1980s. This school sought to increase the pertinence of theoretical frameworks by taking into consideration the institutions that played an important role in the regulation and coordination of agents' actions in a decentralised economy. It contested the models of traditional Walrassian macroeconomics and the market's ability to guarantee the coherence and coordination of the contradictory interests of the various agents involved. This incapacity of the market had its origins in the imperfect character of information and competition which reduced the rationality of agents' choices. In this perspective, intervention on the part of the state and other institutions became necessary in order to correct imperfections in the market.

In the early 1990s a plurality of institutionalist schools emerged in development economics (Israël, 1996; Yong, 1994). For these schools, the models of Walrassian equilibrium were not capable of grasping and analysing the specific characteristics of accumulation and actors' behaviour in underdeveloped countries. In the Third World, markets are less harmonious, labour markets are more segmented and the behaviour of economic agents reveals a gap separating it from the maximising rationality of the basic models

(Stiglitz, 1988). Thus in underdeveloped countries we see large migratory movements from the countryside to the cities, despite vast urban unemployment. In addition, the modalities of distribution are governed more by rules of sharing and communitarian norms than by the norms of productivity in the traditional microeconomy. These behaviours do not conform to the postulates of neoclassical theories, but they are rational from the point of view of the actors, according to the neo-institutionalist school, insofar as they allow agents to deal with the uncertainties created by the imperfections of the market.

Alongside the criticism of these theoretical foundations, the neo-institutionalist school challenges the recommendations of the Washington Consensus's and the liberal strategies of the SAPs. These economists believe that state regulatory intervention is necessary for the regulation and functioning of decentralised economies. In addition, the setting up of stable and coherent dynamics of growth requires, according to the neo-institutionalists, structuring a series of institutions through which the various economic agents, and notably the state and private enterprises, can discuss, negotiate and make decisions. These institutions allow a greater participation for the various actors in the management of the economy and guarantee that these choices and options will be internalised by the actors.

However, this criticism of the theoretical foundations of the Washington Consensus and of its strategies does not mean that there was a complete break with the model of general equilibrium. On the contrary, neo-institutionalism seeks to extend the explanatory scope of the neoclassical school by giving a microeconomic content to institutions. Thus, according to this school, institutions arise from the maximising behaviour of economic agents. These institutions allow the various agents to minimise the uncertainty connected with imperfect information and competition. This conception breaks with the holistic conceptions of the founding fathers of institutionalism, such as J.R. Commons.

The institutionalist school is interested in Southeast Asia's experiments with development. Moreover, Stiglitz, one of the main representatives of this school, helped prepare the World Bank's studies on the Asian experiments and he played a crucial role in aspects of the resulting report concerning the financing of development (Wade, 1996). But the neo-institutionalist interpretive schemas differ from the market-friendly approach by emphasising the importance of imperfect information and the imperfections of the market in a more significant way.

Stiglitz (1996) believes, following Debreu and Arrow, that the functioning of markets requires the fulfilment of three essential conditions: the absence of external factors and public goods; perfect competition; and the existence of a complete system of markets. Stiglitz's examination of the situations of underdeveloped countries allowed him to specify the following characteristics of their economies:

- markets are narrow or nonexistent, which makes it impossible to see prices as indices of scarcity;
- the weakness of the markets also indicates that prices cannot play their coordinating role and presupposes state intervention in the coordination of the various economic activities;
- the acquisition of new technologies is associated with risks that discourage businesses in underdeveloped countries;
- companies are relatively small in size and this does not allow them to profit from benefits of scale;
- businesses do not have the ability to negotiate strategically and this requires state intervention in order to help them in difficult negotiations.

Hence the low level of market development and the imperfect character of information and competition limit the validity of pure approaches based on the general equilibrium, according to Stiglitz (1996), and require that the state and the various institutions be taken into account in regulating decentralised economies. These institutions have as their function not to contest the superiority of market regulation but to correct these imperfections. On this view, the 'Asian successes' proceed from the ability of these economies to set up effective institutions that have actively contributed to the regulation and continuity of these dynamics of growth. However, the failure of socialist experiments in Eastern countries shows, according to Stiglitz, that a high degree of state interventionism is not necessarily synonymous with great effectiveness.

Above all, Stiglitz (1996) maintains, the Asian experiments have demonstrated the state's ability to organise competition. In fact, the various states in the region succeeded in establishing relationships of cooperation among business circles, between entrepreneurs and labour, between small enterprises and large enterprises. From this point of view, the business councils played an important role in the development of this collaboration. But this cooperation does not preclude a certain level of competition among the various actors.

Neo-institutionalism also accords the state an important role in promoting exports, particularly by creating the organs necessary to supply the information indispensable for these activities (Stiglitz, 1996). Exporters in underdeveloped countries encounter difficulties in identifying potential markets for their exports and the products sought on these markets. From this point of view, the creation of institutions specialising in the collection and diffusion of the necessary information made it possible to develop Asian countries' export capacities. In addition, these activities benefited from infrastructures put in place by the state, from preferential access to financing and from foreign currency.

But Stiglitz accords a special role to financial institutions in the successful experiments in development in Southeast Asia (Stiglitz and Uy, 1996). In this analysis, the authors emphasise that Asian governments intervened intensively in the functioning of their financial systems. Public authorities helped create banks and specialised financial institutions, and strongly regulated their functioning by directing credit towards some sectors at the expense of others and by subsidising them.

Governments created different means of regulating financial systems by asking banks to gauge their risks (Stiglitz, 1994). In addition, in most Asian countries the central banks supervised the loans granted by the commercial banks and thus discouraged speculative loans. The public authorities reduced competition in the financial systems by protecting banks that engaged in financing strategic sectors, by making it difficult to enter this market, particularly for foreign banks. Neo-institutionalist studies have also emphasised the state's role in directing credits towards strategic sectors, or, for political and social reasons, towards certain categories of the population, such as peasants. Among the sectors that have benefited from policies of state financial support in Japan and Korea, we can mention steel production, heavy industry, naval construction and the chemical industry.

Financial systems in Asian countries sought especially to develop and increase saving. Such saving, neo-institutionalists emphasise, guarantees the financing of productive investments and thus nourishes processes of growth (Stiglitz and Uy, 1996). For its part, economic growth makes it possible to increase saving and this broadens new dynamics of accumulation. Thus a virtuous circle of growth is created that has its origins in the mobilisation of saving. From this point of view, neo-institutionalists encourage Third World governments to develop structures which increase saving in order to increase investment and relaunch growth.

Generally speaking, the neo-institutionalists emphasise the role played by the various institutions, and especially by the state, in the Asian experiments by correcting the imperfections of the market. According to Stiglitz, these experiments should inspire the various Southern countries in revising their perceptions of the state and of its role in development. Among these functions, Stiglitz lists six:

- the promotion of education;
- the development of activities for the acquisition of new technologies;
- support for the financial system;
- the development of infrastructures, including roads and systems of communication;
- the prevention of the deterioration of the environment;
- the satisfaction of basic needs, including health.

However, these authors' interest in the institutions which have played an important role in Asian successes is not limited to the state. Other studies have shown that Asian countries have succeeded in structuring a complex network of institutions which have made it possible for different economic agents to respond to the problems of imperfect information and its asymmetry.[1] Some authors have maintained that, alongside various interventions by the state, Asian countries, despite the diversity of their experiments, have constructed the stability of their dynamics of growth on a series of institutions, including a stable constitutional order, an organised and qualified bureaucracy, organs for negotiation and deliberation between the government and business circles and the dynamic sectorial institutions that accompanied the development of new industrial activities (Cheng, Haggard and Kang, 1996).

The neo-institutionalist school became increasingly influential in the field of development economics, especially from the mid-1990s on. Moreover, the declining influence of market-friendly approaches allowed the neo-institutionalist approach to dominate studies of the Asian experiments and to make itself the dominant interpretative mode in the Bretton Woods institutions. From this point of view, its microeconomic conception and its view of institutions close to that of the neoclassical school made the task easier.

This view deviates from the Washington Consensus's analyses and strategies in that the latter cannot grasp the imperfections of the market in underdeveloped countries and the resulting specific characteristics of the actors' behaviour. Thus this school emphasises the institutions that play an important role in regulating decentralised economies and allow maximising agents to reduce the uncertainty connected with imperfect information and competition.

Despite these criticisms, this mode of interpretation does not break with Walrassian microeconomics. Instead, it seeks to enrich it by allowing it to grasp situations of imperfect information. In this perspective, it promotes a microeconomic conception of institutions and reduces them to rules and arrangements among economic agents. This view excludes from the field of its analysis collective behaviours and especially the relationships of force and power that run through institutions. Thus in its analysis of competition in Asia, the neo-institutionalist school stresses the relationships of cooperation among governments and enterprises without emphasising the power relationships that govern them. Many studies have now shown that Asian governments were not simple coordinators in the service of large Asian groups, but on the contrary forced them to adhere to their major choices for development in exchange for financing and protection (Amsden, 1989). The groups that refused to participate in the strategies defined by the state, and to undertake certain functions, were no longer able to enjoy the protection of the state, and especially its support and goodwill in the domains of financing and tax deductions. In Asia, these relationships of struggle and collaboration between the state and private groups certainly played an important role in the formation of a 'nationalist' and industrial bourgeoisie, whereas in the rest of the Third World profit-oriented behaviour remained the main characteristic of private firms. These aspects are not examined by the neo-institutionalist school, because its view of institutions is limited to relationships of cooperation and collaboration.

In addition, the neo-institutionalist school limits itself to a descriptive study of institutions, without being able to analyse the dynamics of their evolution. Thus at no time does the school offer an explanation of the processes of generating and forming institutions in underdeveloped countries and their role in the dynamics of accumulation. This school is not interested in comparative studies of the dynamics of institutions in various Third World countries in order to understand why they function effectively in Asian countries but are unable to play the same role in other countries. Thus it is easy for the neo-institutionalist school to emphasise the role played by institutions in 'successful' experiments in development, but it is difficult for them to understand and analyse the reasons for the ineffectiveness of institutions in other underdeveloped economies.

From an analytic point of view, the neo-institutional way of interpreting Asian experiments, especially in Stiglitz's studies, puts the accent on questions of financing development and the major role played by the mobilisation of saving. This thesis can be criticised both from the point of view of its theoretical foundations and from that of its concrete recommendations. From the theoretical point of view, by defending the hypothesis that saving is a precondition for financing, the neo-institutionalists break with Keynesianism and reconnect with the neoclassical view. However, recent theories of the monetary economy of production and studies of the experiments in financing development in Asian countries show the fundamental role played by credit, whether or not there is previous saving. From this point of view state intervention is important to guarantee the completion of the circuit and the destruction of money created *ex nihilo*.

Moreover, by recommending that states increase saving in order to finance growth, the neo-institutionalist school adopts the theses of financial repression that constitute one of the theoretical foundations of SAPs. These theories maintain that underdeveloped countries have significant savings that they cannot mobilise because of their repression by low interest rates. In order to make these savings available for accumulation, these theories recommend that interest rates be raised and financial markets liberalised. However, the financial reforms undertaken in Third World countries have resulted in decreased investment and a depression of productive economic activity along with a rise in speculative activities as a result of the rise in interest rates.

Finally, the neo-institutionalist school does not refer to the international context that has favoured these experiments in development. On one hand the context of the Cold War and American support, both financial and economic, played an important role in setting up these dynamics of economic growth. On the other hand, the explosion of the crisis at the end of the 1960s created room for manoeuvre for Asian countries that allowed them to improve their dynamics of growth.

Ultimately, the neo-institutionalist approach remains descriptive in its analysis of Asian experiments with development. It does not succeed in penetrating these experiments in order to analyse and explain their dynamics. Thus the genesis of institutions is not analysed. Moreover, the conditions of institutions' historical development and efficacity are not explained.

Theories of Late Industrialisation and the Asian Experiments

Theories of late industrialisation appeared in the 1940s, in the work of P. Rosenstein-Rodan and A. Gerschenkron (Ferrand, 1993). These theories sought to analyse the conditions that economies that are less advanced or late in industrialising have to fulfil in order to structure a coherent and effective process of industrialisation. From this point of view, the process of development differs from one country to another and from one period to another, insofar as less advanced countries invent new ways of catching up.

Rosenstein-Rodan (1943) was one of the first to develop the hypothesis that there was a different path to industrialisation and development for new industrial countries as compared with older nations. In a study on industrialisation in Eastern and Southeastern Europe, he emphasised certain conditions, such as a greater concentration of production, the opening of borders to direct foreign investment in order to gain access to new technologies, and strong state intervention in getting industrialisation started. In less advanced countries, the fulfilment of these conditions, along with strong state intervention in, could lead, according to Rosenstein-Rodan, to a 'big push' that would allow them to start up and accelerate development.

However, Rosenstein-Rodan notes that the conditions fulfilled by these countries differed from those fulfilled by the older industrialised nations in Europe. State intervention in economic planning and in directing productive investments appeared in the old capitalist powers only in the 1940s. Moreover, this intervention remained indicative, and did not have the obligatory character it assumed in the new industrialised countries. Thus this comparative analysis was the source of the central hypothesis of theories of late industrialisation. This reinvention of the paths towards development is explained by the fact that underdeveloped countries are faced from time to time with new difficulties that require new responses.

This basic hypothesis was adopted by A. Gerschenkron in his study of the history of industrialisation in nineteenth-century Europe.[2] He sought to identify the specific characteristics of the various experiments in development. For him, there is no single, indispensable path to economic development; instead, underdeveloped countries seek to structure substitutes for the missing links in their development. He classified underdeveloped countries according to their 'relative degree of backwardness', which depended on qualitative factors such as the level of education, the extent of industrial activities, the level of urban development, etc. These distinctions are important, for they make it possible to explain the scope and the specific characteristics of the processes of development.

Basing himself on experiments with industrialisation in nineteenth-century Europe, Gerschenkron (1962) defines six characteristics of the models of development. In his view, in countries with a significant degree of backwardness:

- industrialisation will begin with a great leap forward and will achieve very high rates of growth;
- industrial development will be carried out by very large enterprises;
- industrialisation will give priority to the means of production at the expense of consumer goods;
- the pressure exerted by the population on the levels of consumption will be very strong;

- arrangements and mechanisms for financing industrial development will be more important;
- the agricultural sector will not be able to provide the necessary outlets for manufactured products.

From a methodological point of view, Gerschenkron seeks to study the specific characteristics of development in each country without trying to construct a general model of industrialisation for underdeveloped countries on the basis of his observations and historical studies.

Gerschenkron's studies led, in the 1960s and 1970s, to a great deal of further research on late industrialisation. This research pursued three directions (Ferrand, 1993). First, a series of studies sought to test Gerschenkron's hypotheses. For example, Barsky (1969) verified these hypotheses by using econometric modelling and tried to construct the concept of a relative degree of backwardness. Good (1973) studied in greater detail the role of the banking system in experiments with late industrialisation. Gregory (1974) used this mode of interpretation to analyse Russia's development.

Other authors undertook to develop Gerschenkron's analytical method. For instance, Robinson (1972) studied social tensions and conflicts in processes of industrialisation. In addition, the notion of 'catching up' that Gerschenkron borrowed from Veblen gave rise to an important debate. Some authors contested the hypothesis of an international convergence of the levels of labour productivity with the transfer of technologies and foreign direct investments (FDIs) from developed countries towards underdeveloped countries (Findlay, 1978).

Finally, other authors sought to apply the initial model to new experiments in development. In this perspective, a series of studies focused on the historical evolution of the Japanese economy (Rosovsky, 1961; Cole, 1978). Hirschmann (1968) analysed Latin-American experiments in development by using the interpretive schema of late industrialisation.

However, theories of late industrialisation declined in influence after 1980, following the crisis in development in most underdeveloped countries and the rise of the Washington Consensus. Pure models of general equilibrium were opposed to theories of late industrialisation and challenged their methodological foundations as well as their theoretical contents. From a methodological point of view, the Washington Consensus did not adopt the idea that underdeveloped countries were different in ways that required specific solutions. On the contrary, the Bretton Woods institutions maintained that there was only one, universal path to development, the one it recommended to underdeveloped countries without regard to their specific characteristics. Moreover, the Washington Consensus rejected the idea of structural action and strategic intervention on the part of the state in order to promote development. Instead, the liberalisation of internal markets and making them more open to the international economy are the watchwords of the Bretton Woods institutions and the SAPs applied by underdeveloped economies as a group.

However, at the end of the 1980s there was a turnaround in the ideological and intellectual context. Neo-liberal theses lost their hegemony, as a result of their inability to provide adequate responses to the crisis and the rise of unemployment in most underdeveloped countries. Moreover, the SAPs did not allow underdeveloped economies to re-establish their macroeconomic equilibria and to resume growth. Finally, at the same time, new Asian powers emerged on the international scene and became genuine rivals of the old industrial powers. In this context, there was a resurgence of studies on late industrialisation with the emergence of a new generation of studies that sought to understand the Asian experiments in order to improve the basic model. The revival of this school of analysis in the 1990s is characterised by a plurality of approaches. In the following section, we will examine these various interpretive schemas for studying Asian experiments in development.

The 'Flight of Wild Geese' Model and Asian Experiments

The 'flight of wild geese' model was developed by the Japanese economist K. Akamatsu (1962) in the 1930s, in order to explain Japan's development. This theory describes the evolution of the industrial structure in each economy in passing from labour-intensive industries to capital-intensive industries. According to this theory, each industrial activity goes through a life cycle characterised by a period of expansion followed by a decline in its competitiveness. This evolution follows an inverted V-curve that reminded the author of the 'flight of wild geese' (Korhonen, 1994). This theory explains in the same way the phenomena of delocalisation of industries from one country to another.

This school experienced a major revival in the 1980s, thanks to the resurgence of theories of late industrialisation. Thus K. Yoshihara (1986) adopted this model to analyse Japan's development. In his analysis, he showed that the structure of Japanese exports went through great transformations between the end of the nineteenth century and our own time. Japanese exports at the end of the nineteenth century were dominated by products such as silk and cotton. Starting with the economic crisis of the 1930s, Japan started exporting textiles and labour-intensive manufactured products. In the 1950s,

Japan began to export capital-intensive products such as equipment. In the 1970s, Japanese exports consisted of products intensive in new technologies, such as automobiles and computers. The evolution of the structures of exportation reflects the evolution of Japanese industry's structures of production and the transformation of its competitiveness. According to Yoshihara, the evolution of the structures of production in Japan resembles the 'flight of wild geese' model insofar as the decline of an export sector leads authorities to promote a new sector by protecting it and according it the necessary advantages. For Yoshihara, transfers of technology, foreign direct investments and trade within a region make it possible to generalise the development of the richest countries towards those who are less well off.

This model was also adopted at the end of the 1980s to explain the dynamics of growth in the region of Southeast Asia (Rowthorn, 1996). These analyses start out from the observation that the dynamics of growth in the Japanese economy allowed rapid development in Southeast Asia and the emergence of the first generation of NICs (Korea, Taiwan, Singapore and Hong Kong). In addition, the development of these countries favoured the appearance of the second generation of NICs (Indonesia, Malaysia and Thailand). The enlargement of these spaces of growth made it possible to bring other countries such as China and Vietnam into this process.

This transmission of growth led some authors to adopt the hypothesis of the 'flight of wild geese' to explain the dynamics active in this region, which involved a relocalisation of industries that were losing their competitiveness from the more developed countries towards the less advanced countries. In this perspective, trade is a means of transferring goods and technologies among countries. In fact, exports of merchandise from developed countries towards underdeveloped countries made it possible to introduce new goods. Moreover, commerce allowed the transfer of the equipment and technologies necessary for the production of this same merchandise in underdeveloped countries once they had attained maturity. This transfer allowed developed countries to specialise in the production of new, capital-intensive goods and to export them to less developed countries, whereas the latter, having attained maturity, began to export products to the former.

Transfer through trade was strengthened in recent years, according to this school, by FDIs and transnational firms (TNFs). Thus TNFs used FDIs to delocalise to underdeveloped countries the activities that were labour-intensive and losing their competitiveness in developed countries. This delocalisation allowed developed countries to restructure their industrial activities and to redirect them towards activities intensive in capital and technology.

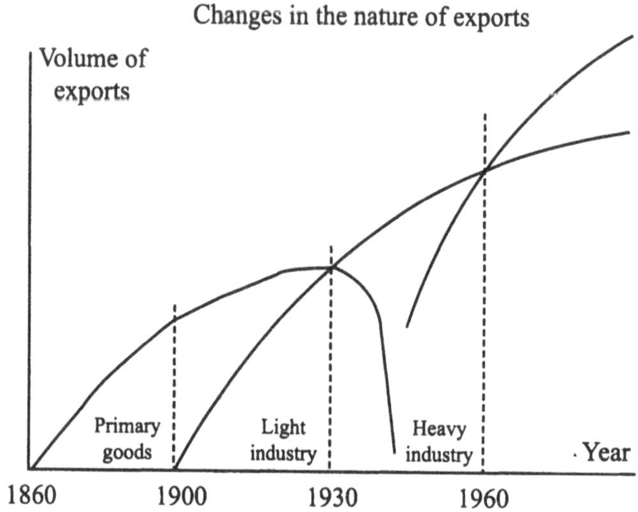

Figure 2.1 The 'flight of wild geese' model in the development of Japan's exports

Source: Yoshihara, 1986.

This analytical schema explains the dynamics of growth in the region as resulting from these processes of the localisation and delocalisation of industrial activities from one country to another. In Southeast Asia, Japan, and, in a second stage, the second-generation NICs, these localisations and delocalisations were central to the process of transferring activities among economies and in the emergence of the second-generation NICs.

This school has been subjected to a number of criticisms (UNCTAD, 1996a, 1996b). First of all, some authors emphasise that the delocalisation of Japanese industrial activities, and a few years later, those of the first-generation NICs, in the region was not a natural process, as the 'flight of wild geese' theory suggests. On the contrary, this transfer required strong intervention by the Japanese government in order to help firms delocalise their activities, notably through various programmes of cooperation, and also a high degree of intervention in the host countries in order to accept the delocalised industries and fulfil the conditions required to make them profitable again. This transfer of activities allowed the Japanese government to reproduce in various other countries in the region the mechanisms of intervention and the specific instruments of its industrial policy.

In addition, this school does not take into consideration the conflicts to which this transfer of industrial activity can give rise. In fact, the 'flight of wild geese' theory presents an idyllic, harmonious view of transnational firms' delocalisation of industrial activities from the more developed to the less developed countries. UNCTAD's experts remind us that this process of transfer can lead to conflicts of interest among producers in underdeveloped countries who try to completely master the new activities and to break away from the firms in the developed countries and the transnational firms that are trying to supervise and keep control over the delocalised activities (ibid.).

The 'flight of wild geese' thesis assumes that FDIs, and especially those made by Japan, played an important role in the transfer of activities in Southeast Asia. This recycling of comparative advantages is supposed to be the source of the strong dynamics of growth in the region. However, this thesis has to be qualified for several reasons. First of all, we must observe that while second-generation Asian countries have received large amounts of FDI, Japan and the NICs of the first generation have received only small amounts of FDI. Moreover, we must emphasise that Japan did not start making substantial FDIs until 1985 (Aykūz, 1996). In fact, up to that time, the total of Japanese FDIs did not exceed $84 billion. However, starting in the second half of the 1980s, Japanese FDIs reached an annual average of $45 billion before decreasing to an annual average of $38 billion in the 1990s.

We examine the structure of Japanese FDIs, we see that primary activities were important in 1980, and constituted almost 25 per cent of the total. However, starting in the mid-1980s, there was a decrease in manufacturing activity, whose share dropped from 35 per cent to 25 per cent of the total, and an important rise in tertiary activities, which represented more than a third of the total. The latter activities were essentially commercial in nature, in order to help distribute Japanese products abroad. In addition, from the geographical point of view, the FDIs in the manufacturing domain in Southeast Asia did not exceed $1 billion in 1985. But from 1985 on, Japanese manufacturers' FDIs in the region greatly increased. This development was closely followed by South Korea and Taiwan, which sought to delocalise their activities in the region. However, despite this significant increase in FDIs made by the Japanese and first-generation NICs in the region, extra-regional FDIs remained larger in some second-generation NICs. Thus in Indonesia and Malaysia, extra-regional FDIs represented almost 60 per cent and 42 per cent, respectively, of the total FDIs (UNCTAD, 1996a, 1996b). In addition, the total of extra-regional FDIs reached almost 40 per cent in the SEATO countries.

Thus, according the 'flight of wild geese' schema, foreign direct investment began to play an important role in structuring a zone of regional growth and delocalising comparative advantages only in the second half of the 1980s. This delocalisation of Japanese FDIs in the region followed the rise in the yen after the 1985 La Plaza accords among the governments of the developed countries. But even in this period, FDIs made by the Japanese or by the first-generation NICs were not dominant in the total of FDIs. These empirical observations make it possible to put this theoretical school in perspective. Moreover, we must note that the dynamics of growth in Southeast Asia considerably preceded the year 1985, and in fact dated from the end of the 1970s and from the 1970s.

The 'flight of wild geese' theory accords an important role not only to FDIs but also to trade in the transfer of comparative advantages from the developed countries to underdeveloped countries in the region of Southeast Asia. However, this hypothesis also seems to be contradicted by the evolution of the facts. If we consider the case of Japan, we see that the Japanese trade surplus with other countries in the region had a tendency to increase rapidly, contrary to the hypotheses of this theoretical school, and the development of these partners did not decrease their dependency on Japanese exports. This surplus rose from $6 billion in 1985 to $27 billion in 1994. Moreover, the share of Japanese imports of the labour-intensive products of the region remained small. In fact, despite the growth of Japanese imports from the region, Japan represents only a secondary market for countries in the area, since per capita it is about as important as the United States or Western Europe. Exports from these countries to Japan represent no more than 10 per cent of the total (ibid.). However, the first-generation NICs played a more important role in creating an intra-regional trade process that promotes growth.

Ultimately the 'flight of wild geese' theory runs up against limits in its attempt to analyse the dynamics of growth in Southeast Asia. The harmonious and coordinated transfer of competitiveness from the more developed countries, Japan and the first-generation NICs, towards less developed countries, the second-generation NICs, China and Vietnam, played only a limited role in Asian experiments. Manufacturing FDIs made by developed countries were not directed towards countries in this region until late in the game. Before, Japanese and Korean FDIs in the region had as their goal to acquire the supplies of raw materials necessary for their economies to function. From the trade point of view as well, if Japan's role remains relatively marginal, the second-generation NICs reoriented themselves towards the region in a significant way only starting in the second half of the 1980s.

Taken together, these observations lead us to qualify the role of trade and FDIs in explaining the dynamics of growth in Asia and to examine in much greater detail the internal conditions, and in particular the role of interventionist policies on the part of the state.

Governing the Market in Asia

One of the most important schools of thought that led to the revival of theories of late industrialisation is the one developed by Wade and Amsden around the hypothesis of the 'governed market'. For Wade (1990), the study of Asian experiments with development shows that the state played an active role in the dynamics of growth through:

- the redistribution of land through agrarian reform, especially in Japan, Taiwan, and Korea;
- control over the financial system and the direction of credit according to the needs of industrial financing;
- the maintenance of the stability of prices (interest rates, rates of exchange, price levels) that affect the profitability of investments;
- protecting national enterprises from foreign competition, and putting foreign currency at their disposition for the needs of the economy;
- aid accorded by the government to certain strategic industries.

These interventions and the 'successes' to which they led put in question, according to Wade, both liberal and market-friendly theories. In fact, in the Asian experiments it is a matter of neither coexistence nor synergy, but rather of domination and governance of the market by the state. The 'governed market' approach hypothesises that strong state intervention in Asian countries was the source of their strong dynamics of growth and the structuring of productive networks having a relatively high degree of coherence. This intervention is necessary to ensure an allocation of resources that can increase accumulation and improve the competitiveness of national economies.

The governance of the market is located, according to Wade (1990), on three levels:

- the state's conception of large, productive public and private investments in strategic sectors and in the acquisition of new technologies. However, these investments should not be completely protected from internal and

external competition. In fact, the state undertakes to organise competition in such a way as to avoid purely profit-oriented behaviours;
- strong state intervention through subsidies, aid and access to credit, in order to decrease the uncertainty regarding investments. But these interventions affect prices and, in particular, they make it possible to promote a different allocation of resources from the one that the free play of the market would have favoured. This new allocation of resources ensures that the strategic sectors will develop and that new, productive sectors will emerge in underdeveloped economies;
- the development of a large number of institutions for discussion, negotiation and coordination of the state's activities and those of public and private enterprises.

State intervention is one of the characteristics of contemporary late industrialism. The experiments in development made in the eighteenth century by the first capitalist nations did not require this kind of intervention and the industrial bourgeoisies, together with banking capital, were able to begin the development of new industrial structures and trade relationships. State intervention became necessary with new generations of capitalist development after the economic crisis at the end of the nineteenth century. Moreover, its importance was proportional to the degree of the country's backwardness. Thus in our own day, state action in Southeast Asia is even more important, according to the theoreticians of late industrialisation, than it was in Germany at the end of the nineteenth century or in Japan in the 1930s.

The governed market thesis was also defended by Amsden, who overtly subscribed to the late industrialisation theory initiated by Gerschenkron (Amsden, 1990). Amsden explains that his goal, following Gerschenkron's model, is to determine the general properties of late industrialisation. This analysis is supposed to make it possible to define and comprehend the differences between countries undergoing industrialisation.

The first characteristic of the new processes of industrialisation, in relation to those studied by Gerschenkron, is the primacy of activities of technological apprenticeship and imitation (Amsden, 1989). From this point of view, underdeveloped countries have an advantage with respect to the old industrial powers to the extent that they do not have to repeat the history of technology and create already existing techniques. In fact, whereas the first capitalist industrial powers, such as England and France in the eighteenth century, gained access to technology by inventing it, the new industrial powers, such as Germany and the United States, resorted to innovation in order to gain access to new technologies a century later. Today, the NICs acquire access to new technologies by importing them and transferring them from the developed countries. However, this transfer has given rise to intense efforts on the local level to master and learn this technology. The new industrial nations have neither the means nor the scientific and technological structures required to develop new technologies. Hence imports remain the chief means of acquiring technology. The state helps enterprises to import new technologies and especially to develop the local structures for mastering and learning it in order to increase productivity.

Alongside the modes of access to new technologies, Amsden, like Wade, believes that recent experiments in late industrialisation are characterised by strong state intervention. Amsden emphasises three kinds of state intervention in Southeast Asia. The first of these is connected with the state's role in conceiving and formulating strategic scenarios for development. The state decides which new industrial sectors to develop in order to maintain and increase the national economy's competitiveness. In South Korea, despite opposition by the World Bank and foreign investors, the state decided in the early 1970s to develop major capacities in basic and intermediary industries such as steel-making, chemicals, and petrochemicals.[3] During the same period, these sectors were strengthened by the development of a sector producing equipment. In addition, from the end of the 1970s, Korea diversified its production base by extending it into electronics and this was not limited to electronic devices for the general public, but also included electronic components and equipment.

The state, through its industrial policy, planned and organised the development of these strategic sectors. It also supported them by protecting them from foreign competition and by helping them with financing. The development of these sectors allowed Korea to improve its position in the international economy. The rise of these new sectors, which provide the basis for the new technological paradigm in gestation, permitted the Korean economy to increase its competitiveness. The role of the state in formulating strategic scenarios is not peculiar to South Korea. In all these countries the various government departments, and especially those that are in charge of industrial development and technology, are in the vanguard of thinking about options and alternatives in order to promote a process of structural changes that can support these countries' dynamics of growth and their competitive participation in the international market.

Amsden also emphasises the role of the state in organising competition in Asian countries (Amsden and Singh, 1994, 1989). In this context, Amsden points out that a high level of competition does not promote growth and industrialisation. Moreover, the absence of competition, as the experience of the former socialist countries showed, does not aid the construction of an effective and competitive industrial system. Thus the whole question, Amsden says, is how to determine the optimal degree of competition capable of ensuring a maximal rate of growth industrial production and productivity over the long term (Amsden and Singh, 1994).

According to Amsden, Asian countries were able to combine a certain level of competition with the coordination of the various groups necessary in order to maintain a high level of economic growth. The state played an important role in organising and structuring this competition. Thus, in Japan, the state very quickly challenged the antitrust legislation inherited from American domination and tried to reconstitute the old Zaibatzu. Several forms of cartelisation were favoured by the MITI. However, the MITI also encouraged competition among the large Japanese groups and, 'in a general manner', Amsden and Singh (1994, p. 647) note, 'competition is encouraged or limited in relation to the branch and the stage of its development'. The state's role in matters of competition is not limited to internal competition but involves also international competition by guaranteeing national groups the protection necessary for them to develop. However, in exchange for this protection, the MITI required all groups to produce results in the area of exports.

In South Korea, the state encouraged the establishment of large industrial groups, or Chaebols. However, it prevented any agreement among the groups and urged them to behave as competitors. In addition, the state supported national groups in international competition. Thus Amsden and Singh observe that:

> these two countries [Japan and South Korea] tried to encourage through competition a dynamic rather than static efficacity; instead of letting maximal competition operate, the two countries deliberately restricted competition by limiting it in many sectors in order to increase their rates of investment and to accelerate their technological development. But competition, understood in a sense different from that used in the manuals, was also very much encouraged: both Japan and Korea promoted an oligopolistic rivalry between conglomerates in the various branches (ibid., p. 654).

Thus, according to Amsden, a high level of concentration of economic activities is central to experiments in late industrialisation. Even Taiwan, whose industrialisation simplistic analyses see as the result of small enterprises, has large groups that played, despite a certain decline in concentration, an organising role in industrialisation.

These experiments differ from experiments with industrialisation at the dawn of capitalism, when the size of enterprises was limited. Since the nineteenth century, the size of enterprises in countries that have been candidates for industrialisation has steadily grown in order to deal with international competition and to acquire the means necessary to implement a major policy of investment and an ambitious industrial strategy. States have tried to aid the formation and concentration of large industrial groups. But these states, alongside the support they provided for the formation of large groups, also promoted competition in order to discourage profit-oriented behaviours and to encourage the various groups to adopt dynamic strategies in the industrial domain.

The third domain of state intervention in Southeast Asia concerns, according to Amsden, the regulation of prices. State intervention in prices occurs through several mechanisms, including:

- tariff protections for the internal market;
- subsidies for exports;
- investments and support for the acquisition of new technologies;
- making foreign currency available to enterprises involved in exports;
- the maintenance of different rates of exchange.

These different kinds of intervention act on prices and are basic for the establishment of relative systems of prices different from those that would have resulted from the free play of the laws of the market. According to Amsden, these are 'wrong relative prices', insofar as they respond more to the requirements and needs of the productive system than to the laws of the market (Amsden, 1989, 1991).

State intervention of this kind is explained by the differing productivity of countries. The differential in productivity leads to the establishment of a structure of relative prices favourable to countries whose level of development is more advanced. The maintenance of this structure of relative prices will not promote the development of industrial activities in less advanced countries, which will be limited in the international market to exporting the agricultural products for which they have a natural advantage. Facing the difficulty of acting on productive structures because of the obstacles to the transfer of technologies, state intervention regarding prices makes it possible to diminish the gaps and helps less advanced countries to begin experiments in industrial development.

The new formulations of the theory of late industrialisation differ with respect to the work of the founding fathers in this field in the status they accord their theory. Whereas Gerschenkron limited his analysis of experiments with industrialisation, and did not attempt to formulate recommendations for underdeveloped countries, the new theoreticians of late industrialisation go further and give their work a normative aspect by setting as an objective, on the basis of the lessons learned from experiments with industrialisation in Southeast Asia, to formulate a series of proposals for Third World economies. Thus Wade (1990) makes the following recommendations:

- the use of national policies to promote national industrial development and to direct it towards industries whose growth is important for the economy's future;
- the use of protection to construct international competitiveness for industrial activities;
- granting priority to export activities;
- welcoming multinational corporations and directing them towards exports;
- the promotion of a system of bank financing controlled by the government;
- the promotion of gradual financial and commercial liberalisation in accord with well-defined stages;
- the establishment of an agency or council charged with thinking about the future of growth;
- the development of solid political institutions before attempting democratisation, and the development of corporatist institutions in order to ensure greater cooperation among the various actors;
- the promotion of reforms in interventionist countries in order to construct institutions capable of conducting a modest industrial policy.

Ultimately, in its analysis of Asian experiments with development, this school of late industrialisation emphasises the role of state intervention in the success of these experiments. This intervention is necessary in order to construct productive coherences and to guarantee them an active participation in the international economy. In a second phase, these authors recommend reducing state intervention in matters of industrial policy, and letting the market and complementary institutions take care of the allocation of resources. In addition, they recommend that underdeveloped countries orient their development towards the promotion of exports in order to construct the competitiveness of the industrial sector and to ensure the maintenance of the main macroeconomic balances.

Thus, these new theorists of late industrialisation, by moving from analysis to a normative discourse, are only recommending a capitalist mode of development insofar as the long-term objective of their recommendations is to ensure the growth of production and productivity and to correct the imperfections of the market by means of state intervention. The role of the state is supposed to diminish as the countries develop and succeed in structuring the mechanisms for trade regulation in their process of growth. The divergences between these theorists and the neoclassical and institutionalist schools have to do with the means of constructing a coherent structure of trade. In actuality, for the various schools of late industrialisation, capitalism remains the sole horizon of humanity, and differences arise only concerning the most effective means for achieving this stage of development.

Profit, Saving and Investment in Asia

Other authors return to the hypothesis of state intervention in Asia in order to show that it seeks to guarantee profits for high-level firms in order to encourage saving and investment (Akyüz and Gore, 1994). These authors emphasise the role of profit and investment in the analysis of the dynamics of growth in Asia. They explain that high levels of investment played a major role in the dynamics of growth in Asian countries. These investments are related to high rates of saving proceeding from the increase in profits and growth. According to these authors, the state played an important role in all this by creating guaranteed incomes for the large groups, and by ensuring that they would enjoy conditions allowing them profits greater than those that a free market could provide.

This hypothesis assumes that profit, savings, and investment in relation to the GDP are proportionately greater in Asian countries than in other underdeveloped countries (Singh, 1996). In addition, this hypothesis may have important consequences on strategies for development. In fact, since the WTO's new rules prohibit state intervention in matters of industry and trade, governments can no longer intervene in order to support the development of certain strategic sectors, as Asian governments did for several decades. In addition, governments can no longer support their exports nor limit or apply high tariffs on their imports. These new restrictions are such as to reduce underdeveloped countries' room for manoeuvre. However, the WTO accords do not prohibit state intervention on behalf of enterprises in fiscal matters, saving, or investment. From this point of view, the state's action regarding profit and saving makes it possible to get around the WTO accords and provides state with an opportunity to intervene in favour of their enterprises in order to construct and strengthen their competitiveness.

However, this mode of interpretation is challenged by an examination of Asian experiments and a comparison of these economies with other economies. It is true that if we examine the situation of the Japanese economy, for example, we see that the series profit–saving–investment during the period 1950–75 can only confirm the hypothesis defended by these authors. In fact, during this period, state intervention allowed enterprises to make high profits and achieve large savings, and this permitted them to make major investments. But macroeconomic studies have demonstrated that Japanese firms' profit rates and margins were lower than those of American firms, even though their rates of investment were higher (Blaine, 1993). In addition, if we examine the case of Korea, we see that profits declined after 1978, whereas investments continued to increase (Singh, 1996).

Experiences in other developing countries, particularly in Latin-America, have shown that a rise in enterprises' profits and saving does not necessarily lead to a rise in investment. In fact, during the 1980s, large Latin-American enterprises achieved, after major restructuring, large increases in profits and saving. However, in a context of uncertainty and financial liberalisation, this surplus in saving was directed essentially towards the financial markets at the expense of the productive sphere (Palma, 1996).

More fundamentally, these analyses minimise the role played by banking systems in the various Asian countries in financing the dynamics of growth. This hypothesis assumes that enterprises made these investments using their own funds. However, several studies have shown the important role played by the banking system in financing the investments made by Japanese enterprises. Kojima (1995) estimates that between 1966 and 1970 the share of bank credits in financing Japanese activities was 49 per cent of the total investments, whereas it was 12.4 per cent in the United States, 20.3 per cent in Great Britain, 29.6 per cent in Germany and 27.4 per cent in France. Between 1970 and 1989, whereas the share of internal investments in the main developed countries represented more than 60 per cent of the total financing, it was only 40 per cent in Japan and 30 per cent in Korea. The share of bank financing in these investments in Japan is explained by the close relationships existing between enterprises and banks, which allowed the latter to hold part of the enterprises' capital. In Korea, the banks are run by the state, and therefore adopt policies for financing enterprises that are in accord with the government's general scenarios for development.

Ultimately, it seems that if state support for enterprises allowed them to achieve greater profits and led them to adopt a dynamic policy in matters of investment, it is difficult to put the series profit–saving–investment at the centre of the processes of growth observed. In fact, as various proponents of the late industrialisation thesis have emphasised, several other factors have played an important role in Asian countries' experiments. These authors have stressed the role of the state in regulating prices or in organising competition. Others have also emphasised the role played in these 'successes' by efforts to master and learn new technologies. These various analyses force us to reconsider the basic Walrassian model by emphasising the influence of state intervention on experiments in development. Proponents of the theory of late industrialisation present Asian models as an alternative to the Washington Consensus and to the SAPs that the Bretton Woods institutions have continued to recommend.

However, beyond the analysis of the special weight of certain elements in the dynamics of growth in Asian countries, theories of late industrialisation do not provide a general theoretical framework capable of analysing these experiences. On the contrary, like the supporters of the profit–saving–investment triad, they erect these particular points and these partial explanations into a general thesis regarding Asian development. In addition, the combination of facts with a multitude of observations cannot make it possible for this school to formulate the general theoretical framework it lacks. The supporters of this theory have carried important research on Asian experiments with developments that have allowed them to better understand it, and to refine our perception of development in this part of the Third World. However, the accumulation of this critical mass has not resulted in the development of a more abstract reflection in order to construct a general line of analysis and overall concepts capable of grasping the specific characteristics of these various experiments. On the contrary, observations and empirical studies have been used much more in a normative way in order to define avenues and strategies for developing capitalism in the Third World.

In addition, as a whole these schools analyse experiments which develop in Asia without paying any attention to outside conditions. Instead, they emphasise the internal conditions for development. But today it is difficult to study Asian development without taking into account the international context and without gauging its role in Asian 'successes'. First of all, the context of the Cold War after World War II led the United States to support these countries and grant them substantial aid. Moreover, the explosion of the economic crisis at the end of the 1960s offered these economies freedom and room for manoeuvre that allowed them to strengthen their dynamics of accumulation.

Theories of late industrialisation seem to be unaware of the external conditions and to neglect their importance. This neglect is explained by their conception of underdevelopment as a kind of backwardness, and this keeps them from reflecting on the relationships of domination exercised from the outside on underdeveloped economies and on the importance of this domination in underdevelopment. In this conception of backwardness, underdevelopment is only a historical stage that will be transcended by underdeveloped countries (Bernis, 1973). However, while for neoclassical theories the necessary catching up is to take place through the liberalisation of internal markets and opening up to the international market, for theories of late industrialisation it requires, at least at first, a certain amount of state intervention and a certain level of protection with respect to the outside.

The International at the Heart of the Asian Model

Another way of analysing experiments in development in Southeast Asia is situated in the Marxist tradition of analysing underdeveloped economies. More particularly, this mode of analysis starts out from the hypothesis that it is difficult to analyse and understand underdeveloped economies without taking into consideration the influence of the international economy. The disconnected and dominated character of productive structures in the Third World decreases these countries' room for action and autonomy at both the political and economic levels. In this way, according to these authors, the international is overtly present at the heart of the national in the Third World. This school seems to be gaining ground today, with the pressures of globalisation on Asian economies and the explosion of the Asian crisis since July 1997.

The first studies produced by this school go back to Karl Marx, who analysed capitalism as a historical stage that would be transmitted to other backward countries through free trade and colonisation. In order to resist the pressures to decrease their average profits, the developed capitalist countries are led, according to Marx, to promote exports of capital and to increase trade with pre-capitalist societies, and this results in the development of capitalist relations of production in these societies. From this point of view, the development is analysed as a process of destruction/replacement of pre-capitalist structures by capitalist structures, which leads to the emergence of new capitalist countries. Thus the classical Marxist thesis took form by maintaining that the capitalist expansionism of the advanced countries was a progressive factor for pre-capitalist societies insofar as it was part of the development of productive forces and the deepening of the movement of the socialisation of labour.

This thesis was adopted by Lenin in 1899, with the publication of his study on the development of capitalism in Russia. In this study, Lenin showed that although it moved relatively slowly in comparison with other developed capitalist countries, since the end of the nineteenth century Russia had experienced a development of capitalism that was to accelerate after the revolt of 1905. Ultimately, C.P. Oman and G. Wignaraja (1991) note:

> for Lenin as for Marx, Luxembourg, and other classical theoreticians of imperialism, the expansionist tendencies of capitalism in developed countries are, despite their brutality, a progressive factor for pre-capitalist societies, and lay the foundations for the development of capitalism on the global scale.

The international communist movement challenged this thesis in the 1920s by adopting Otto Kunsinen's ideas. During the sixth congress of the Second International, the communists criticised the classical Marxist–Leninist thesis and maintained, following Kunsinen's study on the development of capitalism in India, that the capitalist expansionism of the centre blocked industrial development in backward economies and consequently slowed the process of structuring autonomous productive apparatuses.

In explaining the blockage of accumulation in backward countries, the theses adopted during this congress lent priority to the hypothesis of a class alliance between imperialism and feudalism that prevented the development of a national bourgeoisie in these countries. This alliance had its origin in a convergence of interest between a feudal oligarchy for which the transformation of pre-capitalist structures meant the disappearance of the social foundations of its power, on one hand, and the bourgeoisies in advanced countries, which saw in the development of capitalism a new source of competition that could lead to a restriction of their international market and accelerate the tendencies to reduce their rates of profit.

These new theses regarding the impossibility of an autonomous capitalist development at the periphery, and its necessarily dependent character, were to mark more than half a century of Marxist analyses of underdeveloped economies. They were readopted in the 1950s and 1960s by the American Marxists grouped around the *Monthly Review*. In particular, Baran and Sweezy analysed the blockage of accumulation and capitalist development in backward countries as the result of the extortion of the surplus operated by imperialism in these countries (Baran, 1957). Baran's studies have exerted a considerable influence on the theory of the development of capitalism, especially in Latin America, where they led to the appearance of theories of dependency.

During the 1960s and 1970s, theories of dependency were central to thinking about development, and made a significant contribution by studying the mechanisms of dependency linking the home countries and the satellites. However, this theory was very quickly reduced to the school of developing underdevelopment, to the thesis of the stagnation of peripheral economies following the 'inevitable crisis of dependent capitalism', and to the impossibility of developing an autonomous capitalism at the periphery.

However, the resumption of growth and the performances registered by underdeveloped economies in the early 1970s resulted in a reconsideration of this theoretical framework. Throughout the 1970s, there was an acceleration of the process of industrialisation in underdeveloped countries, along with the emergence of new industrial powers in Southeast Asia and in Latin America. Taken together, within the radical school these evolutions led to a broad rethinking of the theory of development and the methodology of theories of dependency, as well as a revival of studies on the development of capitalism at the periphery. This revival took place in the early 1970s, on the basis of a thoroughgoing criticism of theories of dependency carried out by authors such as Laclau (1971), Brenner (1977), Barone (1982), Ben Fine (1978), Chilcote (1981) and Chinchilla (1981).

From this point of view, Barone's studies on South Korea and the debates he has conducted with supporters of the dependency theory are fairly indicative of the revitalisation of analyses of the development of capitalism on the periphery and the challenging of the theses of stagnation in the Third World and the impossibility of autonomous capitalist development (Yaghmain, 1990). In the debate concerning the evolution of accumulation in Korea, Ch. Barone defends the hypothesis that this country experienced an attempt at autonomous capitalist development through mastering the process of structuring an autonomous productive coherence (Barone, 1983, 1984; Landsberg, 1984). This hypothesis opposes the theory of dependency asserting that Korea participates in the international division of labour in a dominated way. In his interpretation of the development of accumulation in Korea, Barone adopts Brenner's conclusions concerning the development of capitalism, emphasising class contradictions and their dynamics in the establishment in new capitalist relations of production following the destruction of pre-capitalist relations.

However, starting in the mid-1980s the debate underwent important changes. While in most Third World countries the debt crisis of the early 1980s led to serious economic depression and marginalisation in the world economy, the countries in Southeast Asia continued to register very high levels of growth, and improved their competitiveness and consequently their share of the international market. The Asian NICs established themselves on the inter-national scene and became genuine competitors for the older industrial powers.

In this context, it was increasingly more difficult to deny this evolution, and various authors sought to understand the role of the international in the emergence of these experiments in development. Thus there was a new turnaround in this debate, insofar as the international was no longer seen as a blocking factor in the emergence of new industrial powers, but instead constituted a factor explaining these evolutions.

Several authors emphasised the American contribution to the development of these countries. J. Hersh hypothesised that the context of the Cold War, and more particularly the Communist threat in Asia, led the United States to show goodwill towards Asian countries and to encourage strong economic growth in order to decrease poverty and therefore the risks of revolutionary contagion (Hersh, 1993). Hersh points out that there was strong concern in the United States as a result of Soviet and Chinese advances in the Far East after the defeat of Japan and the destruction of the regional order that it guaranteed. To deal with these dangers, under Harry Truman's presidency American experts conceived a plan for reconstructing Japan. This plan, drawn up in 1948 by a group of experts that had also participated in the reconstruction of Germany, set three primary objectives:

- stopping Japan's reparations payments to former colonies in the region;
- setting up a programme of stabilisation in order to reduce inflation;
- developing an industrial base connected with exports.

But beyond reconstructing the Japanese economy, the American project also sought to create a zone of prosperity linking Japan, Southeast Asia, and the United States. This zone allowed the creation of a market for Japanese light industry and guaranteed that Japan would have access to the raw materials it needed.

At the economic level, in 1946 the American administration imposed on Japan a radical agrarian reform that led to the expropriation of properties held by absentee owners and to the distribution of land to two million small peasants. With this reform, more than 90 per cent of the land became the property of peasants (Hersh, 1993). Alongside this reform, the American administration defined an aid plan for Japan, the *Economic Recovery in Occupied Areas Act*, whose goal was to reconstruct the economy.

However, the Japanese economy really took off only after 1950, when its potential was used for the war effort in Korea. In 1954, American purchases in Japan for the Korean war reached $3 billion (Hersh, 1993). Along with these purchases, American forces called upon Japanese enterprises for the large, infrastructural works in the region that allowed them to gain access to American technologies and savoir-faire. In addition, the United States opened the American market to Japanese export and thus provided an important market for Japanese groups.

Thus the United States played an important role in reconstructing the Japanese economy and in relaunching Japanese industrial potential after World War II (Aseniero, 1995). In the same way, American aid was crucial in constructing and relaunching the economies of Korea, Taiwan, and most Southeast Asian countries (Finan, 1992). These countries were situated on the periphery of the continent of Asia, and thus were included in the American geopolitical strategy of isolating China and setting up a zone of expansion in Japan. The United States aided the political powers in these countries both politically and militarily. Moreover, in most of these countries, and particularly in Korea, the United States imposed far-reaching agrarian reforms that allowed a rapid increase in agricultural production and productivity (Sunoo, 1988).

At the financial level, American economic and military aid and assistance in Korea and Taiwan between 1946 and 1976 are estimated at $15 billion and $5.6 billion, respectively. In addition, the American authorities opened their market to exports from Korea and Taiwan. However, the normalisation of Japan's relations with its former colonies and its return in the region starting in the 1960s allowed these countries to escape American domination and to develop major economic relationships with Japanese enterprises. Moreover, the war in Vietnam helped Korean and Taiwanese enterprises, who carried out the large-scale projects the American army needed in the region. These enterprises acquired a great deal of experience in executing such projects, and during the 1970s they became major contractors for large-scale projects in the Third World, particularly in oil-exporting countries.

Taken together, this financial, economic, and institutional aid allowed these economies to quickly resume growth. From this point of view, the international element that was blocking development in underdeveloped countries can, for these authors, play a dynamic and favourable role in relaunching the dynamics of growth and development in the Third World.

This hypothesis was adopted by theories of regulation and included within a general framework for analysing the dynamics of historical evolution (Ben Hammouda, 1997). These theories distinguish periods of instability and periods of stability in the functioning of capitalist economies. In the latter, capitalist economies succeed in structuring coherent processes of growth and modes and procedures of regulation capable of reducing and managing large imbalances. During periods of stability, accumulation is not limited to the framework of the national economy; on the contrary, developed economies seek to integrate underdeveloped economies into their logic of functioning. This integration allows developed countries to impose their norms on underdeveloped economies and to reorient their productive structures in relation to their needs. The flow of trade and capital is the source of this loss of the autonomy of productive structures in underdeveloped countries, because it imposes on them systems of prices, technologies, and structures of financing incompatible with the requirements of their structures of production. In this context, the international element plays an important role in blocking accumulation in underdeveloped economies.

However, in underdeveloped countries the periods of crisis correspond to a deep challenge to the old structures of accumulation and a disintegration of their regulatory mechanisms. This instability extends to the international, crating a major destabilisation of the spaces in which developed countries function and of their spheres of influence. This opens up elbow-room for the countries formerly subjected to the asymmetrical influence of developed countries, and gives them an opportunity to redirect their priorities and strategies for economic development.

It is in the context of the crisis of developed economies and the instability of the international economy that theoreticians of regulation have tried to analyse and understand experiments in development in Asia. Thus Borrelly (1991) has developed the notion of room for manoeuvre opened up by the crisis, and has given it a much more precise content. This notion is defined as the substitution for a mechanical and reductive interdependence the freedoms of a network of relationships constitutive of growing liberty for every individual. Thee freedoms were exploited by Asian countries to structure the dynamics of accumulation that have allowed them to diversify their economic structures and to diminish their dependency on the outside.

In addition, Lipietz (1986) has analysed industrial activities in underdeveloped countries in the context of the explosion of the crisis in the mode of regulation and the decline in the profitability of labour-intensive activities. The crisis of Fordism at the centre has led to a major delocalisation of labour-intensive activities towards underdeveloped countries. According to Lipietz, this delocalisation was facilitated by the segmentation of the productive process into three levels: conception and engineering, fabrication by highly trained workers, and execution and assembly by untrained workers. In this perspective, if developed countries have retained control over the capital-intensive sectors and new technologies, the underdeveloped countries have become privileged spaces for delocalisation and labour-intensive activities.

This first generation of regulationist studies on the Asian experiments led to a second generation of studies that has tried to deepen the general line of analysis by taking an interest in concrete experiments. Thus many studies on Korea have shown the structuring of a relatively stable mode of accumulation and specific forms and procedures of regulation that have made it possible to guarantee the stability and maintenance of the dynamics of growth over a relatively long historical period (Cordova, 1994; Lanzarotti, 1992).

Thus, this school is interested in the international context, and more particularly in the mutations of the international economy that create the conditions permitting the relaunching of growth and development in the Third World. However, the different ways of making use of these new conditions at the national level is the source of the fragmentation of the Third World and of the plurality of avenues and trajectories taken by underdeveloped economies. From this point of view, Asian countries have succeeded in exploiting these conditions in order to improve their dynamics of accumulation and their participation in the international economy. However, the elbow-room opened up by the crisis, which Asian countries had succeeded in exploiting in order to structure their dynamics of growth, seems now to be shrinking. Today, the globalisation of the economy and the pressures to liberalise national economic structures are subjecting Southern economies to a level of competition that they are no longer able to sustain!

Ultimately, despite their plurality, these analytical schemas challenge the Washington Consensus's theoretical model and its recommendations regarding development. Asian experiments in development demonstrate the primordial role of state regulation and coordination of the dynamics of growth in the Third World.

Economic disequilibria and the debt crisis led to the Washington Consensus that dominated the field of development economics in the 1980s. From a theoretical point of view, this consensus revived the pure model of general equilibrium, and maintained that the market was capable of ensuring a correspondence between the plans of different agents and of providing regulation for decentralised economies. At the strategic level, the Washington Consensus defined SAPs, whose objective was to reduce large macroeconomic imbalances and to establish new dynamics of growth.

However, the SAPs weak results and the Asian experiments have caused the Washington Consensus to be reconsidered, and since the middle of the

1990s, they have opened a new era in the field of development. It is an era dominated by the practices of inventing and defining new theoretical conceptions and strategies for development that are resolutely situated in a perspective that goes beyond programmes of structural adjustment. *The post-adjustment era has begun in the South.*

Notes

1 See Chu (1987), Haggard (1990), Chang (1993) and Kang (1995) in the CNUCED (UNCTAD) document by T. Cheng et al.

2 Gerschenkron's most important article, 'Economic Backwardness in Historical Perspective', was written in 1951 and reprinted in his book *Economic Backwardness in Historical Perspective* (Cambridge: Harvard University Press, 1962).

3 Moreover, the state supported enterprises that had committed themselves to the 'plan for heavy industry and the chemical industry' by declaring a moratorium on their debts in 1972.

Chapter 3

The Orthodoxy and Post-Adjustment

At the end of the 1980s and throughout the 1990s the field of development economics underwent far-reaching changes. The failure of attempts at structural adjustment in most Third World countries challenged the theoretical foundations and the proposals for development of the Washington Consensus.

Development theory steered progressively away from the strict model of general equilibrium, which had dominated thought and practice in development throughout the 1980s. Consequently, a new theory of development economics, which can be described as post-adjustment development economics, took the place of the Washington Consensus. This new development economics includes all those theoretical approaches that diverge from the Walrassian model by recognising the imperfections of the market and the inability of orthodox stabilisation and adjustment policies, which are inspired by this basic model, to bring about the changes that are necessary for a return to sustained growth in the Third World. Development theory could thus not continue to remain indifferent to the social problems of the people of the South, which were the result of the stabilisation programmes and the weakness of growth produced by the reforms. These trends sounded the death knell of the triumphant liberalism of the 1980s, and led to the development of a new era, concerned with rebuilding the 'empire of chaos' (Amin, 1991), which took over from the neo-liberal obsession in the early 1980s with destroying the old order.

The renewal of development theory was also influenced by new trends in economic theory and the decline of rational anticipation theories in favour of a new synthesis of different theoretical approaches and schools (Hammouda, 1997). Indeed, neoclassical theory progressively abandoned the basic Walrassian model, developing a methodological neoclassicism, which recognised the place and role of contractual procedures in regulating societies, and attempting to integrate them into its analysis. Along with its abandonment of the normative character of the basic model and an increasingly keen desire to test its relevancy, the neoclassical movement confirmed its methodological preference for microeconomics and for the importance of analysing inter-individual relationships between actors. At the same time, it could be observed that the principal rivals of the neoclassical movement had abandoned holistic methods and sought to discover the contributions of methodological individualism to heterodox analyses. This evolution brought the heterodox movements closer to the neoclassical movement. Certain authors even referred to a new synthesis (Abraham-Frois, 1993). The synthesis influenced work on development economics, and is responsible for the continuing changes in the field of economic analysis.

Post-adjustment development economics includes a number of theoretical movements and approaches. While these different movements may agree on the failure of the strict model of general equilibrium in the field of development, they are, however, far from sharing the same analysis of the causes of this failure and the perspectives for research that are open to development economics. According to some scholars, the crisis affecting development economics, and in particular the Washington Consensus, is due to its normativeness from an epistemological standpoint. The neoclassical movement advanced the hypothesis that unrestrained competition and interaction between the plans of different economic operators would ensure the regulation of the market system. Consequently, this movement could not grasp and understand the imperfections of the market and its inability by itself to ensure the socialisation of individuals in a decentralised society. This analysis led to the development of new theoretical approaches that were stimulated by the research in progress. More precisely, it would attempt to break away from the normative nature of the basic model and increase its ability to explain, in particular by modifying the basic hypotheses (Bardhan, 1993).

According to other writers, the failure of structural adjustment was not merely the failure of a specific movement in development economics, but also the bankruptcy of a project to Westernise the world that had formed the basis for this policy. According to this cultural approach, the West had used development economics to impose its own blueprint of society on the different countries of the Third World. The West's universalist claims led it to destroy traditional communities and grassroots solidarity. By its development of trade relationships, the West had imposed its model of social organisation and political modernity, which was based on the individual becoming independent from the community and on the introduction of specific forms of political and economic rationalisation. From this point of view, the crisis of the Washington Consensus was only a further sign of how impossible it was to transpose the standards of Western culture and civilisation onto other worlds, and should induce the North to reconsider its universalist positions and to adopt more relativistic attitudes, which were more in keeping with the principle of the right to be different.

Four main approaches can be discerned in the move to renew development theory in the post-adjustment period:

- the first seeks to look for new inspiration by returning to the work of forerunners in the field, such as Hirschman, with his unbalanced growth theory, or Rosenstein-Rodan, with the Big Push theory. This approach has also been influenced by the theoretical findings of work on endogenous growth (Krugman, 1993);
- the second approach to development problems concentrates on elements linked to market imperfection, and to the place and role of institutions in coordinating the activities of the different economic operators. This approach challenges the ability of any auction system to ensure the convergence of the contradictory interests of different economic operators and gives more importance to the different institutions that play a role in the regulation and running of decentralised economies (Antonelli and Raimondo, 1992; Guillaumont, 1995);
- the third approach involves the renewal of the structuralist approach, which has been able to use criticism of the orthodox approach to stabilisation, in order to make a new and heterodox presentation of development problems;
- the fourth approach takes the opposite tack from the three preceding ones. It regards the crisis of the Washington Consensus as a proof of the failure of development economics. This approach calls for an end of the attempt to Westernise the world, which has been undertaken since the end of colonisation by the North.

The present chapter attempts to study the rise of post-adjustment development economics through a critical presentation of the different approaches, which have changed the analysis of underdeveloped economies. However, despite these changes, we shall advance the hypothesis that these different schools of thought have been unable to overcome the crisis in development economics. From a theoretical viewpoint, the recent changes have not provided economists with the theoretical tools and grids they need to analyse the transformations and transitions in the Third World since the end of the 1980s. Different analyses in recent years have stressed the breakdown of the unity of the Third World and the different routes followed by national economies. The evolution of Third World countries from the mid-1980s on is different from their course in the 1960s and 1970s. During the first few decades of independence, Third World countries undertook large-scale economic and social modernisation programmes. This effort enabled them to organise relatively strong economic growth dynamics, and to form a united group at the international level, in order to negotiate better integration into the international economy. However, with the debt crisis and depression of the 1980s, the context changed completely. Deflationary problems extended to underdeveloped economies, and the unity of the Third World broke down. Some countries, such as those in Southeast Asia, were able to maintain their growth rates and pursue their efforts to build competitive national economies. Other countries, such as the majority of African countries, have declined into marginalisation and chaos. Finally, other countries, such as those in Latin America, maintained, with difficulty, a status quo position in the international economy, without managing to establish a more dynamic participation (Toye, 1987). *Thus, the multiplicity of transitions currently seems to be the fundamental characteristic of the accumulation of capital in the Third World. However, the new approaches to development economics do not enable us to understand and analyse the changes in progress in all underdeveloped economies.*

Furthermore, since the failure of attempts to modernise, based on the nation-state, Third World countries have been torn between the option of globalisation and international integration, and the temptation to turn inwards and to cut themselves off from the world. *From this point of view as well, the new analyses of development have not been able to formulate new strategies to help underdeveloped countries to manage change.*

The two limitations to the different schools of post-adjustment development economics, which we have just described, are due to their static conception of development. *From this standpoint, we put forward the hypothesis that the principal schools of post-adjustment development economics do not have a dynamic conception of the realities of underdeveloped countries, and thus they cannot understand, and even less explain, the diversity of changes in the South.* Certainly, most scholars have taken an interest in the recent changes in the Third World. But it seems to us that most of their analyses do not go beyond the level of empirical observation and are unable to explain the evolutions and changes that are going on.

In the present chapter we shall attempt to examine the orthodox approaches to post-adjustment development economics. The first part of this chapter focuses on recent economic debates that have influenced current trends in development theory. The second part examines the schools of thought which, following Krugman's analyses and research on endogenous growth, have sought to renew recent conceptions of development economics by returning to the work of the pioneers. In the third part, we examine recent work by the institutionalist.

The 1990s: A New Context in the Field of Economics

The strict Walrassian model depends on the two basic principles of perfect competition and the rationality of economic operators. In a world governed by these two principles, consumers and producers meet in the marketplace and exchange goods and services. They respect the rules of market operations and the creation of an equilibrium. This equilibrium is established in all markets, and the economy as a whole can be seen as a system of interdependent markets in a position of equilibrium.

The basic Walrassian model thus regards the economy as a space which is by definition free from conflict, and in which operators have access to complete information in order to make their plans. This basic model describes a 'virtual' universe characterised by perfect competition, an atomicity of participants, a homogeneity of products and free entry into the markets. As Cahuc (1993) notes: 'It is a market with a very large number of buyers and sellers, all fully informed but not acting in concert, exchanging exactly similar goods, at prices that are determined by the market itself.'

This model can be strongly criticised for its lack of realism and its normative content. Increasing criticism at the beginning of the 1980s led neoclassical economists to adapt their work with a view to improving the relevancy and explanatory power of the Walrassian model. This adaptation of pure theory was essentially constructed around three themes:

- challenging the exogenous nature of growth in traditional models and seeking endogenous factors of growth;
- abandoning the hypotheses of perfect competition and complete information in the model of general equilibrium, and developing research on market imperfections;
- a further look at the role of institutions and conventions in coordinating the plans of different economic operators in a decentralised economy.

Heterodox thinkers echoed these new themes of study in the new microeconomics. From a microeconomic standpoint, the neo-Keynesians were increasingly concerned with market imperfections linked to price rigidities. Furthermore, regulation theories reviewed by conventionalists increasingly sought to understand economic situations that diverged from the pure and perfect competitive market. These shared concerns among the three approaches to economic theory have developed into a research programme that has exercised a wide influence on post-adjustment development economics. Its major themes have been market imperfections, the limited rationality of actors and the place of institutions in the regulation of the economic system.

The Nature and Factors of Growth

A new view of traditional economic growth theories began to be taken in the mid-1980s, with the emergence of endogenous growth theories (Amable and Guellec, 1992; Artus, 1993; Henin and Ralle, 1994; Lordon, 1991). Contrary to traditional conceptions that analysed economic growth as the product of an increase in the working population and exogenous increases in productivity, these new approaches took into account the endogenous character of the process of economic growth. According to these theories, the explanation of growth should not be limited to increases in the factors of production, but should take other aspects into consideration, such as the quality of human capital, increasing returns, and the importance of internal learning processes and endogenous technical progress. This theoretical reconsideration had consequences for traditional recommendations in terms of economic policy and more particularly on the hypothesis, championed by the new classical macroeconomics, of the ineffectiveness of government action on economic regulation.

Since their emergence, endogenous growth theories have examined the principal factors explaining growth dynamics and their self-sustaining characteristics. In keeping with this, the first model of endogenous growth, formulated by Romer (1986), stressed the importance of investment in the economic growth process.

Romer modified the hypothesis of constant returns of scale, but located them outside the firm, in order to maintain the context of pure and perfect competition. In more recent work, Romer examined the role of technological innovation and of spending on research and development in economic growth (Romer, 1990). In this model, Romer put forward a multiple-sector economy, in which capital is not homogeneous but belongs to different generations of inputs. In this context, new inputs, manufactured with increased returns, make it possible to improve the productivity of the end goods sector and to increase the general efficiency of the economy.

Lucas (1988) gives special weight to the accumulation of human capital by individuals as an explanation of endogenous growth. The issue was also examined by Becker, Murphy and Tamura, who looked again at population growth, which according to Solow, was an exogenous source of economic growth. They considered that it was in the best interest of economies to restrict population growth, so as to ensure a better standard of human capital that was more able to support a process of sustainable growth (Becker, Murphy et al., 1990).

Other models of endogenous growth have studied the importance of public infrastructures in the growth process (Barro, 1990, 1991; Barro and Martin, 1992). According to these authors, these public assets make it possible to improve the productivity of private agents and increase the process of growth.

Theories of endogenous growth thus break with traditional conceptions and see economic growth as a self-sustaining process, which may be influenced by increasing returns and various types of externalities, such as technological innovation, know-how or public assets.

Market Imperfections

The hypothesis of pure and perfect competition holds a central position in the pure model of general equilibrium. This hypothesis has been abandoned by the new microeconomics in order to increase the relevancy of the basic model. Baumol thus challenges free entry to the market with the theory of contestable markets (Baumol et al., 1988, 1991). According to this line of thinking, a contestable market is defined as one that can be entered or left without incurring any costs. According to Baumol, this concept is a better reflection of the monopoly that exists in certain areas and is an extension of pure and perfect competition. Contestable markets are beneficial for national economies and businesses, to the extent that they ensure:

- non-excessive prices;
- limited waste;
- elimination of subsidies;
- optimal pricing.

Baumol recognises, however, that the scope for contestable markets is currently limited. Because of this, businesses are only interested in actual competition within their fields, and do not worry about potential competition that could come from the entry of new firms into the market. This situation enables businesses to implement suboptimal pricing and obtain quasi-monopoly profits.

The issue of operators' information is also at the heart of the argument about market imperfections. This has led to the development of a movement known as information economics, whose aim is to study the rational behaviour of economic operators facing difficulties in obtaining information on products.

This new discipline deals with the study of strategic interactions between economic operators with asymmetrical access to information.

Akerlof's research on the dependency of prices on the quality of goods was the foundation of information economics (Akerlof, 1970). In his article, Akerlof studied the used car market and formed the hypothesis that sellers had information on the quality of the cars, while buyers only had expectations. In that context, buyers refused to pay high prices because they knew there were 'lemons' on the market. At such a price, however, sellers only sell lemons and withdraw good quality cars. This is a case of *adverse selection*, in which good quality products are driven off the market. This phenomenon can lead to a reduction of trade or even to a market collapse if agents believe that only poor quality goods are placed on the market.

Akerlof's groundbreaking article led to a proliferation of research demonstrating that the freedom of operators in the market can lead to the disappearance of quality products, and recommending the establishment of procedures to reveal the quality of products or to ensure recourse against poor quality goods (Stiglitz, 1987; Belloc, 1987; Orléan, 1991).

In addition to adverse selection, information economics has studied the problem of *moral risk or moral hazard*, related to the fact that a certain number of operators can reduce the amount of risk they take in trading, by actions that cannot be observed by other operators. In moral hazard situations, incentive procedures should be established, so that operators with private information act in an optimal manner for those who do not have such information, while in adverse selection situations, incentives should enable economic operators to obtain information on the quality of goods. Thus, means and procedures need to be established in moral hazard situations, to ensure an equal sharing of risks by traders (Laffont, 1987).

Moral hazard is generally apprehended through *principal-agent* models in which the principal performs an action for an agent or representative, against payment. This action may take the form of production in relationships between employers and employees, harvests in relationships between landowners and farmers, or court decisions in relationships between clients and lawyers. This type of contract poses difficulties when an agent's action is not perfectly transparent, and is consequently difficult for the principal to assess. In such cases, both parties must define a mini-institution enabling them to share the risks and encourage the agent to act in the best interests of the principal.

New microeconomics work on market imperfection was followed by neo-Keynesian work. The neo-Keynesians postulate an economic universe characterised by four basic hypotheses. First, that the behaviour of economic operators is rational and obeys the principle of optimisation under constraint. Furthermore, markets are imperfect and do not follow the rules of pure and perfect competition. Information is incomplete, which means that it cannot be acquired without cost. Finally, markets are incomplete, i.e. there are procedures or contracts extraneous to the market that govern relationships between economic operators.

Within that universe, the best known model is that of R.J. Gordon, who examines the elasticity of prices. This model is used by Gordon to study the evolution of price elasticity in various economies over the 1873–1987 period. The study showed that in the American economy, price elasticity remained constant between 1954 and 1987, and between 1873 and 1914. With some nuances, Gordon's findings for the other economies he studied (United Kingdom, Japan, France and Germany) were quite similar (Gordon, 1990). This research shows that the elasticity of prices was no greater during the Great Depression than it was during the three decades of prosperity following World War II. From a theoretical standpoint, this means that price adjustments were common, but that their impact on the markets was not immediate.

Against this background, the neo-Keynesians have taken an interest in the reasons for low elasticity and the nature of the price rigidities that caused them. However, before introducing rigidities, the neo-Keynesians formed the hypothesis that firms are price-makers, which differentiates them from the Walrassian universe in which they are price-takers. If they are price-makers, then firms can rationally refuse to change prices, despite information received from the market. This behaviour leads to rigidities, which make price adjustment sticky. At this level, there is a distinction to be made between nominal rigidity and real rigidity (Romer, 1993). Rigidity is said to be nominal when an operator's behaviour does not promote flexibility in the price of a good, but has no impact on the price of other goods. Rigidity is real, however, when the relative pricing system is disturbed.

Neo-Keynesians argue that nominal rigidities are the result of imperfect competition in the market, which may encourage firms in a monopoly position to fix prices. Parallel to this explanation, the neo-Keynesians also refer to the menu costs hypothesis to explain price stickiness (Mankiw, 1985). Thus, a firm can refuse to change its prices, despite variations in demand, if the material costs of changing prices are high and the image of its product can be affected.

Real rigidities may stem from the mark-up method used by businesses to calculate their costs. According to this method, sales prices are calculated by increasing the average cost by a fixed amount known as a mark-up. In such a case, if the average cost covers payment of labour input and intermediary products, the mark-up represents capital costs and profits. This method of calculation is a major source of real rigidity, since it makes it possible to avoid sales price increases aimed at maximising profits. Furthermore, it enables firms to disclaim responsibility for price changes.

Okun's distinction between auction-type markets and clientele markets provides another explanation for real rigidities (Okun, 1981). In auction-type markets, operators alter prices whenever demand changes. However, in clientele markets, relationships between economic operators are governed by an implicit contract, so that businesses fix their prices and undertake to guarantee their stability and the quality of their products.

These rigidities led the neo-Keynesians to form the hypothesis of near rationality, which is slightly different from the traditional hypothesis of rationality, since it does not involve perfect price flexibility. Under these conditions, equilibrium is generally below optimum, compared with the Walrassian equilibrium (Akerlof and Yellen, 1985).

In addition to the study of price rigidities in markets for goods, the neo-Keynesians have also shown an interest in studying the labour market. In their analyses of the labour market, they rework the traditional framework with the hypothesis of rational operators. This allowed for adjustment between labour supply and demand through flexibility in real wages. Beyond a certain natural unemployment rate, unemployment was said to be voluntary. However, this proposition is refuted by the neo-Keynesians, who demonstrate that rigidities in real wages block labour market adjustments and are therefore responsible for involuntary unemployment. The contribution of the neo-Keynesians at this level, particularly through implicit contract and efficiency wage theories, has been to demonstrate that rigidities are the result of rational behaviour by economic operators.

Institutions and Conventions at the Heart of Coordination

In addition to market imperfections, recent work in economic theory has examined the different institutions that play an important role in coordinating the actions of different operators and regulating the decentralised economic system. The Hobbesian criticism of liberal society makes it necessary to consider institutions, together with the difficulties in the coordination among operators in situations of strategic interaction and in the absence of any central authority (Villé, 1990). Indeed, in an individualistic society, guided by profit maximisation, operators might defraud and cheat, so as to serve their interests more effectively. Such an approach could lead to social disorder and breakdown. To ensure the coherent functioning of society, Hobbes proposed the introduction of a supra-individual authority, Leviathan, to which individuals would give up part of their prerogatives in order to ensure the preservation of the whole. These philosophical and economic reflections prompted the new microeconomics to introduce institutions into their analysis of decentralised economies.

Considering institutions and agreements is not a new approach in microeconomic theory (*Economie Appliquée*, 1990; Brousseau, 1993). As early as 1987, Coase diverged from the basic model by considering the firm as a locus of coordination outside the market (Coase, 1987). This school of thought, known as neo-institutionalism, has extended in recent years to examine the complementarity between organisations and markets (Alchian and Demsetz, 1972; Williamson, 1975, 1985). In addition, North sought to explain historical phenomena by taking into account the knowledge gained through the neo-institutional approach (North and Thomas, 1973; North, 1990). While their studies recognise the importance of institutions in the running of decentralised economies, however, the neo-institutionalists follow the neoclassical line in holding that institutions are a result of rational choices by operators (Guerrien, 1990).

Coase's transaction cost theory has an important place in the neo-institutional line of thought (Gillis, 1987). In his work, Coase sought to understand the reasons that motivated firms to develop their own internal organisation and avoid recourse to the market. According to transaction theory, this internalisation can be explained by the cost of outsourcing, especially when the market is imperfect. In this way, a firm can save on market costs, and a boundary is established between it and the market. Relationships between internalisation and the market are governed by the principle of marginal costs. This theory has long been criticised and has been accused of being descriptive and lacking an operational definition of transaction costs.

Despite this criticism, however, Coase's analysis is still influential in the field of political economy. For instance, Arrow (1974) takes up Coase's thinking when he argues that the firm and the market are alternative forms of economic organisation. Hymer (1976) also uses Coase's analyses in his study of direct foreign investments. In his research, Hymer explains that the development of multinationals is linked to the imperfection of international markets and firms' desire to internalise their activities in order to reduce risks. Finally, Williamson (1975, 1985) extends Coase's research by developing organisation theory, which uses a neoclassical framework to analyse forms of coordination outside the market as vertical integration processes within firms.

In the end, by setting aside the limitations of the hypothesis of the auctioneer, the new microeconomics is able to study a world much richer than the Walrassian world. Despite its increased relevance, however, the new microeconomics is obliged to accept the market's inability to explain the phenomenon of socialisation in its entirety. Hence its recognition of the importance of standards and institutions in regulating decentralised economies.

These concerns are also shared by the French 'conventionalists'. Convention theory is a new approach that developed in France in the 1980s. The research is motivated by the difficulties of the neoclassical framework in understanding economic situations that diverge from the pure and perfect competitive market. However, the goal of the economists adhering to this movement is not to correct and extend the framework of standard theory (Dupuy et al., 1989). Instead, as Orléan explains, it is:

> a collective work under way for some time, which focuses on analysing capitalist economies, and which recognises the essential role played by non-market forms of coordination, production and resource allocation (Orléan, 1994, p. 13).

The development of this school of thought meets a series of methodological and theoretical requirements. The first lies in the development of a multi-disciplinary approach combining economics with sociology, in order to analyse various forms of joint action and coordination. The second concern of the conventionalists is to go beyond what they view as the sterile opposition between orthodoxy and heterodoxy in the field of political economy. This presupposes that convention theory must take account of the contributions of extended standard theory to the study of organisational and institutional phenomena and must recognise the importance of methodological individualism. Opposition is outdated and it is time to draw closer or even for a synthesis, since, as Orléan writes, 'there is now a pervasive feeling of belonging to the same scientific community faced with difficult problems' (ibid., p. 15).

Despite this common will to develop a broad eclectic framework, which would provide for a broad gathering of non-orthodox approaches, different conceptions of conventions exist among economists. According to one view, a convention can be defined as:

> a mechanism constituting an agreement of wills, like its product, having a mandatory normative force … and should be understood both as the result of individual actions and as a framework that constrains its subjects (Dupuy et al., 1989).

This relatively abstract definition is set out more precisely by followers of convention theory in specific fields of analysis. For instance, Salais (1989) uses the notion to study labour relations. The point of departure of his analysis is the neoclassical model's inability to account for labour relations, since they are established between employers and employees before work is carried out. Indeed, according to Salais, labour relations depend on two principles: the making of a contract when labour is hired and the carrying out of labour in production. These two principles correspond to two logical equivalencies: an equivalency between wages and the future length of work, and an equivalency between the actual working time and the goods produced. According to Salais, this ambivalence in labour relations gives rise to uncertainties over the production and the quality of goods. This uncertainty is permanently eliminated from the real economy, according to Salais, by the establishment of two conventions:

- a 'productivity' convention, that makes it possible to replace nonexistent labour with an alternative standard at the time of exchange;
- an 'unemployment convention', which constitutes a procedure for the evaluation after the event of the productivity convention and allows employers to make adjustments between forecasts and actual production.

On this basis, Salais defines labour relations as:

> a compromise, which generates tension, between two equivalency principles, one which, when a bargain is struck between an employer and an employee, establishes an equivalence between future working time and wages, and one that, creates an equivalence, in the subsequent course of production, between the actual working time and the goods produced (Salais, 1989, p. 237).

Uncertainty arising from the destructuring of growth dynamics in capitalist economies in the current crisis is also a factor in Orléan's ideas on conventions. He argues that uncertainty is a manifestation of the inability of the Walrassian market to ensure the coordination of individual actions in a decentralised economy (Orléan, 1991). Even though neoclassical theory recognises uncertainty, according to Orléan it reduces it to a calculable risk, which makes it unable to explain the evolution of modern economies. Thus, uncertainty should mean that economists accept the idea of the appearance of new elements that cannot be incorporated into previous data. This uncertainty creates situations where there is a general lack of confidence in the constraints of the social order (Orléan, 1989).

This widespread lack of confidence can lead to generalised risks for socioeconomic organisational systems, which cannot be overcome by agreements or private assurances. Conventions are, therefore, a necessity, and their legitimacy, according to Orléan 'stems from the specific existence of coordination imposed on the social system by uncertainty, i.e. a widespread withdrawal from arrangements' (ibid., p. 244). The author gives two examples of this type of convention: lenders of last resort, and savings insurance. However, more than studying individual forms of coordination, convention theory should make it possible 'to understand how collective reasoning is constituted and what resources need to be mobilised to establish it' (Orléan, 1994, p. 16). Convention theory economists should:

> have access to formal tools enabling them to understand the interrelations of various market, organisational, institutional or ethical resources and how their interrelations can be made coherent despite the apparent diversity of the reasoning behind them (ibid.).

This search for general coordination mechanisms can also be found in the work of Favereau (1989). His analysis of conventions is founded on a criticism of standard theory, which reduces the rationality of individual behaviour to the optimisation and coordination of individual behaviour towards market regulation. Furthermore, extended standard theory, which includes such approaches as transaction theory and incentive, agency and contract models, reduces non-market forms of coordination to individual agreements between agents. However, the relevance of the basic model can only be enhanced at the expense of a certain loss of general coherence. From this point of view, the advantage of convention theory, according to Favereau, resides in the fact that it attempts to account for the existence of 'collective cognitive mechanisms', in addition to individual contracts and rules, which are capable of ensuring the coherence of individual decisions in a decentralised economy (ibid.). By taking these conventions into account, Favereau is able to give an alternative presentation of the decentralised economy, conceived as a population of organisations (in the sense of internal markets), structured by the play of reproduction and coherence.

The elements presented in these different conceptions of convention theory help us come to grips with the principal characteristics of this new theoretical approach. The theory is born of criticism of the Walrassian model that reduces coordination between economic operators to market regulation – hence its claim to heterodoxy. Furthermore, the theory is not satisfied by the extended standard theory's adjustments to the basic model, since consideration of non-market forms of coordination remains limited to individual contracts and agreements. From this viewpoint, convention theory aims to provide an alternative approach by establishing conventions arising from collective behaviour by economic operators as a regulating principle in decentralised economies.

Despite these statements of principle, it should be noted that convention theory comes back in concrete analysis to extended standard theory. This connection forms the foundation for a new broad synthesis that conventionalists strongly favour, hoping to get beyond the sterile opposition between orthodoxy and heterodoxy. This connection is immediately apparent in methodological choices, including the abandonment of holistic approaches and the choice of individualism, despite the claims of conventionalists on the necessity of maintaining a global approach to economics.

This concordance between the two lines of thinking is also visible in the conventionalists' use of the theory of uncooperative game theory to analyse interactions between economic operators. Although this theory enables us to abandon the auctioneer hypothesis of the traditional model, it has difficulty in explaining the viability of decentralised economies. Finally, the link between the two theories can also be observed in their conceptions of institutions. On this level, despite a reference to J.R. Commons, one of the founding fathers of American institutionalism in the 1920s and 1930s, the conventionalists seem much closer to the vision of the new American institutional economics. While this new institutional economics styles itself as a descendant of American institutionalism, the two movements seem to have diverged over a number of issues (Dutraive, 1993). The difference between the old and new American institutional approaches lies in their conception of institutions. While an institution, according to Commons, provides a series of rules and standards to which operators can conform, in the view of the new institutional economics, institutions are reduced to the forms of coordination generated by market imperfections. Furthermore, institutionalism recognises and seeks to integrate the action of structures in the definition of coordination institutions, whereas the new institutional economics restricts its study of institutions to individual arrangements and agreements. This opposition stems from the methodological opposition in the two approaches between holism and individualism.

In summary, recent research in economic theory has led to a broad and eclectic synthesis of heterodox approaches, such as conventionalism, the new Walrassian microeconomics and the neo-Keynesians. This evolution has come about through an abandonment of holistic methodological positions and the rejection of the idea of constructing an alternative hypothesis to general equilibrium in the case of Keynesians and heterodox theories, and the aim of the new microeconomics to develop a grid to explain the functioning of economies. This convergence has made it possible to outline a new research programme in the field of economics, focusing on the study of market imperfections and aiming to improve analysis of coordination phenomena between economic operators in decentralised economies. This research programme has considerably influenced post-adjustment development economics.

The Return to the Founding Fathers

The work that aimed to return to the thinking of development pioneers began by noting the decline of their approach from the middle of the 1970s, in favour of orthodox analyses (Krugman, 1993). According to these analysts, this decline can be explained by the failures of development and by the low standard of formalisation in the founding models of development theory (Krugman, 1995).

Recent economic research findings, however, are tending to confirm the intuitions and the recommendations of several pioneering studies on a number of issues. Regarding international trade, the research of the early development theorists demonstrated that international openness and integration into the world economy were unfavourable to underdeveloped countries. For instance, Myrdal (1957) showed that the spread of technical progress and growth from developed countries to underdeveloped countries, which could be inferred from the Hecksher-Ohlin model, was cancelled out by holdback effects. During the same decade, ECLA studies, particularly by Prebisch and Singer, on the deterioration of terms of trade in underdeveloped countries, because of their participation in international trade, exercised considerable influence on development theorists, and justified the elaboration of import-substitution strategies aimed at the domestic market.

These ideas were strongly criticised with the return in force of neo-liberal thinking and the comparative-advantage approach in the 1970s. More particularly, research on 'effective protection rates' and 'domestic resource cost' sought to demonstrate that protection of industrial sectors, especially heavy industry, penalised them, by keeping them out of global competition, which could have motivated them to increase their competitiveness. Furthermore, according to the critics of introverted growth models, protectionism also penalised exports, agriculture and light industry (Balassa, 1971; Little et al., 1970).

Neo-liberal criticism was strengthened in the 1970s with the difficulties and limitations that affected import-substitution strategies. A number of studies increasingly stressed the positive correlation between exports and economic growth (Michaely, 1977; Balassa, 1978). The introverted approaches of the pioneers of development theory were particularly challenged in the 1970s in studies by Krueger (1978) and Bhagwati (1978). Their research examined the effects and consequences of exchange rate liberalisation policies and the reduction of customs duties in 10 countries between 1952 and 1972. It also demonstrated that devaluation does not have an inflationary effect, and that liberalisation is necessary to encourage exports. These studies, and the debt crisis, had a major impact on development strategies in the Third World from the early 1980s onward. The recommendations of the early pioneers were set aside in favour of more liberal policies that encouraged international integration according to the comparative advantages of underdeveloped countries.

Recent research on international trade, however, diverges from the presentations of neo-liberal theories. The point of departure of the new theories on international trade is a criticism of comparative advantage theory and its inability to make sense of international relations. More specifically, the traditional theory of international trade does not provide a satisfactory explanation for the fact that the bulk of trade takes place between developed countries with comparable levels of technology and factor endowments, and involves similar products (Hellier, 1993).

This criticism of the traditional comparative advantage theory has given rise to what is commonly referred to as the 'new theory of international trade' (Greenaway, 1987; Helpman and Razin, 1991; Krugman, 1990). Although the early work of this new trend dates back to the end of the 1970s, these developments only became the new dominant paradigm in the debate on international trade in the mid-1980s. In this body of work, Krugman looks into the effects of non-constant returns on international specialisation and uneven development between countries (Krugman, 1981). Krugman develops a model based on two countries and two sectors (agriculture and industry), and considers economies of scale, external to the firm, in the industrial sector. The two countries begin to trade with each other, according to the principles of comparative advantage. However, economies of scale give the country with the most capital stock a cost advantage, which promotes the accumulation of capital and strengthens its initial advantage. According to this model, economies of scale are responsible for cumulative growth and competitiveness, which leads to a monopoly in industrial goods. In the longer term, the country with more capital stock specialises in industrial production, while the other is locked into an agricultural-exporting economy.

Other authors have examined trade policies on international markets with imperfect competition (Brander, 1981; Brander and Krugman, 1983; Brander and Spencer, 1985). They recommend that economies adopt strategic trade policies aimed at increasing foreign markets for national firms. Authors such as Brander and Spencer favour strong government intervention in favour of national enterprises, by means of taxes and export subsidies, and by defining a fiscal policy that penalises foreign exporters. The new theories of international trade criticise traditional theories and demonstrate that free trade is not an optimum solution for economies.

These conclusions are, however, qualified by Krugman, who considers that it is difficult to define an alternative policy to free trade, and that support for free trade should continue, even though it is a second-rate solution (Krugman, 1993). Thus, while free trade may be no better than protectionist strategy, it is easier to implement and leads therefore to fewer distortions. So, while he departs from the neo-liberals in his analysis, Krugman and the other adherents of the new international trade theories join comparative advantage theorists in recommending the implementation of free trade policies in international trade.

In addition to work on international trade, the return to the work of the founding fathers also concerns the issue of economies of scale. We should point out that early work on development economics stressed the importance and role of economies of scale in the dynamics of economic development. With his 'Big Push' theory, Rosenstein-Rodan was one of the first authors to consider that economies of scale on the microeconomic level and the supply of labour in underdeveloped countries could lead to strong growth dynamics (Rosenstein-Rodan 1943, 1961). Economies of scale are also stressed in the work of Hirschman (Hirschman, 1964). In his reflection on unbalanced growth, he points out that the idea of economies of scale is central to inter-industrial liaisons. During the same period, the issue of economies of scale was also studied, to varying extents, by development theorists such as Nurkse, Scitovsky, Lewis and Myrdal, who were interested in understanding how to transform economies of scale at the microeconomic level in underdeveloped economies into increasing returns at the level of the national economy (Krugman, 1993).

From the middle of the 1960s, however, the issue of economies of scale was set aside, with the return in force of neoclassical theory and the hypothesis of increasing returns in traditional growth theories. The neoclassical model of growth was based on Solow's work, which sought to construct a model of stable growth based on Walrassian hypotheses (Solow, 1956). According to that model and its extensions, growth can only proceed from population growth and from increased labour productivity, stemming from exogenous technical progress. In these models, investment does not influence growth since, as stipulated by neoclassical theory, physical capital has diminishing incremental returns and constant returns to scale; in this framework, the profitability of investments decreases along with capital stock. From this point of view, the rate of accumulation cannot overtake the growth of the workforce and its level of efficiency.

These models of growth faced considerable criticism from the middle of the 1980s, because of their inability to explain the evolution of growth dynamics in recent years. In the first place, these theories cannot explain the catch-up phenomena at work in the world economy, and more particularly the fact that even if a certain number of developed and Third World countries have not succeeded in organising coherent production systems, they have still experienced strong growth in productivity, which has enabled them to approach American productivity levels (Henin and Ralle, 1994). Furthermore, the traditional framework is unable to explain the slowing down of productivity in the present crisis, despite the increased rate of technical progress. Since the beginning of the 1970s, there has been a sharp rise in research and development expenditure in developed countries, along with the progressive establishment of a new technological paradigm, following the decline of the Ford technical model. However, despite these changes, productivity has not resumed the strong growth it enjoyed in the 1950s and 1960s.

For these reasons, there was a revival of growth theories in the mid-1980s, concentrating notably on increasing returns, which marked a return to the work of the founders of development economics, such as Rosenstein-Rodan and A. Hirschman. Neoclassical theory cannot by definition include increasing returns in its theoretical schema. Factor increases cause higher than proportionate increases in the volume of production, and producers have no reason to restrict production, since they are sure to be able to sell their products. Based on this, production will tend towards infinity, and in situations of pure and perfect competition, it becomes difficult to resolve the producers' optimisation problem.

Since it is difficult to sustain this hypothesis, Romer (1986) modified it by introducing increasing returns, using Marshall's logic. Romer argued that the internal conditions of production within enterprises are conditions of nonincreasing returns. He envisaged increasing returns from the size of the market or the national economy, which had a positive external effect on capital and encouraged firms to invest. This accumulation of capital led to an increase in the firm's productive capacity; this is the effect on capital. In addition, it had beneficial effects on the acquisition of skills and on increasing know-how within the firm (something that Romer refers to as 'learning spillover'), which is transmitted to the rest of the economy through inter-business links. The hypothesis of increasing returns is introduced into the analysis in this way, while preserving the fundamental principle of pure and perfect competition.

In this model, the growth path closely depends on the elasticity of production and total knowledge. If elasticity is less than one, the model retains the basic properties of Solow's model and growth tends towards zero. However, when elasticity is equal to 1, Romer demonstrates the possibility of a growth path at constant rates, relatively close to the growth path resulting from exogenous technical progress. Finally, if elasticity is greater than one, growth will occur at increasing rates.

Romer's model also demonstrates that the situation of competitive equilibrium is suboptimal. Firms do not include the implications of global economic interdependence in their plans and thus do not obtain all the benefits they could from the positive external effect. When they develop their production plans in the context of decentralised economies, firms only consider the marginal productivity of knowledge, equal to f'_k in the production function $f(k,K)$, which is clearly inferior to productivity in social optimum calculations ($f'_k + Nf'_k$) (Amable and Guellec, 1992). Investment stemming from market equilibrium would be lower than investment corresponding to the social optimum. Hence the importance of government intervention to make private interests compatible with collective interests.

A return to the work of the founders of development economics is also seen in the emphasis which endogenous growth theories place on the accumulation of human capital and the importance of access to and mastery of new technology. Romer stresses the role of technological innovations and Lucas focuses on the accumulation of human capital in explaining the dynamics of economic growth. In Romer's model, growth from additional investments is not endogenous to factors of production and constitutes an additional factor that enables economies of scale to contribute to growth. Lucas tries to overcome this limitation by analysing human capital as an aspect of labour, which allows a clear improvement of the productive capacities of the labour force (Lucas, 1988). According to Lucas, the accumulation of human capital may come from learning phenomena, such as 'learning by doing', or as a result of training programmes to which workers devote part of their working time, in order to improve their performance, and thus increase their earnings.

Lucas demonstrates that the combination of an accumulation of knowledge with constant marginal efficiency and the external effect of human capital allows economies to experience sustained growth. However, Lucas observes that the growth rate of human capital in an optimum situation is higher than in an equilibrium situation. He thus observes the same gap between the equilibrium and the optimum, highlighted by Romer's model, which stems from the inability of private agents to incorporate the surplus of social efficiency from the accumulation of human capital into their plans. From this angle, the decisions of economic operators about the accumulation of human capital are determined by private considerations of increased satisfaction, and do not take into consideration the collective consequences of the accumulation of human capital. This gap between optimum and equilibrium justifies government intervention in the form of subsidies for educational systems and training and research organisations.

Lucas' model also offers some explanations for uneven development among nations. His model shows that an initial discrepancy in the endowment of different nations with physical and human capital tends to continue and even widen. These findings focus our attention on the importance of the investments underdeveloped countries should make, to increase physical and human capital and reduce the discrepancies in development, which divide them from developed countries.

Endogenous growth theories that attempt to revive thinking on development by returning to the works of the founding fathers have had a considerable influence on development studies. Barro sought to determine the factors that influenced growth dynamics in 116 economies between 1965 and 1985 (Barro and Lee, 1994). This study demonstrated once again the importance of the factors that have been highlighted by different theories of endogenous growth, such as GDP/per head, education, health, the share of investments in income, the scope of the government and political stability. Other authors have examined growth factors in Africa over the 1960–87 period (Savvides, 1995). Lucas looked into factors that restrict the flow of investments from developed countries to underdeveloped countries (Lucas, 1990). He particularly noted differences in endowment in human capital, market imperfections and political stability.

Endogenous growth theories have thus inspired one school of post-adjustment development economics to seek to renew development theories by returning to the work of the founding fathers. This has enabled these authors to break away from the Walrassian model. Indeed, these new presentations challenge the basic model by recognising the suboptimal nature of equilibrium and by stressing the importance of government intervention to correct imperfections. However, while they may in theory recognise the importance of the role of government in optimising growth, they refuse to include it in their recommendations (Romer, 1993). In fact, all these authors criticise all forms of interventionism in the regulation of underdeveloped economies, because of the difficulty of drawing up and implementing such policies. Laissez-faire remains the best solution for these authors, even though it is only a second best. Thus, despite a profound criticism of the Walrassian theoretical framework, this approach to post-adjustment development economics remains a prisoner of neo-liberal theories in terms of recommendations and development strategy.

The ambiguity in these analyses is also apparent when applied to the newly industrialised countries (NICs) of Southeast Asia. After studying these economies, Krugman (1994) came to the conclusion that we were looking at a myth based on low labour costs, and that these economies would not stand up to international competition and would collapse fairly quickly. This analysis seems to be contradicted by the facts and by recent interpretations of the experiences of Southeast Asian countries, which, on the contrary, despite the recent crisis, stress the profound changes in the productive structures of these countries. These changes are a result of adaptation and mastery of new technologies. Thus, instead of seizing on these economies to demonstrate the accuracy of their views and to justify their theoretical analyses on international trade, the advocates of the new theories of international trade seek to minimise the experiences of the NICs.

The adherents of these new theories deliberately maintain this ambiguity between analyses and recommendations. Although they develop more relevant analyses of international trade and economic growth, these economists do not break their ties with the Walrassian framework and continue to identify themselves with the dominant party in the field of economic theory. These studies thus refuse to analyse and understand the changes and transitions in progress in the Third World and treat the Southeast Asian NICs as exporters of cheap labour-intensive products, like the economies of Tunisia, Morocco or Mauritius. This refusal to understand the uniqueness of these countries' experience cannot even be justified by a desire to preserve links with the neoclassical school, since most neo-liberal theories today accept the role played by various institutions and non-market interventions in the 'success' of the NICs.

The New Institutional Economics

Development economics, like the new microeconomics, has seen challenges to the basic hypotheses of the Walrassian model. The need for increased relevance has led to abandonment of the strict model's hypotheses of perfect competition and information, and development studies have begun to examine the imperfections of the market. These imperfections suggest the need for further research on institutions and mechanisms that correct the market's regulating action in decentralised economies. These concerns were behind the renewal of work on institutions with the new institutional economics (NIE) or new institutionalism. This line of research also developed in development economics and has progressively come to dominate recent work on underdeveloped economies.

The development of this line of thought has been influenced by the neo-Keynesians and the synthesis which they attempted to make between macroeconomic concerns and the microeconomic bases for the actions of economic operators.[1] The development of the neo-Keynesian movement in the 1980s was based on opposition to the theory of rational expectations about the ability of decentralised economies to achieve equilibrium. According to expectation theory, price adjustment ensures market equilibrium, whereas according to the neo-Keynesians, prices are 'sticky', and adjustment of prices to quantities is relatively slow. The neo-Keynesians argue that it is this price 'stickiness' that is responsible for rigidities in the market. However, although initial synthesis economists only point out the existence of rigidities, the neo-Keynesians attempt to give them a microeconomic explanation: they uphold the paradoxical hypothesis that rigidities are the result of rational behaviour by economic agents in imperfect market conditions.

The neo-Keynesian revival is essentially opposed to the theory of rational expectations with respect to two issues. The first point is epistemological in nature and involves the eternal debate between relevance and rigour, and the coherence of theories (Blinder, 1979). While the neo-Keynesian theory recognises the rigour of rational expectations, it nevertheless stresses their unrealistic nature. Certain authors have, therefore, opted for a research problematic aimed at increasing the relevance of the neo-Keynesian theory, through a more in-depth study of rigidities and their macroeconomic consequences. There has been some work to show that, in menu cost issues, rigidities may result from rational behaviour by firms, given the cost of price adjustment. Some research has shown that price rigidity is more generally the norm in capitalist economies than flexibility (Carlton, 1986).

The second issue addressed by the neo-Keynesian economics involves the postulate of the rationality of operators in rational expectations. The neo-Keynesians' criticism of rationality does not apply to the basic core of neoclassical theory, especially equilibrium and the market. The criticism addresses the 'radical' and exclusive nature of the postulate in rational expectations. Through their study of the labour market, the neo-Keynesians point to the considerable complexity of relationships between economic operators, which should lead economists to qualify the postulate of rationality. A number of studies on efficiency wages consider that a real wage higher than the equilibrium wage may have positive repercussions on productivity (Katz, 1986; Krueger and Summers, 1988). Other work on implicit contracts has demonstrated the existence of implicit relationships and strict standards, established among workers or between workers and management, alongside the relationships codified in collective bargaining (Taylor, 1980). Beyond these divergences from rational expectation theory, the goal of the neo-Keynesians is not so much a revival of the *General Theory*, as it is an attempt to reconcile the Keynesian method with the neoclassical model. The methodological choice of individualism and the consideration of contractual procedures in the regulation of societies are at the core of the synthesis between Keynesian and neoclassical methods.

This theoretical evolution has had major consequences on development practices and strategies. Authors increasingly challenge the liberal recommendations of the Washington Consensus. J.E. Stiglitz, the new chief economist of the World Bank, notes that development experiences in Southeast Asia have demonstrated the importance of government intervention in regulating a market economy (Stiglitz, 1997). This new development practice views the market as the most important institution for regulating the projects of different operators in a decentralised economy. According to that conception, however, market imperfections require corrective interventions by the government (Datta-Chadhuri, 1990). In this respect, Stiglitz believes the government should intervene in six areas in modern economies (Stiglitz, 1997). The first area of government intervention is the promotion of education. According to Stiglitz, universal education creates the conditions for a more just and egalitarian society. The government should also play a major role in developing new technologies. Stiglitz points out that in the United States, new technologies, including the electronic communications networks, have been developed by the government.

The third area of government intervention involves the financial sector. Stiglitz notes that, in Asian countries, the government ensured the stability of the financial system and allowed the creation of the necessary institutions to finance growth dynamics. The government should also intervene in the development of basic infrastructures, such as roads and communications systems. Government intervention is also important in preventing environmental degradation. Finally, according to Stiglitz, the government has a role to play in the satisfaction of the population's basic needs, particularly health care.

Alongside these changes and evolutions in development practices and strategies, however, and their divergence from the Washington Consensus on adjustment, theoretical practices have developed which, under the influence of the new microeconomics and NIE, emphasise market imperfections and take an interest in the institutions involved in the regulation of decentralised economies.

A number of theoretical trends and practices, which identify themselves with institutionalism, have emerged in the field of development economics. The point of departure for all these new institutional approaches is the inability of pure Walrassian equilibrium to deal with the uniqueness of accumulation and behaviour of economic operators in underdeveloped countries. According to these authors, markets are less harmonious in Third World countries, the division of the labour market is very deep, and the situation of extreme poverty leads operators to behave in ways that do not conform to the postulates of the basic Walrassian model. Berthélemy, Devezeaux de Lavergne and Gagey note that, 'under the influence of factors that are unusual in rich countries, economic rationality can lead to reactions that appear paradoxical to the pricing system' (Berthélemy et al., 1991).

Stiglitz (1988) lists a series of stylised facts in Third World countries that cannot be analysed by standard theory, including:

- tremendous urban unemployment, which makes it appear that wages are higher than market equilibrium wages;
- considerable wage differences for relatively similar levels of qualification;
- considerable migration from rural areas to urban areas despite urban unemployment;
- modes of distribution based on principles of sharing and community participation, especially in the rural environment, rather than on productivity.

Questioning the ability of the pure model to make sense of concrete realities in underdeveloped countries has not led to a break between the new institutionalism and the basic model. On the contrary, NIE in the field of development is an extension of neoclassical theory, to the extent that it seeks to explain institutions by the microeconomic behaviour of operators (Yong, 1994). From this standpoint, institutions allow operators to maximise their behaviour in a context of imperfect information and competition. NIE can thus be distinguished from J.R. Commons' conception, which seeks the foundations of collective behaviour through an analysis of institutions. In NIE, institutions are restricted to the study of forms of coordination among operators as a result of market imperfections.

The diversity of the new institutional approaches can be observed through an analysis of the different definitions of institutions proposed by different authors. North establishes a distinction between institution and organisation. According to this analysis, institutions represent all the formal rules (laws, etc.) and informal constraints conceived by people, which form the structure of incentives in an economy (North, 1994). Organisations, on the other hand, are conceived by North as individuals or groups of individuals. Interactions between institutions and organisations are the foundation for social change. This distinction between organisation and institution is not taken up by authors such as Nabli and Nugent, who define an institution as a set of rules and constraints that govern behaviour and relationships between individuals or groups (Nabli and Nugent, 1989). From this viewpoint, organisations such as labour unions, various markets, implicit or explicit contracts and codes of cultural behaviour are seen as institutions, since they produce standards of behaviour for individuals or groups of individuals. According to Stiglitz, institutions include rules and operational standards, as well as organisations such as the family or the market (Stiglitz, 1988).

The diversity of NIE resides essentially in the conceptions and aspects, which different authors stress in their analysis of institutions.

Institutionalism and Transaction Costs

Certain authors focus on Coase and Williamson's transaction cost approach, which considers that, in the context of an imperfect market, businesses seek to internalise a great many activities in order to save on costs generated by recourse to the outside (Basu, 1984). This theory has not been much developed, because of criticisms mainly of its descriptive character and its lack of an operational definition of the notion of transaction costs.

Institutionalism and Social Change

This theory is an extension of North's work on economic history. North places institutions at the centre of the evolution of different economies and views them as the foundation for the decadence or the prosperity of nations (North, 1988). According to this conception, development is defined as growth dynamics with effective institutional change.

According to North, relative price changes are the foundation for institutional change, since they lead economic actors to define new contractual and institutional arrangements. North's theory of institutions includes three levels of analysis:

- a theory of the rights of property and organisation, which, according to North, helps the problems of incentives and information in a market economy;
- a theory of government, which, according to North, plays a central role since it defines and implements property rights;
- a theory of ideology that justifies and explains actors' behaviour and especially induces them to control their individualistic actions and makes them more sensitive to equilibrium and social stability.

North's ideas on institutions have led to the development of a considerable body of work in development economics. Ruttan and Hayami (1984), for instance, developed the theory of institutional innovation induced by interactions between supply and demand. Feeny (1979) showed that the rising price of land in Thailand from 1850 onwards and its opening up to international trade led to stronger land property rights and the abandonment of slavery. Other authors, such as Bently and Oberhofer (1981), observed similar developments in West Africa, with increased demand for institutional change following economic development and an increase in productivity under the impact of technical change.

Institutionalism and Imperfect Information

This is the largest school of institutionalist thought, which wields considerable influence in the field of development theory. This approach seeks to understand the formation of institutions through the rational behaviour of economic operators. The imperfect nature of economic information explains imperfections in market operations, which different actors seek to minimise, by implementing a multitude of contracts and microeconomic organisations (Bardhan, 1993).

The most representative work of this school is that of Stiglitz. His theory of imperfect information is based on five central hypotheses (Stiglitz, 1985, 1986, 1988):

- economic operators are rational;
- information has a cost, and therefore, individuals do not have perfect information at their disposal;
- institutions are endogenous and represent the response of operators to problems of access to information;
- the economy is not efficient in Pareto's sense of the word, which means operators adapt and sometimes act in ways that contradict classic rationality;
- in this situation of imperfect information, the government must play a major role to promote the coordination of maximising behaviour by operators and so make up for market imperfections.

In this theory, an examination of situations of imperfect information is the point of departure for studying development problems and analysing the behaviour of economic operators in underdeveloped economies. This approach has shown a particular interest in the behaviour of peasants in Third World countries, which classical analyses viewed as irrational. Contrary to the standard line of thought, institutional economists have shown that the contractual forms developed by peasants at the grassroots level constitute rational responses to market imperfections, and especially to the uncertainty surrounding the rural environment in underdeveloped countries, because of technological backwardness and the lack of any form of support from the public authorities (Bardhan, 1989; Binswanger and Rosenzweig, 1984; Eswaran and Kotwal, 1985; Stiglitz, 1988).

This school has studied other themes, such as the experiences of Southeast Asian countries (Chang, 1993; Haggard, 1990). According to Cheng, Haggard and Kang, the transition towards a system of promotion of exports in Asian countries required the formation of a series of institutions, which strengthened the government and its ability to formulate and implement its strategies (Cheng et al., 1996). According to these authors, despite differences in their development strategies, Asian countries organised four types of institutions, which contributed considerably to their growth dynamics:

- the first institution involves the constitutional system, which defined the connections and relationships between the different political actors. In most

countries, this was an authoritarian system in which powers were concentrated;
- the establishment of an organised and highly qualified government bureaucracy;
- the role played by different negotiating and arbitration organisations involving governments and the business community. These institutions helped solve problems of information and facilitated the dialogue necessary to work out development strategies and policies;
- strong state institutions, which played a dynamic role in these countries' rapid industrialisation, especially industrial development boards and sectorial institutions (heavy industry boards, export councils and other export organisations ...).

Stiglitz also looked into the growth dynamics of Asian countries (Stiglitz, 1996). In his analysis, he stressed the need for government intervention in incomplete and imperfect markets. According to Stiglitz, inadequate markets are important in underdeveloped countries, and require government intervention as the experience of Asian countries has shown, to correct their imperfections and to ensure a greater coordination of the strategic actions of different operators.

Government action has been particularly decisive in the financial sector in Asian countries, because imperfection is more serious in that market and can threaten development efforts. Stiglitz lists a series of imperfections in the financial market that call for regulating intervention by the government (Stiglitz, 1994). Public authorities in Asian countries contributed to the creation of a financial system and various financing institutions. They also closely regulated the operations of financial markets by directing funds to certain industrial activities and not to others (Stiglitz, 1996).

To sum up, this branch of NIE has played an important role in challenging the pure Walrassian model, by demonstrating its inability to analyse and understand the unique behaviours of economic operators in situations of imperfect competition and information. These studies contributed to the criticism of the consensus that had dominated development economics since the beginning of the 1980s. While this branch of NIE criticises traditional microeconomics, it does not, however, cut all ties with liberalism, as its theoretical methods are an extension of the new Walrassian microeconomics and aim to enrich the basic model by giving it the means to understand and analyse market imperfections linked to imperfect information. Institutions are thus analysed as a product of maximising and rational behaviour by those operating in imperfect markets. This is a reductionist view, which limits institutions to arrangements and rules, which operators establish in situations of imperfect information. The approach is marked by methodological individualism, and its analytical scope excludes the collective behaviour, which the founding fathers of the institutional school of thought favoured in the works of J.R. Commons. Bardhan (1989) points out that these analyses ignore the power relationships and struggles within institutions, which lead to an unequal sharing of property rights.

In the field of development, NIE cannot easily explain and analyse the genesis of institutions (creation and renewal). Indeed, most contributions are limited to a synchronic vision of institutions, trying to describe them and understand the role they play in the dynamics of accumulation and economic growth. The dynamics of the creation and evolution of institutions are rarely analysed. For example, with respect to transition dynamics in Third World countries, NIE holds that the efficiency of the institutions set up in Asian countries is responsible for these countries' dynamic and competitive integration into the world economy. This approach does not explain why these economies were able to develop efficient institutions and why other Third World countries have not been able to follow the same pattern. In other words, we need to understand the underlying causes of the inefficiency of institutions in most Third World countries except in Southeast Asia. NIE merely describes institutions which are supposed to function efficiently in certain countries, without proposing means and mechanisms to improve the performance of institutions in other countries, so as to promote a revival of growth dynamics and of dynamic integration into the international economy.

In conclusion, while the new institutional economics allows us to enrich the pure equilibrium model in development studies by increasing its relevance, it does not equip us to analyse the dynamics in progress in the Third World, and particularly the different transitions occurring since the mid-1980s. Nor does this school of thought live up to expectations in terms of development strategies, in the context of the crisis of the nation-state and the increased opening of national economies to the international economy.

Note

1 In this respect, it should be noted that several advocates of the new institutional economics, such as Stiglitz, come from the neo-Keynesian movement.

Chapter 4

Heterodoxy and Post-Adjustment

In this chapter we will continue our study of the post-adjustment theories. The first section is devoted to the conventionalist approaches. The middle section will be devoted to the new structuralist and Keynesian approaches. The last part will deal with the cultural approach.

Relativisation of Rationality

Several works, especially in French, have examined the relativisation of the rationality of economic actors subject to social and economic determinism. This work challenges the ability of traditional microeconomics to grasp these specific modes of behaviour, and attempts to explain the gap between the rationality of these actors and Walrassian rationality. This work has dealt with African economies and has attempted to deal with theories on the irrationality of African economic actors. 'Economic irrationality', according to Hugon (1995), 'is linked to the degree of priority given the symbolic dimension of actions. The value of persons and interpersonal relationships is greater than the value of things'.

These studies have stressed African economic operators' submission to two systems of determination: the community system, which binds them to their home community through a series of obligations, and the individual system, in which economic agents attempt to fulfil their subjective needs. It is against this background that Hugon (ibid.) writes that: 'What is a virtue according to community logic (polygamy, solidarity, respect for ancestors), becomes a vice, according to the logic of efficiency:– nepotism, patronage, tribalism.'

This overlapping of two types of reasoning has major consequences on development studies, particularly about the viability of statistical systems, which are essentially based on individual systems of determination, and do not account for the weight of community logic in actors' behaviour. Indeed, 'The statistical methods used,' says Mahieu (1995), 'are based on an individual representation of social determinations. Individualism in this case is only one method for representing the impact of social factors on individual behaviour.'

This approach makes the community an important social institution, which plays an important role in mitigating the impact of uncertainty and instability in Africa. From a theoretical point of view, this approach is close to the French conventionalist approach, which seeks to move beyond standard theory and extended standard theory and to construct a new conception of the socialisation of actors, by taking institutions and conventions into consideration (Hammouda, 1997). In the study of conventions in underdeveloped economies, Favereau distinguishes three levels of analysis (Favereau, 1995).

- *The first level involves agents' individual rationality*

In this context, Favereau considers that decision-making criteria differ and change from one polity to another. Furthermore, each polity develops its own mechanisms and procedures for the social management of uncertainty. 'We will consider,' writes Favereau (1995, p. 186):

> rules of decision-making to be a priori no more and no less rational in African economies than in European economies, on condition that we admit that decisions are rational within the framework of socially constructed formulations of decision-making problems. The uniqueness of African economies (sub-Saharan Africa) should be sought in the type of socialisation of uncertainty, and more specifically, in the possible preponderance of the Domestic Polity over the other Polities, in the social inscription of individual rationalities.

In African societies, Favereau concurs with Mahieu's hypothesis of the decisive role played by community standards on the behaviour of individual actors.

- *The second level of coordination involves businesses*

Favereau begins by pointing out the principal characteristics of African businesses, including poor management and the prevalence of corruption. These characteristics are a result of the preponderance of social institutions (such as community rule) in motivating the individual behaviour of economic operators. In this context, African businesses are a centre of production, which aims to redistribute the wealth they create rather than to accumulate it. Furthermore, the domination of the commercial polity by the domestic polity can be observed in African businesses, which attempt to reproduce social relationships external to them, thus further weakening them.

- *The third level of coordination involves equilibrium of rules*

In order to analyse coordination as a whole, Favereau uses the conventionalists' idea of a balance of rules, which examines economic operators' rules of adaptation and adjustment. This idea leads him to suggest that the model of operation of African businesses cannot lead to strong growth. In fact, according to Favereau (1995, p. 195):

> African societies' microeconomic modes of adaptation to uncertainty tend to increase macroeconomic uncertainty, by making the economy more vulnerable to conjunctural crises, crises of supply and crises of demand.

In Favereau's view, SAPs, which attempt to reduce deficits, should be reinforced, and local agents should be taught standards of efficiency by organisational reforms, so as to overcome the institutional obstacles, which characterise these societies.

In their criticism of standard microeconomic studies, conventionalist analyses do not stray from their normative methodology. Indeed, their work switches between scientific analysis and normative discourse on development. These analyses advance the hypothesis of the superiority of capitalist management standards over all other forms or standards of management. The objective of the analysis is no longer to understand the underlying reasons for economic crises in Africa, but to demonstrate that the crisis is the result of lack of conformity of operators' behaviour with what is supposed to be the rational standard of behaviour. Seen in this light, the goal of development strategy is to bring the behaviour of operators closer to the capitalist standard, which is seen as an ideal model of efficiency, and to break away from the grassroots solidarity that African societies have been able to maintain, despite the violent penetration of commercial relationships during the colonial period. From this point of view, the violence of adjustment, which sought to reduce social regulation by the state, does not go far enough and should be reinforced by other forms of action against grassroots solidarity, which is viewed as a serious obstacle to development.

The study of the community as an institution that plays an important role in the socialisation of African economic operators is central to Mahieu's research (1990). He considers that:

> economic theory is confronted with particularities in African economic behaviour at two levels: the microeconomic level of the relationship with the community

and the macroeconomic level of the relationship between the state and these same communities.

At the microeconomic level, African economic operators are subject to community constraints, which, according to these analyses, are superimposed on the maximising individualistic logic of the pure equilibrium model. 'Survival thus depends,' according to Mahieu (1990, p. 12), 'not only on individual rights (and the corresponding trade list), but above all on community rights, which are conditioned by obligations towards the self-same community.'

In order to analyse the community, Mahieu introduces the ideas of rights and obligations. From this point of view, the community is made up of a dense network of rights and obligations between individuals. The foundations of the community are not restricted to economic aspects, but also include political, religious and other motivations, which are more closely linked to the imaginary and symbolic world. In this world, each individual has an individual list of rights and obligations towards his or her community. This list gives rise to exchanges and transfers between individuals. From this point of view, African societies appear as societies of a community imposed on its members and of community transfers. These exchanges may lead to disequilibrium, since certain individuals may receive more than they give. 'This situation,' explains Mahieu (ibid., p. 122), 'of credit or debit with respect to the community depends largely on the individual's position in the history of the community.'

This system of rights and obligations draws its strength from the system of sanctions that communities set in place to impose strict respect for community standards on every individual. Furthermore, the community represents for each individual a refuge and a guarantee in periods of uncertainty. According to the author, this conception constitutes a radical criticism of the analyses of the World Bank, which, 'by refusing to step outside the framework of the market, shut themselves up in the economic theory of rational households and totally bypass the reality of the community' (ibid., p. 23).

Community relationships do not, however, stop at the microeconomic level, they also involve a macroeconomic dimension in the relations between the state and the various communities that form the nation-state. There too, according to Mahieu, community constraints and community transfers are central to relations between the state and citizens. According to this, the state's various social expenditures should be analysed through the prism of community constraints and transfers that have to be made to different communities.

Despite its intention of breaking away from the neoclassical framework and from the standard analyses of the World Bank, this approach is still marked by an a-historical and static analysis. In its essentialist analytical grid, community constraints appear as a characteristic outside time, and are therefore unaffected by historical evolution. A number of studies have pointed out the destructuring of community relationships in African countries since colonial times. To introduce export crops, colonial authorities reformed local fiscal systems, particularly by imposing taxes in cash. These economic changes were at the root of the development of commercial relationships, which began to erode community relationships (Hammouda, 1993). This process continued in the post-colonial period, with attempts to reform the modern state and with the emergence of an urban middle class, which began to free itself from its community ties, and formed the core for the emergence of the autonomous individual. Community relations have not, of course, completely disappeared, but in the face of these changes, their impact has become increasingly formal.

The idea of community constraints is not a new one in the study of African communities. As far back as 1957, in his analysis of the historical evolution of societies, Amin was the first to introduce the hypothesis of a succession of three modes of production, the community family, the tributary family and the capitalist mode, as an alternative to the hypotheses of the Asian mode of production or the succession of five modes of production (Amin, 1979, 1996). According to Amin, the succession of these three forms of social organisation occurred through two basic events. The first was responsible for the transition from the community mode to the tributary mode. In community society, land ownership was established on a community basis and kinship ideology dominated society and played an important role in maintaining it. In tributary societies, social power was crystallised within state cores, which dominated economic activities and land ownership. Under community and tributary systems, economic activities are marked by the value of tradition and attach little importance to commercial exchanges. Tributary authorities legitimise their social control in the metaphysical and religious ideological world. The second major change involved the transition from tributary societies to capitalism, with the development of commercial relations and the private appropriation of the means of production and an economic ideology.

The argument developed by Amin was a simple research hypothesis, which we should continue to question, particularly with regards to 'failed' transitions towards capitalism in certain underdeveloped societies, such as the Arab world or Africa. But it has an advantage over the neo-communitarian theories in that it provides a dynamic and historical grid of explanation, which does not stop at a mere empirical observation of the importance of the community in Africa, but attempts to understand and analyse it. In parallel with the difficulties acknowledged by Mahieu (1990) in setting up a community formula to replace the Walrassian formula, the community as a microeconomic constraint has stood the test of time, and despite the mutations and evolutions of African societies and their legitimising world, continues to explain the behaviour of individuals and economic actors.

The analyses of the neo-communitarian macroeconomic school of thought also pose certain difficulties and evoke criticism. It should be pointed out in the first place that this conception of macroeconomic relations is limited to mutual transfers between the state and the different communities. Everything seems to take place in the best of all worlds, to the extent that what the state levies from the different communities is returned through agricultural development programmes or other types of state expenditures, particularly social spending. This interpretation, which does not include power struggles between the state and the different communities, is contradicted by present-day facts. Firstly, democratic openness and the questioning of authoritarian power have demonstrated that African states, after a brief modernist period, have turned inwards to their leaders' ethnic or regional communities, to the exclusion of the other communities. Thus, while certain communities have benefited from certain transfers, others have been totally excluded from the distribution of the fruits of the economic growth of the 1960s and 1970s. This political and economic exclusion partly explains the identity-based nature of the movement protesting against the political monopoly of the African state in the 1980s.

Neo-communitarian theorists seem also to minimise the impact of state levies on peasants, especially since they consider that state transfers feed into community solidarity networks. This analysis is contradicted by precise studies and field surveys in different African economies (Cochet, 1996). This work shows that, on the contrary, levies on peasants have played an important role in setting up state structures and have obstructed accumulation on farms, thus engendering low agricultural productivity. The limitation of the modernisation of agricultural productive structures and low levels of agricultural surplus meant that, from the mid-1970s, African states went into debt, in order to continue to fund growth dynamics. State investment in agriculture was rarely directed at improving agricultural productivity, however, especially that of subsistence crops. On the contrary, agricultural development efforts in the 1970s were aimed at export crops, which produced income to feed government budgets. Relations between the state and the communities have thus nothing in common with the smooth, stable image conveyed by the neo-communitarian theorists. On the contrary, the study of state/community relations places us at the heart of mechanisms of control and social domination exercised by the state over African peasants.

The neo-communitarian theorists explain low agricultural productivity by community constraints. According to these theorists, African peasants attribute greater importance to community time and social activities than to productive activities, which leads to a negative impact on agricultural productivity. Mahieu (1990, p. 86) notes that:

> several perverse effects intervene in the allocation of time for productivity, because of the priority given to community time and the particular value of formal work in relation to the community. Any attack on the distribution structure has chain effects on the substitution of informal activities for formal activities and on reduced productivity.

In this analysis, reduced agricultural productivity and the stagnation of agricultural development are essentially due to the inadequate means of production available on African farms. Equipment is not very diversified, limited as it is to hoes, machetes and a few baskets. The availability of these tools is problematical, since industrial development as envisaged in most African countries after independence, has paid little heed to coordination with agriculture. Furthermore, since transportation equipment is not well developed, in most cases, peasants carry their produce, which is not without consequences on the availability of labour input on farms. In addition, fertilisers and pesticides are rarely used, as they are seldom available and are relatively expensive. Finally, there is little variety in the biological material available to peasants (Hammouda, 1995).

These factors, taken together, are responsible for the low productivity of labour and especially the difficulties reported in many African countries during work peaks, contrary to the affirmations of communitarian theorists regarding the time peasants spend on community obligations. The main consequence of peasants' low labour capacity, because of inadequate equipment, has been a restriction of the surface area farmed per person, which promotes the process of degradation of soil fertility. Furthermore, the low productivity and the precarious balance on farms are accompanied by a broad movement of decapitalisation, in order to maintain the labour force.

The neo-communitarian theory reduces the complexity of relationships and relations in underdeveloped societies, especially in African economies, to community constraints, thus excluding from the field of analysis a number of phenomena that have considerable importance in the recent evolution of underdeveloped economies. Despite the major criticisms they apply to the general economic equilibrium school of thought, institutionalist theories do not on the whole offer us a way out of the crisis in development studies. Throughout this section, we have demonstrated their inability to analyse and understand the mutations and evolutions in progress in most Third World countries. The difference between transitions is a particular blind spot for these theories. Beyond a few ad hoc recommendations, these different approaches have not been able to revive reflection on development strategies. The limitations of the neo-institutionalist theory reside in its methodological choices and the option of methodological individualism. While this methodological choice permits a more detailed analysis of the behaviour of economic actors and challenges Walrassian rationality, it does not make it possible to analyse the differentiated transitions and evolutions taking place in underdeveloped countries. These phenomena are structural in nature and therefore require global visions and comprehensive analytical grids.

Revival of the Structuralist Approach

The structuralist approach has played an important role in the emergence and development of development economics. This approach took shape in the 1940s and 1950s in Latin America with the work of ECLA and Prebisch, in Europe with Perroux and Myrdal and in the United States with Hirschman. This approach differs from the neoclassical approach in that it challenges the equilibrium model and its ability to ensure coherent allocation of productive resources. Influenced by the Keynesian approach, the structuralist approach defends the idea of state intervention in economic regulation and in correcting market imperfections (Oman and Wignaraja, 1991).

The most important contribution of structuralist studies, however, resides in their consideration of structural aspects in analysing Third World economies. Thus, underdevelopment is not analysed as a natural phenomenon, but as an historical situation linked to the breakdown of productive structures and to the phenomena of domination exerted by the international economy. According to structuralist analysis, the global economy is made up of two poles with totally different productive structures. Production structures are thus heterogeneous, to the extent that they include low-productivity traditional sectors and high-productivity modern sectors. Productive structures in peripheral areas are specialised in a number of primary products that are exported to developed countries. Contrary to the peripheral areas, productive structures in developed countries are homogeneous, in that all sectors use the same production techniques. Furthermore, these structures are diversified allowing central economies to operate in a coherent manner.

The impact of these structures is central to structural analysis of the phenomena of underdevelopment. According to this approach, structural unemployment in underdeveloped countries is due to the heterogeneous nature of productive structures. On one hand, labour-intensive traditional sectors cannot employ all the manpower generated by rapid population growth. On the other hand, modern sectors use capital-intensive technologies and provide few jobs.

This approach also views foreign deficits as an expression of the productive structures of peripheral countries. While the elasticity of demand for the import of manufactured goods in peripheral areas is higher than one, the elasticity of demand for the import of primary goods in central areas is lower than one. This difference in elasticity is responsible for the chronic trade deficits of peripheral countries. This situation is further aggravated by the tendency of central countries, thanks to technological progress, to substitute synthetic intermediary products for raw materials and primary products imported from peripheral countries. The difference between the elasticities of demand for imports and the limited number of products exported by peripheral countries is responsible for the steady deterioration of the terms of trade. According to the structuralist approach, these phenomena create a natural trend towards uneven development between the two poles of the global economy and perpetuate underdevelopment in the peripheral areas.

With that background in mind, structuralists have formulated a number of recommendations aimed at breaking out of the vicious circle of underdevelopment and initiating new development strategies in the periphery. First of all, they emphasise the role of the state in correcting market imperfections, especially by setting up a new development strategy aimed at the domestic market. In addition, this approach put forward the idea of unbalanced growth and the need to concentrate investment in strategic sectors capable of stimulating the economy as a whole. The strategies suggested by the structuralist approach sought to replace imported consumer goods by local goods. These import-substitution strategies led to a severe regulation of imports, in order to build up the competitiveness of industrial activities developed throughout the periphery.

The structuralist approach that developed following the end of World War II combined considerable theoretical reflection with a number of proposed development strategies.

According to this approach, through concentrating development on the domestic market and through state intervention, it should be possible to reverse the trend of uneven development between the centre and the periphery and allow growth to take off in underdeveloped economies.

This approach began to be challenged at the end of the 1960s, however. First, the stagnation of Latin-American economies and of all the economies that adopted import-substitution strategies led to criticism of the structuralist approach. This development strategy did not enable the periphery to recover high growth rates and aggravated the external deficits of underdeveloped economies. In addition, at the end of the 1960s, there was the emergence of dependency theories, which criticised the theoretical foundations and the 'reforming' political proposals of the structuralist approach. For the dependency theorists, the failure of import-substitution strategies was proof that structuralist recommendations could develop nothing but further underdevelopment and that the development of the periphery required a radical break with the global economy.

This criticism was responsible for the marginalisation of the structuralist approach in the 1970s. The approach was even more strongly criticised in the 1980s, with the return in force in the field of development economics of the pure general equilibrium model and the Washington Consensus's attack on all forms of government intervention in the running of developing economies.

The decline of the Washington Consensus following the failure of structural adjustment programmes led, however, to a revival of the structuralist approach and to the emergence at the end of the 1980s of a new theoretical model based on that approach. The point of departure for neo-structuralism was a double criticism of the theoretical foundations and the development options of structural adjustment programmes. From a theoretical standpoint, the new approaches criticised the Washington Consensus's concentration on supply issues and the marginalisation of demand in the analysis of disequilibrium in underdeveloped countries. Accordingly, they proposed a rehabilitation of demand as a category of analysis and as a foundation for new development policies (Fontaine and Jacmart, 1993).

In the early 1980s, advocates of neo-structuralism were already criticising the stabilisation programmes of the World Bank and IMF, which they considered ill-suited to absorbing deficits while maintaining growth in underdeveloped countries (Taylor, 1981). The restrictive monetary policy, recommended by the IMF, led to a rapid increase in production costs, which led to a reduction in supply and to renewed social conflicts over distribution. According to the neo-structuralists, this drop in supply and the ensuing inflationary pressures can increase disequilibrium between supply and demand. Furthermore, increased exports are not an inevitable result of devaluation, since they require an elasticity of demand for these exports higher than one. Devaluation does, however, lead to higher prices for imported goods and particularly equipment, which leads to higher production costs and reduced investment. According to the neo-structuralists, the stabilisation advocated by Bretton Woods institutions cannot reduce deficits, but actually increases them and thus perpetuates the dependency of underdeveloped countries.

Neo-structuralists follow the structuralist approach in attempting to revive demand, while criticising the neo-liberal stabilisation policies inspired by the Walrassian model. They also remind us that development studies should take into consideration the specific structural aspects of underdeveloped societies. They pointed to structural rigidities that prevent the spontaneous balance between supply and demand, and they called for government regulation. These analyses also related to both Marxist and classical analyses, since their models included production costs and analysed inflation as the result of conflicts between salaries and profits.

Neo-structuralist analyses differ from the founders of the structuralist approach in opting for a comparative static analysis of equilibrium situations. In their analyses, the neo-structuralists opt for short- and medium-term models, including IS/LM models (Taylor, 1981). They also differ from the founders on the role of the state. While early structuralist analysis stressed the fundamental role of the state in economic growth dynamics, the new analyses questioned state intervention in the dynamics of accumulation, and recommended firm discipline in the management of public funds, by reducing subsidies on basic commodities and by privatising non-strategic public enterprises. It also considered that to rebuild business competitiveness, it was necessary to reduce customs barriers and to improve the capital content of exports (Romo, 1994).

The neo-structuralist approach contains a wide variety of schools and authors. Looking beyond this diversity, we can distinguish two main approaches. First, there is the Latin-American approach, which in keeping with criticism of orthodox stabilisation models, has inspired heterodox stabilisation experiments in Latin America. These models of stabilisation have used administrative control of prices and the suppression of the wage index to fight hyperinflation, especially in Brazil with the Austral Plan and in Argentina with the Cruzado Plan (Grellet, 1994; Salama and Valier, 1990). However, these experiments failed and were unable to control deficits in those countries and effectively to fight inflation.

A second neo-structuralist approach developed out of the work and early models of Taylor. This approach uses a Keynesian perspective to study the impact of various stabilisation scenarios on the economies of underdeveloped countries. This work is theoretical in nature (Ocampo, 1987), but also includes applied research on Third World economies, including African economies (Ndulu, 1991; Lundahl and Ndulu, 1996).

In this section, we present one of Taylor's models, in order to discuss the theses of the neo-structuralist approaches, since all the authors draw on his work. Taylor, like all neo-structuralist writers, begins by criticising orthodox stabilisation models and questions their ability to fight imbalances in underdeveloped economies while maintaining economic growth. Taylor (1988) then emphasises that macroeconomic policies have five objectives:

- to maintain a socially acceptable level of growth;
- to maintain a low rate of inflation;
- to increase wealth creation and to improve its distribution;
- to maintain a certain degree of financial and commercial independence with regard to foreign countries;
- to achieve these objectives in a stable environment, capable of overcoming all shocks.

In his study of macroeconomic policies, Taylor took particular interest in ways of closing models. He distinguished two methods, a stagnationist system based on stimulating demand and an exhilarationist system based on restructuring supply. This distinction coincides with the traditional distinction between Keynesian underemployment, which corresponds to the stagnationist system, and full employment, which corresponds to the exhilarationist system. In a stagnationist system, increased effective demand and progressive income redistribution leads to increased production and higher rates of utilisation of production capacities, thus increasing employment. On the contrary, in a full employment situation, the economy reacts to a regressive distribution of income, which can increase the share of profits in national income, leading to a revival of investment.

Taylor transposes this distinction to underdeveloped economies. He specifies, however, that the two systems can coexist, because of the existence in certain underdeveloped economies of under-utilised resources with rigidity of supply. In that context, IMF stabilisation policies include five types of changes in economic policy (Taylor, 1988):

- austerity, in that the public sector must reduce its deficit;
- revision of the rate of exchange in the sense of a devaluation;
- monetary restrictions;
- liberalisation of the market in order to improve macroeconomic performances in the medium term;
- a new regressive policy, with restrictions on salaries and a reduction in the transfer programme.

IMF and World Bank stabilisation policies are supply-side restructuring policies for underdeveloped countries, designed to address macroeconomic imbalances (Fontaine, 1993). Supply-side restructuring is not based here on increased investment, but rather on improved and increased production, forming the basis for a recovery in exports. In this framework, control of public spending plays an important role, since it makes possible a decision in favour of foreign demand rather than domestic demand.

The supply-side recovery plan in the orthodox stabilisation model is designed to combat major imbalances, particularly in the balance of payments, while maintaining economic growth. In this schema, supply-side restructuring can lead to a recovery in exports that makes possible an increase in growth and employment. Recovery in domestic demand, owing to increased employment, promotes an increase in the use of productive capacity and an increase in investment. This way, supply-side restructuring can improve major economic balances and bring about recovery in the dynamics of economic growth. However, in his study on a series of stabilisation experiences in the Third World, Taylor (1988) notes that this schema comes up against some serious obstacles. Firstly, elasticity of export supply is low in underdeveloped countries, whereas imports have reached an incompressible level, which makes it difficult to achieve equilibrium in the balance of payments. Furthermore, the orthodox stabilisation model, based on supply-side restructuring and recovery in exports, may be blocked by the impact of export composition, reduced global demand and the protectionist attitudes, which have begun to develop in the global economy.

Export recovery does not necessarily lead to a recovery of growth in domestic markets, however, since devaluation can have recessive effects. Furthermore, monetary restriction and higher interest rates increase production costs and consequently reduce investment. Thus, the recessive nature of orthodox stabilisation programmes can block structural reforms aimed at dynamic integration of underdeveloped economies in the international economy.

Taylor (1991) systematised his analyses of stabilisation programmes, using different models. In this section, we examine a series of models he developed in 1991. These models are the result of an eclectic mixture of structuralist theories, the Cambridge School and Marxist ideas. The models are based on a series of stylised facts, which the author attempts to clarify. Among these facts, we can cite the following:

- there is a need to identify the power centres in economies and the price rigidity they induce;
- macroeconomic equilibrium does not necessarily lead to full employment of the factors of production. Macroeconomic balance depends on investment, exports, fiscal pressure, etc.;
- the supply of currency is endogenous, and can be adjusted to the level of economic activity and inflation;
- a structuralist conception of inflation based on social conflicts over distribution;
- relations between real and financial sectors may be illustrated by changes in portfolios;
- the import-substitution strategy entails recourse to foreign countries to import capital goods and intermediate goods;
- development is not a harmonious growth process.

In this model, Taylor considers a closed economy[1] with a single sector. He specifies two versions in this model: a structuralist version and a neoclassical version. The objective of this model is to determine the evolution of the economy following macroeconomic changes. We will restrict our discussion to a presentation of the structuralist version, which is based on demand.

- *The point of departure of this model is macroeconomic equilibrium*

(1) Product = Demand

(!) $PX = PC + PI + PG$

$$PC + PI + PG - PX = 0$$

where X: the product
C: consumption

I: investment
G: government spending
P: prices.

Income distribution can be expressed as follows:

(2) $PX = wbX + rPK$

where w: monetary wage rate
b: labour share in the product
r: rate of profit
K: capital stock.

Total consumption can be expressed as follows:

(3) $PC = wbX + (1\text{-}s)rPK$

workers' savings are equal to zero
capital savings are equal to s.

By combining equation (1), (2) and (3), we obtain the following equation:

(4) $PG + PI - srPK = 0$

This is the equation of macroeconomic balance, which stipulates equality between private saving and government spending.

Taylor makes the hypothesis that:

increased capital due to national saving is equal to:

(5) $g^s = sr\ PK/PK$

increased capital linked to investment demand is:

$g^i = PI/PK$

increased government spending linked to increased capital is:

(6) $\mu = PG/PK$

At this level, equation (4) becomes:

(4) $\mu + g^i - g^s = 0$

The investment function in this model is linked to use of production capacity, measured by

(7) $u = X/K$.

u is a contemporary version of the accelerator that makes investment a response to economic activity over the medium term. Investment is also linked to the rate of profit, r, which can be interpreted as businesses' anticipated future receipts or available cash flow when investment is self-financed in periods when credit is rationed.

(8) $g^i = g^i(r,u) = g^i(\pi,u)$

In this model, Taylor chose to determine prices using the mark-up principle:

(9) $P = (1 + \pi)wb = wb/(1 - \pi)$

which means that prices depend on variable costs (in this example, labour) and a set margin determined by producers.

Taylor adds other equations to define his model

(10) $b = L/X$

the ratio of labour to production

(11) $r = [\pi /(1 + \pi)]u = pu$

In this model, the nominal wage is set by historical conditions, capital stock (K) by expected investment, and government spending (G) by economic policy choices. Prices and profit levels are determined by equation (9). The equations for demand (4), (5) and (8) and the equation for distribution make it possible to determine u and r. The production comes from equation (7) and the level of use from equation (10). Thus, the model allows Taylor to determine the level of employment and production in an economy based on demand. Taylor uses the model to examine the consequences and impact of variations in a series of variables (government spending, monetary wages, real wages, etc.) on levels of employment and production (Taylor, 1991).

Overall, these models enable Taylor to examine the impact of orthodox stabilisation programmes and point out their depressive character in Third World economies. In some cases, these programmes only manage to reduce major imbalances by considerably reducing economic activity. But this deflation does not allow underdeveloped economies to carry out the structural reforms they need for more dynamic integration into the international economy. From this standpoint, the structuralist approach is very interesting, since it makes it possible to grasp the limitations of orthodox approaches to stabilisation.

Despite their interest, the new structuralist models cannot, however, overcome the current crisis in development economics and its inability to analyse and understand the mutations and transformations under way in the Third World. Indeed, owing to their very structure, these models are short-term models and only concern aspects linked to macroeconomic balance. The models cannot and by definition do not seek to understand long-term changes in the Third World. The dynamic transitions that have taken place in Southeast Asian economies, for instance, are the result of strategies and choices operating since the middle of the 1960s and reinforced in the 1970s and 1980s through selective and effective state intervention. Indeed, all Asian governments were characterised by a long-term vision. This vision of the future is even more important during a period of crisis that is marked by deep uncertainty about the future. Their vision enabled the authorities to intervene to favour certain industrial activities over others, in terms of investment, subsidies or institutional support.

Their perception of the future has helped Asian governments to favour strategic sectors over access to financing and credit. On the other hand, economies that did not bother to plan for the future and whose development efforts were limited to managing an agricultural export position inherited from the colonial period, now find themselves on the fringe of the international economy. From that point of view, the changes and transitions facing underdeveloped economies are not the result of short-term macroeconomic choices, but rather the end result of long-term choices and options, which short-term models, such as the neo-structuralist models, can neither understand nor explain.

Furthermore, although they identify themselves with the structuralist tradition, these models have a simplified vision of structures. Their conception of structures stops at an examination of distribution in terms of opposition and conflict between wage-earners and profit-makers. This conception, although not without merit, has its limitations, since production is envisaged in the form of macroeconomic sequences, without paying the slightest attention to productive structures. From this standpoint, the neo-structuralist approach does not seem capable of analysing the changes in progress in underdeveloped countries. Indeed, while distribution issues are not marginal to the differentiated transitions experienced by underdeveloped countries, it appears important to study productive structures, in order to understand them. Analysis of the experience of Southeast Asian economies shows that these economies have paid particular attention to productive structures, since, through strong state intervention, they have sought to develop strategic sectors linked to the development of new technologies in order to improve their competitiveness. Furthermore, the Asian experience demonstrates the close and dynamic relationships in industrialisation between industries linked to the domestic market and export industries. The needs of the population should not be neglected, on the pretext of the demands of globalisation and the need to form part of the global market. This process of 'walking on two legs' requires particular attention to be given to wages. These should not be viewed merely as a cost to be controlled, but also as a market outlet, whose development determines the future of industries linked to the domestic market. Countries on the fringe of the international economy have paid little attention to the evolution of their productive structures, and after their experience of import-substitution, have opened up their economies and sacrificed their national economic structures in hopes of integrating with the globalisation movement. Despite the importance of the issue of productive structures, the neo-structuralist approach only pays limited attention to it.

The Cultural Approach

The structural adjustment crisis was behind the development and confirmation of a new approach to development economics. This is the cultural approach, which is found largely in Francophone literature. It puts forward the hypothesis that the failure of adjustment is simply a manifestation of the crisis affecting the North's attempts to Westernise the South.

UNESCO's work, which sought to give a cultural dimension to development, was at the source of the cultural approach in the 1970s (Kellerman, 1992). This first generation of work was continued by the work of Latouche (1986, 1989, 1991) and Rist in the late 1980s (1994, 1996).

The failure of development strategies in the Third World was the point of departure for the cultural approach. According to Latouche (1986, pp. 7–8):

> Every technique has proved to be ineffective. Whether it was international specialisation, import-substitution policies, focusing on heavy industries, promoting those industries that would lead to industrialisation, specialisation in export niches – every recipe has failed.

This failure led advocates of the cultural approach to challenge the very notion of development. According to these authors, development is a belief in the possibility that through globalisation, the Western myth and model can be extended to the entire planet. From this angle, globalisation is an attempt to impose Western social standards on other societies that have their own specific social standards and constructs. Rist (1996, p. 389) states that:

> the problematic of 'development' is inscribed in the depths of the Western imagination. The idea that growth or progress can develop indefinitely is an assertion that radically distinguishes Western culture from all others.

From this point of view, underdevelopment according to the cultural approach involves 'the extraordinary process of deculturation engendered by the West. Deculturation and Westernisation are two facets of the same phenomenon' (Latouche, 1986, p. 14).

This Eurocentric drive to Westernise the planet is not, however, confined to Westerners alone. It has been reproduced by leaders in the South. Indeed, according to Rist (1996, p. 390), 'the "development" paradigm has become a belief shared equally by all nation-state authorities (and thus by all international organisations), nearly all economic technocrats and a great many populations'.

This criticism of development and Northern expansionist tendencies provides the cultural approach with an opportunity to define the West, which seeks to impose its model of development and its modes of economic and social organisation. Says Latouche (1986, p. 12):

> The West, whose development forms the paradigm, merits description. A geographical space, whose outlines have been more or less definite over the ages, its borders are increasingly ideological in nature. The West was the home of Hellenism, followed by early Christianity, and the triumphant Roman empire, not to mention the Arab-Islamic empire, and its most typical traits can be found between the Mediterranean basin and the shores of the Atlantic.

This definition of the West is relatively vague to the extent that it covers different political entities and civilisations. But the author defines his conception of the West more clearly, when he indicates that it is the space dominated by:

> the belief, unheard of in the rest of the cosmos and in other cultures, in cumulative and linear time, that man has a mission totally to dominate nature, and the belief in reason designed to carry out this action (ibid., p. 13).

It becomes clear that what is being referred to is not so much the West itself as the Western concept of modernity, which has affected European societies at all levels since the French revolution. The first of these levels is the philosophical level, where it has instituted the principle of independent reasoning with respect to religion, following from the works of Thomas Aquinas. Western modernity also established the principle of the separation of politics and religion in managing the politics and affairs of the polity. Finally, this evolution in ideas was accompanied by great scientific and technical progress, which made possible a more rational approach to political and economic structures. This is the heart of the Western model. According to the cultural approach, the function of development is to extend it to the entire planet.

Cultural theorists are opposed to the extension of this model, since they consider that other regions of the world, and the Third World in particular, have their own cultural and social models which should be developed. Cultural writers have an essentialist conception of human societies, to the extent that they consider that every society has a unique culture that forms its world of perceptions and its social imagination. According to these theorists, this cultural universe is stable over time and is not subject to outside influence.

Orientalist studies of the Arab world are an illustration of the essentialist grid of cultural analysts. They consider Arab-Muslim societies to be different from Western societies in terms of the sources of legitimate authority. Indeed, while Western legitimacy is temporal, in Arab-Muslim societies, according to Badie (1987):

> Only God is right, or more exactly his revelation, which is extended to his prophet. This argument for legitimacy, according to certain traditions, can perhaps benefit the first four caliphs, the family of the prophet or his descendants, particularly in duodecimal Shiism, to the twelfth imam.

This version of legitimacy has its source in the conception of the original

Islam of the Muslim community, the Umma, as a totalising community with a universal vocation. This concept allowed the state of Medina to overcome tribal conflicts and political contests over regional leadership and opened up new horizons for the community. Indeed, the Medina model created by the prophet proposed the 'myth of a social order written into divine law' (Camau, 1990) as an alternative to the tribal social order. In this order, authority could only belong to God and could only be exercised by an intermediary (the prophet or the Commander of the Faithful), to whom the community must swear obedience. Legitimacy could only be based on respect for religious precepts.

According to Orientalists, in societies where political life is dominated by religion, the ulama, or religious scholars, should hold a central position in legitimising political authorities, since they determine whether or not political leaders respect religious standards. Thus, as Camau points out, 'allegiance is due to the prince, to the extent that the ulama consider him faithful to the letter of Islamic law' (Camau, 1990, p. 413).

In the view of the Orientalists, this religious legitimacy calls into question all forms of temporal legitimacy in Islamic countries. It compromises any attempt to import elements of Western political modernity. Indeed, in the words of Badie (1987, p. 21):

> to the extent that the state provides the means, particularly territorial means, for its sovereignty, it increases its illegitimacy and makes the prince's effort to achieve legitimisation all the more difficult. If it lays claim to a Weberian political monopoly, it deprives itself of the legitimising function of the ulama; if it concedes them this function, it reduces its political effectiveness.

According to Orientalists, the temporal sphere's obedience to the spiritual sphere in Arab-Muslim societies jeopardises the grafting of elements of Western modernity, and invites these societies to define their own ways of transforming the structures of the exercise of political power.

These analyses have immediate political ramifications in that they devalue the democratic struggle (an avatar of Western political modernity) in Arab societies. Furthermore, according to cultural theorists, the impact of culture leads to specific political behaviour in different societies. The spread and intensification throughout Arab countries of a political practice that draws its inspiration from Islam merely follows the normal course of events. Islam is attempting to revitalise the Medina model and use it as an alternative to the current crisis of the state in the Arab world. According to cultural theorists, who have rediscovered the analyses of political Islam, this crisis is a result of the foreign, imported nature of the reigning political order in Arab societies. According to them, Arab societies must become reconciled with their history and their tradition by a return to and a revival of the model of the Islamic state and the submission of political practice to religious authority.

The spread of the Western model continues to this day, according to cultural theorists, following the crisis of the nation-state, through the myths of globalisation and of integration with the globalisation movement, which are presented as the goal to be achieved by underdeveloped countries. Peemans (1996) points out that this pressure to open up national economies is accompanied by symbolic violence aimed at:

> presenting either as a natural order or as a universal aspiration, even a universal liberation, what is actually a 'world order' that suits the objectives of a new elite, or rather of the new ruling classes that are in process of being formed.

Since its development, the cultural argument has encountered strong opposition and major criticism. The first criticism concerns its conception of culture as an immutable whole, which underestimates the evolutionary dynamics of cultural practices. Bayart (1996, p. 46) points out that, 'cultural theory persists in considering that a culture is made up of a closed, stable set of perceptions, beliefs or symbols that have a strong "affinity" with specific opinions, attitudes or behaviours'. This substantialist conception of culture, which is similar to the German Romantic concept of zeitgeist, encloses individuals in imagined cultural universes. This vision does not take into consideration the perpetual movement of change, experienced by the different cultural sets, through complex mechanisms of innovation and borrowing, which cancel out the 'pure' nature of different perceptions of the world. To take the example of Arab-Muslim societies, which are considered in the cultural argument to be an example of societies where the political sphere is subject to the religious sphere, we can observe a slow yet far-reaching evolution in recent decades, with the emergence of the 'secular' person (Hammouda, 1995). This person, far from rejecting religion, which continues to be a daily practice, is beginning to allow the principle of separation between politics and religion. Certainly, this principle does not find political expression and is not the result of a revolution violent enough to be noticed; but it is at the heart of an insidious evolution in society.

Acceptance of this principle does not contradict either a return to Islam, or individual attempts to seek refuge from the ideological crisis in Islam. The principle is even fuelled by the return to religion, to the extent that holding religion sacred leads individuals to grant it status as the foundation of self-consciousness and to refuse to associate it with the vagaries of the temporal sphere.

The emergence of this new person in the Arab world comes at the crossroads of three major historical developments. The first of these involves the long, slow trend towards the separation of political and religious authority. This separation began during the Abbasid caliphate with the appearance of an important figure: the Vizier. The Vizier was an official who took care of the administrative management of the empire. By the ninth century, his importance had increased and spread to Andalusia, with the Omeyyad caliphs of Spain and the Fatimids of North Africa. The Vizier, who defined the general orientations of the empire and ensured their implementation, with the approval of the caliph, introduced a new sharing of roles between religious authorities and political authorities. In the words of Mantran (1990), 'there was a separation between religious authority – the sphere of the caliph – and political authority – the sphere of the vizier'. With the weakening of the Muslim empires, political authority increasingly took precedence over religious authority.

This tradition was consolidated under the Ottoman Empire from the fifteenth century. Political authority under the Ottomans was personified by the Sultan, who held absolute power and religious legitimacy. The Sultan appointed a Grand Vizier and senior officials in charge of handling the affairs of the empire. This period also saw the beginning of the distinction between public law and religious law. The Ottoman Empire underwent a series of reforms, the most important of which were the Tanzimat reforms, which led to the promulgation of the constitution in 1876. This movement reached its height in 1924, with the end of the caliphate and the establishment of a secular republic by Kamul Atatürk.

This secular political practice was reinforced by a twofold evolution in thinking and theory in the Arab world. The first was linked to the Arab Nahda movement, with such thinkers as Tahtawi, Abdou, Al-Afghani, Abderrazik and others. This movement advocated a series of changes aimed at breaking out of dependency and underdevelopment. The most important was the reform of structures for the exercise of political power through separation from the religious sphere. Parallel to the Nahda movement, the rise of mystical movements from the end of the seventeenth century influenced religious practice in the Arab world. These movements, resulting from the influences of hermetic philosophy on Arab thought, stated that while divinity is inaccessible, it is possible to come in contact with its emanations through prayer and rigorous efforts of asceticism and conjuration. In our view, these movements played an important role in the emergence of the secular person, because they made religion a personal issue involving an individual's relationship with the divinity.

Finally, the emergence of the modern school in the Arab world at the end of the nineteenth century led to the devaluing of Koranic schools and the replacement of traditional elite groups, such as the ulama, by modernist elite groups. These elite groups were further encouraged by the construction of the modern state, which ensured their rapid rise. The conjunction of these three factors explains the evolution of beliefs in the Arab world and the emergence of a 'secular' person, whom the crisis in the modern state only rarely pushes towards a commitment to Islamic political movements. *This is why, in this day and age, it seems difficult to support the hypothesis that political legitimacy in the Arab world is accompanied by religious legitimacy, which forbids all modernisation of political authority in the direction of enhanced participation by citizens.*

The evolution of the relationship between religion and politics is also indicative of the historical changes and mutations that can affect cultural logic and perceptions. Cultures and perceptions evolve and change by following different types of strategies (Bayart, 1996). Among these strategies, we can cite extraversion tactics, essentially linked to colonial presence, transfer practices or authentication procedures. However, openness and the importation of foreign cultural elements are necessarily accompanied by adaptations and reinterpretations of foreign cultural schemas. Bayart (1996, p. 81) describes 'the transfer of meaning from one practice, place or perception, or from one symbol or text to another, because it is, almost by definition, reinterpretation and derivation'.

People thus appropriate and reinterpret foreign cultural practices and perceptions. This permanent reinvention of exogenous cultural contributions and their ownership provides a hybrid picture of local cultural identities.

This act of appropriating exogenous contributions is apparent when we examine the specific relationships each culture creates with the economy and with commercial relationships. The development of capitalism in the periphery demonstrates that this form of social organisation can be adjusted to community relationships and traditional solidarity. As Bayart (1994) states:

> the projection in time of the capitalist economy on the periphery is hardly a linear process. It combines with specific temporalities, which are generally attached to specific places and historical territories: capitalism is obliged to deal with the active memories of the neighbourhood, the bazaar, the chieftainship, the slum and the country.

Indeed, while in Europe and in other countries, capitalism required the dissolution of community relationships and the emergence of individuals who were joined together by commercial relationships, the development of capitalism in the periphery seems to take advantage of traditional forms of solidarity (ethnic communities, regional communities, etc.) and even uses them as the heart and foundation of its development.

It thus follows that, contrary to the claims of the cultural theorists, culture is not a closed and immutable entity; rather it evolves, is transformed and undergoes change in time and space. This evolution is the result of dialogue, borrowing and exchanges between different cultures. These exchanges do not exclude attempts at domination or the wish to exercise hegemony. These dialogues are, however, a source of interbreeding and of mixing between different countries, which means that a 'pure civilisation, whose members are organically linked in an indissociable whole, is a pure fiction' (Shayegan, 1996).

Because of its basic hypotheses on the immutability and the stability of cultural universes, the cultural approach is unable to analyse and understand the dynamics of the evolution of the Third World. In this evolution, it only concerns itself with the marginalisation of certain regions, such as Africa and the Arab world, which it sees as a demonstration of the failure of the North's attempt to Westernise the South. But what can one say of the experiences of other countries, especially in Asia, where for many years the Confucian cultural universe was presented as incompatible with economic development? How can we explain the development, in a great number of Third World countries, of legal and rational forms of political and economic management, the importation of elements of Western political modernity and the relative success of the transplant? How can we understand the important protest movements against political authoritarianism and the calls for democracy in the Third World in recent years? Are these popular movements a negation of their cultural identities? The cultural approach can provide no answer for these important questions.

The cultural approach also comes up against the fundamental question of alternatives to the development crisis in the periphery. Few cultural theorists are interested in that question. Rist (1996) proposes three ways of going beyond the current limitations of the different development projects:

- the first way involves pursuing the growth necessary to satisfy the fundamental needs of the people (Coméliau, 1991). However, the authors recommend controlling the structure of growth and directing it towards essential goods;

- the second way is inspired by the practices of certain social movements in the South, which, faced with the failure of development experiences, have opted for the political struggle of marginalised societies. As Rist (1996) notes, 'Despite "development", the idea is to organise the creation of new ways of life, which lie between modernisation, which brings suffering and yet confers certain advantages, and tradition, which can be a source of inspiration, but which can never be revived';
- finally, the third way is that of radical criticism of the economic vision behind all the presuppositions and concepts that underlie the idea of development.

The alternatives put forward by cultural theorists do not seem to provide ways to create concrete strategies for a different social development. Cultural theorists propose lines for further thought, but no concrete alternatives. Rist (1996) recognises the difficulty of giving a concrete content to his project. Indeed, apart from reorienting the structures and contents of growth, the other proposals of the cultural theorists remain vague and ill defined. The suggestion to reorient growth is not, indeed, completely new, since following the failure of import-substitution strategies in the late 1960s, a number of writers emphasised the importance of giving a new content to economic growth in the South. More specifically, this work considers that development of the domestic market, by enabling a larger share of the population to satisfy its basic needs, could initiate new dynamics of accumulation and growth in the South, and decrease its dependency on international markets. From this standpoint, the cultural approach, which seeks to make a radical break with 'development', merely repeats the traditional proposals of development theory.

Conclusion

The failure of adjustment programmes was the theoretical starting point for the movement criticising the Washington Consensus. The questioning of the general equilibrium in the analysis of problems of underdevelopment was inspired by the continuing changes in the field of economic theory and the emergence of new contributions that sought to increase the relevancy of the Walrassian model by modifying some of its basic hypotheses. Questioning the Washington Consensus and changes in the field of political economy were the source of the new theoretical conceptions in development economics, which we refer to as post-adjustment development economics. In this chapter, we have sought to carry out a critical examination of the different approaches that dominate the field of study of development problems. We have distinguished four different approaches. First, an approach closely related to endogenous growth theories, which attempts to revise development theory by returning to the founding fathers. The second approach, institutionalism, is particularly concerned with market imperfections and studies the role and impact of institutions in the regulation and operation of underdeveloped economies. The third or post-Keynesian approach starts from its criticism of the orthodox foundations of models of stabilisation, and attempts to construct new strategies designed to stimulate internal demand. Finally, the cultural approach considers the failure of development strategies to be above all the failure of the North's attempts to Westernise the world following independence.

Our critical examination of the different approaches to post-adjustment development economics has demonstrated their inability to grasp and explain the mutations and evolutions in progress in the Third World. These limitations require a renovation of development theories and the construction of approaches capable of analysing the current dynamics in most underdeveloped countries, and looking beyond the specific features of each individual economy to the general transitions experienced by Third World economies. This would require economists to take a particular interest in the study of the articulation of concrete modes of accumulation and regulation procedures that make it possible to manage imbalances and to keep tensions at tolerable levels.

Note

1 He envisages open economies in other models.

Chapter 5

Towards a New Post-Adjustment Development Strategy

Introduction

In most Southern countries, SAPs have failed to reduce the deficit and generate new growth dynamics. The failure of these programmes is a reminder that development is a slow and complex historical process which cannot be reduced to observance of certain macroeconomic variables. Indeed, the founding fathers of development economics have defined development as a process of changing economic and social structures in order to create the conditions for a long-term increase in production and productivity.

This failure of the SAPs should spur reflection on *post-adjustment development strategies*. The goal of such strategies should be to repair an economic and social fabric damaged by a decade of SAPs, generate new growth dynamics and increase the competitiveness of Southern economies in order to improve their integration into the global economy. The era of resigned management of underdeveloped societies is behind us, and there is a need to develop new thinking on what types of societies and development strategies can be invented and imagined in the Third World. Development economics should open up a new field of research and broad debates on the choices and options of the Third World, which was reduced to silence by the neo-liberal Washington Consensus.

These new development strategies must take account of the changes and transformations that have taken place in the global economy and in the Third World over the last two decades. Indeed, the globalisation of the economy has led to a weakening of the nation-state which used to be at the heart of the political and economic organisation of the modern world. The crisis of the nation-state has meant the emergence of identity-based movements that regard opening up to globalisation with fear and dread, particularly in the most marginalised countries. Furthermore, some areas have started setting up regional integration mechanisms in order to better resist the transnational flow of merchandise and capital.

A new conception of development should seek to reconcile the imperatives of reconstructing the local, national or regional social and economic fabric in order to lay the foundation for a beneficial integration into global life. At the dawn of the twenty-first century, development experiences that are removed from the international experience are part of the very distant past. Also distant are neo-liberal laissez-faire recommendations as a response to current challenges and as a way of ensuring competitive integration into the international economy. Indeed, more than ever, the stability and consistency of the local, national or regional social and economic fabric form the necessary foundation for dynamic international integration.

The historical experiences of underdeveloped countries over the last four decades demonstrate that development is not an uninterrupted, linear process. Indeed, the will to modernise, which characterised the leadership of post-colonial Africa, has run up against international uncertainties and social impedimenta. *That is why, today, indeterminacy increasingly appears to be at the heart of development processes*. With this in mind, post-adjustment development strategies need to free themselves from the determinism typical of the Bandung development strategies and options, and the unwavering belief in the modernising abilities of the state. This ideological conception was the root cause of the monopolisation of politics and society by a state which was supposed to bring progress and modernity. The failure of the development experiences inspired by the Bandung model has led economists to contemplate the obstacles to development and reflect on a new development philosophy focusing on a more open political and social order and greater citizen participation in the management of development.

In this chapter, we shall seek to reopen the debate on development strategies and make a contribution to thinking on the new choices that need to be made in the South. Our aim is not to establish a general development model that could be transposed on all countries. The objective of this chapter is more modest – it is confined to suggesting a few avenues of thought on how to give a new impetus to development in the Third World. We intend to introduce ideas about the creative distortions that need to be created and structured to develop sustainable growth dynamics in the context of globalisation. Indeed, Third World countries have experienced differing evolutions, which have led to the breakdown of the unity of the Third World, and which create the need for specific responses tailored to each country in light of its individual level of development and its economic or political particularities.

In so doing, we shall also seek to draw on the experiences of Southeast Asia in order to learn from their successes and their limitations. In this chapter, an examination of these experiences will enable us to draw a number of lessons that will contribute to a new, post-adjustment development strategy. We must put into perspective the distortions that have enabled these economies to overcome the obstacles to accumulation and ensure sufficient continuity and coherency in their growth dynamics to enable them to develop competitive productive structures. Our examination of these experiences should help facilitate critical comparative analysis with other development experiences in order to understand certain failures.

Our study of the Asian experiences and our effort to compare them with other experiences in the Third World will allow us to get beyond the normative discourse as we attempt to formulate lines of analysis for a post-adjustment development strategy. Strategies of this kind should be based on the lessons learned from actual experience, and not on *a priori* positions or before-the-fact political or ideological convictions.

In this chapter, we shall examine growth and accumulation dynamics in order to point out their most significant aspects. In next chapter, we shall examine the means that have been used to create stability and growth, and absorb the disequilibria of the development process.

In this chapter, we will also examine the evolution of accumulation mechanisms and the laying of the foundations for the structuring of growth dynamics. This study will attempt to shed light on the mechanisms that facilitate the revival of productive structures. Our study will be based on the Asian experiences, which we shall seek to compare with other development experiences in order develop avenues of reflection towards new, post-adjustment development practices.

However, it should be clear from that start that Southeast Asian development experiences are varied. Indeed, it is impossible to boil down the different Asian experiences to a single model (see Asienero, 1995). These differences are due, first of all, to the varying natural conditions and factorial endowment of the different countries. For, while some Southeast Asian countries are endowed with considerable natural resources, others are obliged to import the raw materials they need for their industries. Individual differences also stem from the differing history of these countries, some of which are former Japanese colonies, whereas others had been colonised by the former European colonial powers. Finally, other differences arise from their post-colonial development choices. Indeed, while the first tier of NICs (newly industrialising countries) promoted exports, along with import-substitution, which was a major strategic axis in the 1960s, second-tier NICs only seriously focused on exportation from the mid-1980s on.

A Variety of Development Experiences in Southeast Asia

In recent studies on Southeast Asian economies, it is common practice to distinguish between four different tiers of countries with respect to their industrial development. Firstly, Japan, which has the oldest industrial tradition. In Japan, the Meiji restoration in 1868 was the starting point for the country's modernisation and the beginning of its industrial development (Yoshihara, 1986). By the early twentieth century, Japan was experiencing strong economic growth and was expanding colonially in the region, particularly in Korea and Taiwan. Japanese colonisation, which was aimed at meeting the country's food needs, took the form of fierce repression in Korea. But Japanese colonisation also allowed a certain number of reforms to be imposed in both countries. Thus, in Korea, colonisation led to the abolition of the royalty and the introduction of the notion of private property (Bouteiller and Fouquin, 1995). In addition, in the 1920s, Japanese colonisation initiated an industrial development policy and set up a relatively strong administration. Japanese colonisation also provided the colonies with considerable material infrastructure and with quality human resources through the imposition of compulsory primary education.

In the 1930s, Japan emerged as a new industrial power. Its success was the work of an authoritarian, industrialising bureaucracy that was highly independent with regard to social classes and private groups (Hersh, 1993). Japan's participation and defeat in World War II reduced its industrial development efforts to naught. However, in light of the threat of Communist expansion in Asia, the Americans, who for a time had envisaged the destruction of Japan's industrial capacity, opted instead for Japan's reconstruction to help it withstand the Communist threat. In 1946, in a bid to promote the recovery of the Japanese economy, the American administration imposed a radical land reform abolishing absentee land ownership and distributing farmland to two million small farmers.

In addition, the American administration set up a recovery plan for the Japanese economy which sought to integrate Southeast Asia into Japan's economic sphere. Thus, the Korean War considerably boosted Japanese businesses and helped them to become major, world-class industrial groups three decades later.[1] Japan's industrial development strategy focused on meeting the needs of the domestic market, and did not integrate a major export focus into its industrial development strategy until the late 1950s (World Bank, 1993). With the end of the American occupation in 1951, and the normalisation of its relations with its former colonies, Japan became an industrial power.

Indeed, the strong industrial growth experienced by Japan since the late 1960s, and its ability to resist the recessive dynamics of the crisis, have enabled it to develop considerable industrial skills, especially in new technologies, which have made it one of the foremost industrial powers of the late twentieth century.

The second group of countries includes the first-tier NICs, which are South Korea, Taiwan, Singapore and Hong Kong (Duharcourt, 1996). Except for Hong Kong (World Bank, 1993), all of these countries launched their economic development through import-substitution strategies. However, beginning in the mid-1960s, they consolidated their growth dynamics through a strong focus on the promotion of exports. Throughout the 1970s and 1980s, these countries continued their high levels of economic growth, which allowed them to increase their competitiveness and thus improve their international integration.

However, despite these common features, there are major differences between the first-tier countries. Indeed, while South Korea and Taiwan were colonised by Japan, Hong Kong, which was only recently turned over to China, and Singapore are former European colonies. These historical differences have heavily permeated their post-colonial political and economic structures. To wit, following the war, South Korea and Taiwan adopted the Japanese model of building a strong bureaucracy to take charge of the industrialisation and modernisation of the political and economic structures. This state bureaucracy was highly independent with regard to both the social classes and the industrial groups (Hersh, 1993). But Singapore and the other ASEAN countries (including Indonesia, Malaysia and Thailand) were marked by European culture and adopted political structures relatively close to European models.

Moreover, from an economic standpoint, whereas South Korea and Taiwan are industrial powers, Hong Kong and Singapore have concentrated on trade, services and port activities for their global integration (Perkins, 1994). These countries and Japan have all received considerable aid and support from the United States, and this American support has taken many forms. First of all, strong pressure in favour of radical land reforms led to a more egalitarian distribution of land and especially a rapid increase in agricultural productivity. In addition, until the early 1970s, the United States provided considerable economic and military aid for these countries. The Americans also opened up their market to industrial exports from these economies. Finally, the American engagement in the Korean and Vietnam wars was a boon to the Japanese, Korean and Taiwanese companies, which supplied the American army with equipment and carried out the necessary infrastructure work.

The third class of countries includes the second tier of NICs: Indonesia, Thailand and Malaysia. Malaysia is a former British colony which was specialised in tin mining and export and rubber extraction and export. Following independence, the authorities set up an industrial development programme based on local processing of raw materials. With the rise in prices of raw materials in the 1970s, the programme was consolidated by the development of industrial activities linked to the domestic market. However, from the mid-1980s onward, the authorities promoted the development of export promotion activities, and took advantage of the delocalisation of labour-intensive industries, especially from first-tier NICs. Despite this, the agricultural and natural resource export niche was not abandoned, with the development of new crops such as cocoa and the discovery of large natural gas deposits. Malaysia experienced strong growth in the 1980s, and has pledged to change the structure of its exports to manufactured products by the year 2020 (Bouteiller and Fouquin, 1995).

Thailand is richly endowed with natural resources. It has been exporting rice, fruit and vegetables since the nineteenth century. In the 1970s, the authorities developed an industrialisation programme based on the processing of agricultural products and the development of import-substitution activities. Finally, in the mid-1980s, Thailand experienced considerable development of export promotion activities.

As for Indonesia, by the 1960s the country had developed an industrial sector aimed at meeting domestic demand. From 1973 onward, its industrial development took advantage of the rise in oil prices, which enabled the state to set up an important state industrial sector and protect it from foreign competition. However, with the drop in oil prices in the early 1980s, industry sagged. In the mid-1980s, the state launched a policy of reforms and opening up to the international economy. Against this backdrop, industrial exports developed rapidly (Bouteiller and Fouquin, 1995).

This brief introduction enables us to point out the differences between the first- and second-tier NICs. Firstly, there is the influence of history to the extent that Japanese colonisation in South Korea and Taiwan marked the local elites and largely influenced the structures and mechanisms of industrial development. On the political level, second-tier NICs have been the scene of serious ethnic conflicts between the Chinese minority and the local elite in each of these countries (Malaysia, Thailand and Indonesia) (Harrold, Jayawickrama and Bhattasali, 1996). The authorities of those countries reacted by trying to help the local elite and repressing the Chinese minorities. However, beginning in the mid-1980s, with the development of export promotion strategies, the Chinese minorities returned to favour and local authorities relied on these minorities and the strength of their ties with the Chinese diaspora to develop exports (Jomo, 1996).

These economies also had different economic histories. While the first-tier NICs refocused their development strategies on export promotion in the late 1960s and early 1970s, the second-tier countries continued with import-substitution strategies until the early 1980s. In this regard, the supply of natural resources and raw materials in the latter countries allowed them to sustain an industrial development strategy focusing on the domestic market for a longer time (UNCTAD, 1996). However, the first tier of countries, which lacked raw materials to export, soon focused their industrial development on exports in response to the macroeconomic disequilibria generated by the import-substitution strategy.

In addition, while the first tier NICs began exporting new-technology-intensive goods in the mid-1980s, second-tier countries were still confined to the export of labour-intensive products. Furthermore, part of the foreign direct investments (FDIs) made in second-tier countries came from first-tier countries delocalising their labour-intensive industries. But the advantage due to low labour costs in these countries began to fade with the rise of new exporting countries such as Vietnam and some Chinese provinces. In light of this, beginning in the early 1990s, the second-tier NICs sought to create new competitive advantages by making the transition to goods with a high technology content. This transition is not without problems, though, and seems to be held up, among other obstacles, by the level of education, training and qualification which is much lower in these countries than in first-tier countries.

In Thailand, Indonesia and Malaysia, these transition problems have revealed themselves through a drop in productive investments and their redirection towards investments in real estate or on the financial market. This blocking of the transition has led to an increase in external disequilibria which has in turn caused speculation on their national currencies. These elements largely explain the financial crises which have struck Asian countries since mid-1997, and which have spread throughout the world's financial markets.

The fourth class of countries includes former socialist countries that have begun to liberalise their economies and to focus their productive activities on exports, such as China and Vietnam. Indeed, since the beginning of the reform programmes in 1978, China has experienced strong economic growth and rapid development in FDIs and exports. Two-thirds of FDIs are made by Chinese from Hong Kong, Taiwan and the diaspora. Despite their low levels of employment and production, these FDIs account for over a quarter of all

Chinese exports. The opening up of the Chinese economy and the liberalisation of its internal resource allocation procedures have been conducted in an authoritarian manner by the state, which has retained strict control over the workings of the country's political and economic life (Amin, 1996).

Vietnam opened up much more recently, in the late 1980s. This opening up was further reinforced by the withdrawal of Vietnamese forces from Cambodia and the return of Vietnam to the international arena with the end of the American embargo in 1994 and the re-establishment of diplomatic relations with the United States in 1995. As a result, FDIs have grown, especially in labour-intensive industries. Thus, China and Vietnam have become direct competitors with second-tier NICs due to their low labour costs.

Thus, the different Southeast Asian countries present different profiles. Their particularities can be explained by their political and economic history, their endowment in terms of production factors and the qualifications of their human resources.

These differences reflect those in Southern countries, where some countries have a longstanding industrial tradition and others do not. Certain countries have tremendous raw material resources, especially oil, which enable them to finance their industrial activities more easily. Others are obliged to turn to international aid to launch their industrial development processes. Politically, these countries present characteristics disparate enough to reflect practically all the political contexts found in Third World countries, where the population is relatively ethnically homogeneous and the political regimes more or less authoritarian.

Thus, the Southeast Asian countries present a fairly wide range of experiences, which make it possible to compare them with other development experiences in the Third World. This group of countries does not share strong particularities that would make it difficult to compare them with other countries. From this standpoint, an analysis of the broad outline of the development strategies of Asian countries and their discussion in the light of other development experiences will be extremely useful for the development of post-adjustment development strategy guidelines. This methodological choice is aimed at avoiding the pitfalls of normativism, since the elements of the strategy will be based on concrete experiences and not on the findings of an ad hoc position.

Strong Growth Dynamics in Southeast Asia

Despite the differences in their accumulation dynamics, Southeast Asian countries have experienced very high levels of growth. Indeed, according to World Bank estimates, from 1965 to 1990, these eight Asian countries (Japan, South Korea, Taiwan, Hong Kong, Singapore, Malaysia, Thailand and Indonesia) experienced the highest levels of growth in the world (World Bank, 1993). More particularly, while the rest of the world experienced a serious recession in the 1980s with the rise of monetarism and deflationist policies, Southeast Asian countries continued to grow. Indeed, while Japan's annual growth did not exceed 3.9 per cent, between 1979 and 1992, this figure respectively reached 8.1 per cent in Korea, 7.6 per cent in Taiwan, 6.7 per cent in Hong Kong and 7.3 per cent in Singapore (Bouteiller and Fouquin, 1995).

Furthermore, in the late 1970s in South Korea, the richest 20 per cent of the population took in between 41 and 47 per cent of national income and the poorest 40 per cent between 15 and 20 per cent. During the same period, the shares of these two segments of the population were 56 per cent and 11 per cent in Mexico, while in Brazil, the richest 10 per cent of the population had more than 50 per cent of national income and the poorest 40 per cent of the population only received less than 9 per cent (Page, 1994). This growth has meant a quicker reduction of absolute poverty in Asian countries than in other Third World countries. Indeed, while in the mid-1970s, absolute poverty affected only 8 per cent of households in South Korea and 5 per cent in Taiwan, it stood at 15 per cent in Brazil, 14 per cent in Mexico, and 19 per cent in Columbia (ibid.).

However, distribution is much less egalitarian in the second-tier NICs, which explains the problems and the crises affecting their import-substitution sectors. Furthermore, the more egalitarian distribution of income in first-tier NICs should not mask the tough management conditions of the labour force in these countries.

On the whole, the data shows that from the mid-1960s to the mid-1990s, and especially after the mid-1970s for the second-tier NICs, Southeast Asian countries experienced strong growth dynamics. Industrialisation was at the heart of this growth. Industrial development helped these countries make far-reaching changes in the structure of their exports by directing them away from traditional products and towards goods with a higher technological content. Thus, these economies were able to position themselves better internationally. These performances were even more significant in that they were achieved in an international context characterised from the early 1980s onward by rising deflationary tensions in developed countries combined with a decreased demand for exports from underdeveloped countries. Furthermore, over that same period, most underdeveloped countries, caught up in the debt crisis, experienced serious economic depression and were pushed to the fringes of the international economy despite the application of SAPs.

However, beginning in the early 1990s, Asian economics began to liberalise due to the pressures of globalisation. This opening up meant a loss of local control over their growth dynamics and caused the outbreak of the biggest crisis in the recent economic history of the region.

Asian Crisis and System Risks

The Asian financial crisis which began in June 1997 in Thailand has taken an important turn, spreading to countries such as Japan and South Korea, which were supposed to be more stable and have greater control over international capital movements. Indeed, South Korea, on the brink of suspension of payments in December 1997, decided to call upon the International Monetary Fund, which agreed to provide it with emergency aid in the amount of $20 billion to face its growing deficits. Observers view this aid as insufficient, since over $100 billion would have to be mobilised to restructure Korea's banking and financial sector. In Japan, the Yamaichi securities company, one of the biggest Japanese financial institutions, filed for bankruptcy. Throughout the country, this bankruptcy caused the same sort of panic among investors as was witnessed around the world during the 1929 crisis. Interventions by the Japanese government and more particularly by the Central Bank were unable to ease investors' minds and persuade the different actors to adopt more rational positions. Of course, there had been endless rumours of enormous losses by banks and financial institutions following the fall of the stock market. Observers consider that the collapse of Yamaichi may be the beginning of a great saga that could bring down the entire Japanese financial system and drag down the international monetary and financial system with it.

The Asian financial crisis began in 1997 with the drop of the Thai stock market, which then spread to a series of core Asian growth countries. These initially included Indonesia, the Philippines and Malaysia. The outbreak of the crisis was partially due to the hard times experienced by those countries. In recent years, they had run up large internal and external deficits. The trade deficits were due to the problems their economies faced in making the transition from specialisation in low labour costs to specialisation based on capital- and technology-intensive products. As a result, most of these countries began losing their shares of the international market to newly rising economies such as Vietnam or China, where labour costs were even lower. These conjuncture-related difficulties were accentuated by the fact that the countries' currencies were tied to the dollar, which had risen considerably over the last year. In that context, faced with sizeable deficits and overvalued national currencies, these countries were hit with massive speculation by a number of speculators including American financier George Soros, who was openly named by the Malaysian prime minister as being responsible for the outbreak of the crisis.

This crisis, which observers predicted would be limited to the peripheral countries to the Asian boom area, dragged on and by late September 1997, it struck other, supposedly more stable countries, such as Japan, South Korea and Hong Kong. Indeed, the Tokyo and Seoul stock markets were affected by the region-wide drop in stock market values and the phenomenon soon caught up with them. The 'snowball phenomenon' in the regional financial crisis can be explained by several factors. The first is the psychological factor, due to the fact that the drop in the first countries led to pullouts by international investors, who began to fear an accentuation of the downward trend, and whose future growth prognostics for the region were revised downward. In addition, Japanese and Korean financial institutions had been very active in the region in recent years and thus were affected by the crisis in the first countries to suffer. These institutions sought to withdraw into their own financial centres to minimise their losses. It should also be pointed out that the Japanese and Korean financial and banking systems were very fragile. Indeed, economic development and growth dynamics in these countries were financed by heavy reliance on essentially state-run financial systems in Korea and strongly linked to business firms in Japan. Thus, the businesses in these countries were highly indebted and the banks were considerably weakened in terms of responding to and resisting the shock wave from the rest of the region.

This crisis affected different Asian countries in different ways. China, Vietnam and Taiwan were much less heavily affected by the downward trends associated with the crisis. The difference in these countries lies in their attitudes and their regulations regarding international capital movements. The countries with a more open attitude to international capital movements were the most heavily affected by the financial crisis for the simple reasons that in many cases, portfolio investments were made in a short-term gain perspective without any commitment to production. These investors withdrew their capital as soon as higher profits were available elsewhere. From this standpoint, China and Taiwan, despite their openness, had a more restrictive attitude towards international investments aimed at promoting productive investments.

However, the Asian crisis was not merely the result of temporary deficits facing Asian countries. Indeed, more structural elements linked to the global economy were at the root of these upheavals. This economic configuration dates back to the beginning of the implementation of inflation-fighting policies known as 'competitive disinflation' by developed countries in the early 1980s. This group of countries sought to fight inflation by raising interest rates in order to control prices and increase the competitiveness of their business firms. Higher interest rates lead to a significant drop in internal demand for investments and consumption by both households and businesses. This depression in productive activities led to the rapid development of the financial sphere, which became the principal sphere of investment. The rise of the financial sphere was furthered by the deregulation of the circulation of international capital movements. Thus, an international financial market was created where surplus international capital and savings migrated from one financial centre to another in search of the best profit-making and earning terms. According to some economists, the development of financial markets led to the creation of a financial bubble totally divorced from the real sphere, which, if it bursts, could bankrupt the international system and entail a serious system risk for the international economy.

On the whole, the Asian development experiences are fairly indicative of the margins of freedom opened up for most Third World countries in the 1970s. Asian countries used this leeway to develop stronger growth dynamics in order to negotiate a more competitive entry into the international economy. But these efforts were obstructed by the pressures of the economic globalisation movement. Indeed, the Asian countries were unable to withstand the opening up of their economies and their entire economic and industrial potential was threatened. These experiences pose significant questions for analysts regarding the future of development and of the nation-state in the Third World with the rise of globalisation.

The Asian development experiences, with the rising power of their economies throughout the 1970s and 1980s and the outbreak of the crisis in 1997, form an important basis for comparative analysis of development strategies with a view to developing new lines of thought for post-adjustment strategies.

A Strategic Vision behind the Asian Successes

One of the first lessons that should be learned from these experiences is the long-term vision shared by all the Asian governments. This vision of the future was particularly important in that it took place in a crisis environment in which the future was highly uncertain. This vision enabled the authorities to promote industrial activities in relation to other activities in terms of investments, subsidies and institutional support. Furthermore, this view of the future allowed Asian governments to emphasise access to funding and credits for strategic sectors.

This strategic vision of the future can be perceived on three levels. The first involves the *choice of priority sectors for public and private investment. Most of these countries made sectors at the heart of the technological paradigm (such as electronics) their priority.* Most of these countries are active in the electronic industry. Indeed, while Japan and the first-tier NICs specialised in high-end components and electronic equipment, second-tier NICs sought to penetrate and/or consolidate their position in mass-produced electronics, especially by promoting delocalisation of the activities of Japanese firms or firms from first-tier NICs. Furthermore, Japan and first-tier NICs sought to develop their production capacities in industries involving new material and new products such as synthetic fibres. The development of these industries was important for these countries because they enabled them to build up competitive production capacities within the technical system and in industries that were still in their infancy. This attitude contrasts with those of other countries, such as Latin-American countries (Brazil and Argentina) which, after having made significant efforts to support new technologies, abandoned these industries. Furthermore, most other underdeveloped countries lack both the necessary production capacities and even a coherent strategy for the introduction of these technologies into the workings of the administration or the industrial sector.

Alongside these industries, the Asian countries sought to develop industries corresponding to a *move upstream*. Thus, after having developed branches downstream from the textile industry in the 1960s, in the 1970s, development efforts turned to intermediary products such as threads from man-made fibres. In the electronics industry, a similar trend could be observed from downstream sectors towards intermediary sectors. Indonesia followed the same pattern in the chemical industry with a progressive evolution towards agro-chemistry. Finally, *sectors meeting particular needs in strategic sectors of the economy were also supported by Asian governments*. In that respect, we can point to the production of fertilisers and various types of input for the agricultural industry.

State interventions and the support provided by Asian governments were not based on theoretical grids. They were not balanced, and were not directed to all sectors with the same intensity. Indeed, they did not seem to be directed in priority at sectors viewed *a priori* as strategic sectors. In fact, the very notion of a strategic sector varies according to the dynamics of accumulation.

Thus, electronic components, which were a strategic sector for first-tier NICs, were not strategic in second-tier NICs, which had a greater mastery of mass-produced electronic industries. State interventions in this area were pragmatic and aimed at meeting the concrete needs of growth dynamics, sustainability and consistency. In that respect, the industries they promoted and developed essentially included sectors at the heart of the technological paradigm, upstream industries, the replacement of imports with local production and sectors meeting specific economic needs.

The Asian countries' strategic vision of the future was also apparent *in the relationship between the foreign and domestic markets in the growth dynamics of Asian countries*. Indeed, most of these economies sought to maintain strong coordination of domestic growth factors and more particularly domestic demand and recourse to the international market. Indeed, if we examine the Korean experience, we note that the country began with an import-substitution strategy in the late 1950s. In the late 1960s, this option was combined with the promotion of exports in order to absorb the imbalances caused by import-substitution. From 1973 onward, Korean development was reoriented towards domestic demand and significant capacity for basic and intermediary production was built up (iron and steel, chemical and petrochemical industries) (Bénabou, 1982). When these growth dynamics ran out of steam, they were reinforced, in the late 1970s and especially the 1980s, by a new strategy of promotion of exports focusing on products with a high content in new technologies such as electronic components. The same evolution can be observed in Indonesia. The government set up an import-substitution strategy in the 1970s. When this strategy lost momentum, it was combined with the development of labour-intensive exports.

This coordination between national and international markets in the structuring of growth dynamics is important because it reduces underdeveloped countries' dependency on international markets and enables them to find new foundations for growth when these markets are depressed. The experience of African countries in this regard is highly indicative of the consequences of pegging growth dynamics on international prices of basic commodities. In this case, growth rises and falls with the fluctuations of international prices without the African countries having enough room to manoeuvre to moderate the recessive effects of a large drop in these prices.

This coordination enabled the Asian countries to experience strong growth dynamics in the 1970s and 1980s in a context of rising deflationary tension and international recession. But the coexistence of these two trends demands a specific distribution policy according to which the payroll is not seen merely as a cost that must be reduced absolutely, but also as an important component in the development of domestic demand.

The third level on which the Asian countries' strategic vision of the future can be perceived is the support of their governments *with regards to the management of transitions from one type of international market niche to another*. Indeed, a study of the history of growth dynamics in Japan reveals that in the late 1960s Japanese firms made the transition from labour-intensive products to technology-intensive products with the support of the government. First-tier NICs also received considerable government support to manage the same transition in the late 1970s and early 1980s. Today, second-tier NICs are keenly feeling this problem.

In this regard, it should be emphasised that state support is important to help businesses make this transition. Government assistance may take several forms including direct aid and various types of subsidies and funding for businesses. The state can also assist in the transition by discouraging domestic competition in new industries and protecting them from international competition (Singh, 1996). The state also plays a fundamental role in this transition by developing the human resources needed to master technology-intensive industries through the development of education, training and access to new technologies. Indeed, second-tier NICs are currently facing serious difficulties in making the transition and building competitiveness in the export of high new-technology content products due to their shortage of qualified human resources. In addition, these countries are experiencing a freeze in productive investments as investors turn to real estate and financial investments. This freeze is responsible for the outbreak of the crisis in these economies.

The transition from one type of niche in the international market to another more capital-intensive one is currently at the heart of the loss of growth momentum in countries which chose to develop the labour-intensive export sector in the early 1970s and jumped on the bandwagon of delocalisation of these industries by developed countries. This failure was compounded by the fact that, due to increased productivity stemming from technical changes, some of these industries moved back to developed countries beginning in the early 1990s in order to be closer to their markets (Ben Hammouda, 1995b).

In light of this failure, some countries, such as Chile, abandoned the project of a more dynamic integration based on the export of products with a high technology content and returned to a more traditional niche in the export of raw materials. Others sought to rationalise and restructure their labour-intensive industries without implementing a transition strategy.[2] Several factors can be cited to explain the difficulty of this transition, including state support and the existence of qualified human resources to master new technologies. The rentseeking attitude of Third World bourgeoisies, which refuse to take risks by investing in new sectors, should also be mentioned. The profitability of such investments is uncertain and more long-term than investment in labour-intensive sectors. In light of this, the bourgeoisies choose to continue operating in traditional niches that provide immediate profits. From this perspective, the Asian experience is interesting because the public authorities managed to incite major groups to invest in new specialisations. The public authorities encouraged international and national competition in mature sectors, and reduced support for them (Singh, 1996). These governments also succeeded in creating new 'rents' or conditions for capital development in new sectors.

Thus, this strategic vision in terms of the choice of sectors, of the coordination of national and international markets and the transition from labour-intensive sectors to capital-intensive sectors is central to the debate on post-adjustment strategies since it can be used to enhance growth dynamics in Southern economies.

Agricultural Modernisation in Development

Agriculture has played an important role in the Asian development experiences. An interest in agriculture emerged rapidly following World War II, in response to political and strategic concerns. Indeed, under pressure from the American administration, Japan and South Korea developed radical land reforms in order to halt the progress of the communist parties, whose propaganda essentially centred on a more egalitarian distribution of the land. Thus, land reform in Japan meant the abolition of absentee land ownership and the distribution of land to over 2 million small farmers. After that reform, nearly 90 per cent of the land became the property of the farmers.

In Taiwan, the Americans put strong pressure on the defeated Kuomintang troops, which took over after the departure of the Japanese colonists, to redistribute the land. The new government implemented a land reform in the late 1940s (Wade, 1990). In Korea, land reform was implemented in 1950 under pressure from peasant revolts. The reform restricted ownership to 3 hectares and abolished sharecropping (Sunoo, 1988). This reform led to a more egalitarian distribution of the land. Indeed, in 1944, nearly half of all rural families owned no land and 48.5 per cent of families held an average of 0.8 hectares per family, while 2.9 per cent of families farmed an average of 26 hectares per family. By 1956, nearly 97 per cent of families held no more than

1 hectare per family (Lanzarotti, 1992). However, while the distribution of the land became increasingly egalitarian, the average farm area was very small, which posed problems in terms of the modernisation of the farms and the introduction of technical progress.

However, while Japan and the first-tier NICs implemented far-reaching land reforms, second-tier NICs resisted change despite strong political pressures from peasant movements and communist parties and only made marginal modifications in land ownership. By maintaining an inequitable land distribution system and a high number of landless peasants, these countries created considerable political instability. Furthermore, this type of land-ownership structure is not unrelated to the problems of their import-substitution industries in the 1970s, linked to the soft domestic market in these countries (Hersh, 1993).

Land reform promoted rapid growth in agricultural production in Korea. Between 1955 and 1961, agricultural added value increased by 4.5 per cent per annum. This growth further increased in the 1960s and 1970s with an annual increase of 5.1 per cent between 1962 and 1967 and 10.3 per cent between 1968 and 1979 (Kim, Hajiwara and Watanabe, 1984). The growth of per capita production was much higher in Korea than in other underdeveloped countries such as Argentina and Brazil or even the United States. Indeed, whereas the average growth rate of per capita production between the late 1960s and the late 1970s was 4.2 per cent in Korea, it was only 1.7 per cent in Argentina, 1.9 per cent in Brazil and 1.5 per cent in the United States. In addition, there was a rapid increase in agricultural yields in Korea, with average rates of 3.1 per cent for wheat, 33.6 per cent for soybeans, 4.6 per cent for rice from the mid-1960s to the late 1970s. Increases in yields were much lower in other underdeveloped countries, notably in Latin America (see Lanzarotti, 1992).

Alongside the rapid increase in production, there was an evolution in the structure of production in most Asian countries, particularly in Korea. There was a rapid increase in the production of fruit, vegetables, meat and dairy products due to increased income. Thus, the share of fruit in agricultural production reached 27.9 per cent in 1980, while the share of cereals dropped from nearly 70 per cent in the 1960s to less than 50 per cent in the 1980s. However, despite this trend, cereals were still predominant in agricultural production and rice, which weighed in at over 40 per cent of agricultural added value, remained dominant (Kim and Joo, 1982).

The increase in agricultural yields made it possible to free a large segment of the rural population for industrial activities. Thus, it is believed that in

Korea, the increase in agricultural productivity and industrial development has meant a decrease in the rural population of nearly four million inhabitants. The percentage of agricultural workers in the labour force has considerably declined in most Asian countries. Indeed, between 1950 and 1993, it fell from 49 per cent to 5.5 per cent in Japan, from 74.1 per cent to 21.7 per cent in Korea, and from 56.1 per cent to 11.5 per cent in Taiwan. Despite a relative decrease, the percentage of agricultural workers remains relatively high as a share of total employment in second-tier NICs. It dropped from 84 per cent to 62.3 per cent in Thailand, from 62 per cent to 29.5 per cent in Malaysia and from 79 per cent to 45.8 per cent in Indonesia (Bouteiller and Fouqin, 1995).

Agricultural growth has played a decisive role in the Asian development experiences because it promoted food self-sufficiency in the countries concerned and thereby reduced disequilibria due to the import of food commodities. Furthermore, this form of growth led to the development of rural income and hence to demand for the industrial sector. The impact of agricultural development on national development leads us to emphasise land reforms and a better distribution of the land. We should also determine the other factors behind the increase in agricultural production.

Agricultural price policies have played an important role in agricultural development in Asian countries. In this regard, the Korean experience with agricultural price policies is highly instructive. Like most underdeveloped countries, from the 1950s up to the mid-1960s, Korea practised a policy of low agricultural prices. The aim of this policy was to redirect the agricultural surplus towards industrial development. In this context, the import of agricultural products and particularly the import of American cereals under law PL 480 exerted downward pressure on domestic agricultural prices. This policy discouraged agricultural activity and led to a decline in rural income. However, while Korea rapidly learned its lesson from the consequences of this policy, most underdeveloped countries waited two decades before changing their agricultural options and strategies.

Indeed, as early as the late 1960s, Korea changed its agricultural pricing policy and rapidly increased the prices of rice and barley. Indeed, between 1970 and 1979, the annual increase in rice prices stood at around 20 per cent, while the increase in barley prices was much higher, at around 25 per cent (Kim and Joo, 1982).

To support this change in the pricing policy, the state undertook a huge programme of buying rice from peasants at higher than world prices. Several purchasing mechanisms were implemented by the state, including direct purchasing from peasants, trading of fertiliser for rice, granting of mortgage loans pledged against rice production and payment in kind of tax on income from farmlands. Between 1965 and 1979, the percentage of barley and rice purchased directly from peasants by the state respectively increased from 5 per cent to nearly 40 per cent of the total and from 9 per cent to nearly 25 per cent. The state focused its support for agricultural prices on rice and barley because they represented 42 per cent of total income from farms and 34 per cent of food expenditures by working urban households (ibid.).

A study of rice supply and demand enabled the state to determine the level of food commodity imports (ibid.). However, these imports were highly regulated and food commodities were subject to a system of partial restriction of imports. Furthermore, national production was protected in relation to imports and according to estimates, by the late 1970s, the nominal rate of protection on cereals was over 100 per cent. However, due to an increased demand for agricultural goods and their diversification, there was an increase in agricultural imports beginning in the mid-1970s. Rice and barley imports did not resume until the late 1970s and the early 1980s, due to poor harvests and unfavourable weather conditions.

State purchases were used to meet the needs of urban consumers. There were two marketing pipelines: the official pipeline, which monopolised nearly 43 per cent of the rice marketed, and the free market, where prices were aligned with the official market. Household sale prices were lower than the purchasing prices paid to producers. In 1980, the price difference (loss for the state) was 11,726 wons per sack of rice (80 kg), which represented 32 per cent of the purchasing price, and 21,498 wons or 98 per cent of the purchasing price per sack of barley (76.5 kg) (ibid.).

In 1980, this twofold government intervention resulted in a 32 per cent loss by the state on rice and a 98 per cent loss on barley (ibid.). Between 1970 and 1979, the deficit of the cereal management account totalled 7.3 billion wons. Public financing of cereal transactions was conducted through long-term overdrafts granted to the state by the Central Bank. This deficit was a controversial issue for economists, especially regarding the inflationary consequences due to the fact that it was financed by overdrafts at the Central Bank. However, the inflationary effects seemed to be limited since the subsidies also contributed to maintaining the stability of consumer prices.

Government intervention regarding agricultural prices had two aims. Firstly, it was aimed at increasing rural income in order to enable rural people to purchase manufactured goods, thus broadening the domestic market. Secondly, subsidising of urban consumer prices was aimed at controlling the cost of reproduction of the labour force and maintaining it at low levels in order to preserve and develop the international competitiveness of Korean exports of manufactured goods.

In addition to price subsidies, state interventions in agriculture provided other forms of support for farm production. More specifically, the state helped peasants obtain the fertiliser they needed to compensate for the poor quality of the soil. In this case as well, the state set up a two-tier price policy on fertiliser (ibid.). The state purchased fertiliser at a set purchasing price from producers and sold it to farms at a price lower than the purchasing price. This policy led to a significant deficit in the fertiliser account which the state sought to make up by gradually increasing the sales price of fertiliser to peasants.

This state support was translated by a rapid increase in the consumption of fertiliser by Korean farms. Fertiliser consumption increased from 170 kg per hectare to 380 kg per hectare between the mid-1960s and the late 1970s. Consumption in other underdeveloped countries, particularly in Latin America, was much lower. Indeed, over the same period, average fertiliser consumption per hectare in Latin America rose from 17.5 kg to 39 kg. In addition, there was a rapid increase in mechanisation, as the number of tractors increased from 61 in 1970 to 2664 in 1980, and the number of threshers increased from 41,038 to 219,896 over the same period. However, there was less mechanisation than in other Third World countries due to the small size of the farms.

Alongside these commodity and fertiliser price subsidy policies, the state also developed a research and extension system aimed at helping farms intensify their labour and increase productivity.

As we have already pointed out, these combined measures led to a rapid increase in agricultural production in Korea. Furthermore, the nutritional status of Koreans improved, with an increase in the average daily calorie ration per inhabitant from 1,943 calories in 1962 to 2,599 calories in 1979.

However, agricultural self-sufficiency was not achieved due to the poor quality of the soil and the increasing urban and industrial demand for agricultural produce. In the early 1970s, the rate of self-supply was only 81 per cent. And beginning in the mid-1970s, there was a significant increase in the import of agricultural commodities.

This increase in imports led to a decrease in the self-sufficiency, particularly for cereals, which fell to 60 per cent in 1979. According to estimates, this level is likely to continue to fall to 40 per cent, due to population growth and the shrinking supply of farmland. The food deficit and the cost of state support for the agricultural sector have led developed countries, and also some local industrials, to pressure the state to completely liberalise agricultural imports. According to these industrials, by opening up Korean markets to rice imports, they could take advantage of much lower international prices and increase the competitiveness of Korean companies, especially in terms of labour-intensive exports.

However, despite some slight liberalisation of agricultural commodity imports, the state seems to have rejected a wide opening of its borders to rice imports. In order to face the growing deficit of the agricultural sector, the state developed a new strategy to increase agricultural production. This strategy sought to establish increased agricultural productivity, through more intensive farming, as an alternative to agricultural price subsidies. The state tried to achieve this aim by regrouping the land to encourage greater mechanisation of farms, improving research and extension services, using new technologies, making greater use of fertiliser and pesticides, and developing high-yield crops (Kim and Joo, 1982).

However, food self-sufficiency was not the only objective aimed at by the state's massive support for agricultural development. In fact, it expected agricultural development to stimulate industrial development by providing it with outlets for its production and intermediary goods for certain industrial activities, especially agricultural produce processing industries. This development sequence was successful in a great many Asian countries. In South Korea, for instance, demand from agricultural households played an important role in certain industrial activities. In the late 1970s, rural demand for clothing made up around 30 per cent of the total demand for the product, rural demand for food products made up nearly a quarter of total demand and rural demand for tobacco was around 10 per cent. Rural consumption also contributed to the growth of certain industrial sectors. Its contribution is estimated at around 20 per cent for the clothing industry and food production and 7 per cent for tobacco between 1967 and 1978. Thus, higher farm incomes due to increased prices for agricultural products and higher productivity beginning in the late 1960s promoted rural demand and enabled peasants to play an important role as purchasers of agricultural products. Nominal family income from agriculture increased 33 times between 1965 and 1979.

Sales from the manufacturing industry to the agricultural sector increased between 1970 and 1983. Indeed, the share of intermediary agricultural consumption of manufactured goods increased from 37 per cent to 57 per cent of total. However, at the same time, intermediary consumption of agricultural goods by the manufacturing sector dropped significantly from 12 per cent to 4 per cent of total. In light of the general evolution of production structures, agriculture was increasingly dependent on industry for its intermediary consumption and for its outlets, whereas the dependency of industry on agriculture tended to decrease. 'As a result', notes Lanzarotti (1992, p. 113, our translation), 'between 1970 and 1983, agriculture benefited from considerable offer and growth effects duc to its exchanges with the industrial sector, while the reverse was not true'. In certain production chains, such as cereals, fruits and vegetables or industrial crops, the link between agriculture and industry was very strong.

This data on the Asian experiences, and the Korean experience in particular, have allowed us to point out the dynamic role of agriculture in economic development. What is interesting is that these experiences sought to lay the foundation for development through agricultural modernisation. This modernisation was implemented through a broad movement of distribution of the land to peasants, which led to a rapid increase in agricultural production and productivity. This transformation of production structures was reinforced by state intervention in the form of accompanying measures, and particularly through the implementation of twofold support for agricultural prices. The double price system made it possible to increase rural purchasing power without affecting the competitiveness of manufacturing exports.

This agricultural modernisation strategy laid the foundation for a rapid increase in agricultural production and productivity, which enhanced the development of food self-sufficiency. But the dynamic agricultural sector also laid the foundation for industrial development by providing it with additional demand for the distribution of its production. The development of mechanical and chemical industries met agriculture's needs for machinery and intermediary products. In addition, certain industrial activities, particularly the agro-industries, obtained the necessary raw material for their development from agriculture.

This effort to modernise agriculture contrasts with other experiences in the Third World where the government maintained very inequitable landownership structures and refused, as in many Latin American countries, to undertake the redistributions needed to give landless peasants access to farmlands. In other countries, where the landownership structure was more egalitarian, peasants lacked government support to make the necessary investments to intensify and increase agricultural production. In many underdeveloped countries, the archaism of their agrarian structures meant high levels of food dependency. In addition, low agricultural income constituted a major limitation on the import-substitution strategies set in place by most Southern countries in the 1960s and 1970s. Indeed, in countries with a dominantly rural population, urban demand was well below the threshold necessary to make import-substitution industries profitable.

However, while the modernisation of the rural world was necessary and even fundamental for development, its difficulty and complexity should not be ignored. In Africa for instance, a variety of avenues of rural modernisation have been implemented. Certain countries, such as Côte d'Ivoire, have followed the avenue of small agrarian capitalism with the clearing of the Eastern forests and the development of small coffee plantations. In other countries, particularly in the Sahel, modernisation efforts were focused on the construction of large hydro-agricultural complexes for the production of subsistence crops for local consumption or export.

Other countries sought to explore different avenues of modernisation, especially the former socialist countries. Thus, the Ujamaa experiences in Tanzania tried to revive the agricultural industry through a return to traditional solidarity and community farming. In Ethiopia, peasant pressures caused the 1974 revolution to undertake one of the rare agrarian revolutions in Africa.

But despite the variety of avenues pursued, most rural modernisation experiences failed, thus creating increased food dependency in African countries, impoverishing the rural population and increasing population drift to the cities despite high urban unemployment. There are several reasons for this failure, including high dependency of peasant farms on international basic commodity prices and the authoritarianism of the post-colonial states, which tried to impose sudden reforms on rural social structures. Indeed, as Coquery-Vidrovitch writes, recent African history has shown that:

> sudden imposition of modernisation measures, whether they take the form of mere accelerated mechanisation, which cannot be assimilated over the very short term, if only for social reasons, or generalised collectivisation, can only led to catastrophe (Coquery-Vidrovitch, 1985, p. 208, our translation).

These failures demonstrate that while the modernisation of agrarian structures remains an important objective in a development strategy, it is difficult to design a single, abstract pattern for the transformation of rural spaces in the Third World. Modernisation efforts should innovate and define new methods adapted to the concrete situations of rural areas. The transformation of social and productive structures should be progressive and take the concerns and demands of the peasant population into account. Thus, as Coquery-Vidrovitch explained, 'rural development can only be self-centred, i.e. carried out with and by the peasants and not for them' (ibid., p. 207).

Industrialisation at the Heart of Post-Adjustment Strategies

It should be emphasised that industrialisation played a fundamental role in Southeast Asian growth dynamics. Thus, in Japan, the percentage of employment in manufacturing rose from 15.4 to 24.1 per cent of total employment between 1950 and 1990. The other Southeast Asian countries experienced similar trends. During the same period of time, manufacturing employment as a percentage of total employment in first-tier NICs progressed, respectively, from 7 to 26.9 per cent in Korea, from 12 to 32 per cent in Taiwan and from 19 to 29.5 per cent in Singapore. Only Hong Kong saw a regression of manufacturing employment with the delocalisation of its manufacturing activities to China and the rapid rise of tertiary commercial and financial industries.

This strong industrial growth caused a rapid transformation of the structure of exports in these countries, with the rise of manufactured exports at the expense of traditional exports. In Japan, for instance, the percentage of manufactured exports rose from 93.4 per cent in 1967 to 96.8 per cent of the total in 1993. Among the first-tier NICs, only Korea and Singapore experienced a strong progression of manufactured exports as a percentage of total exports during the same period, respectively from 67.3 per cent to 93.7 per cent in Korea and from 21 per cent to 87 per cent in Singapore. In Hong Kong and Taiwan, the share of manufactured exports in their total exports remained relatively stable, at over 90 per cent of total.

But the second-tier NICs experienced the most spectacular change in the structure of their exports. Indeed, between 1967 and 1993, the percentage of manufactured exports in their respective total exports rose from 3.7 to 50.5 per cent in Indonesia, from 12.6 to 65.5 per cent in Thailand and from 24.9 to 68.4 per cent in Malaysia (Bouteiller and Fouquin, 1995). However, there were differences in the structure of manufactured exports in the different countries. Indeed, while the share of raw materials and labour-intensive products only represented 30 per cent of total exports in first-tier NICs, it was closer to 60 per cent in second-tier NICs (UNCTAD, 1996).

Industrial development in Asia presents a series of characteristics whose identification and comparison with other Southern countries can be used as a basis for reflection on a few avenues for post-adjustment strategies. The first of these characteristics is linked to their will to coordinate the development of industries focusing on the domestic market with the development of industries focusing on the foreign market. This effort was especially significant in Japan and in the first-tier NICs. After the war and in the 1950s, these countries developed import-substitution strategies focusing on domestic markets. However, as early as the mid-1950s in Japan and in the mid-1960s for the NICs, these strategies were combined with export promotion activities in response to external deficits linked to the import of capital goods and intermediary goods. Export promotion activities focused on labour-intensive products.

These strategies underwent significant changes in the 1970s. Indeed, the increase in oil prices in 1973 caused an increase in imports and an economic recession in Korea and Taiwan. In light of this, the governments in both countries decided to emphasise the development of industrial activities aimed at the internal market. Thus, Taiwan adopted its fourth development plan focusing on capital goods, electronics, petrochemicals and electrical machinery. At the same time, Korea adopted a plan for the development of heavy industries, chemical industries and steel and iron. These plans enabled those two countries to revive their economic growth dynamics based on internal demand and its ability to provide outlets for their industrial sectors (Wade, 1990).

The substance of the industrial development strategy underwent further changes in the 1980s. A further rise in the price of oil prompted the first-tier NICs, and especially Korea and Taiwan, to develop a new focus and promote the development of less energy-intensive and more new-technology-intensive industries. Thus, by the late 1970s, Korea and Taiwan had adopted plans for the promotion of exports focusing on new industries, such as machine tools, automobiles, semiconductors, computers, telecommunications, robotics and biotechnologies. These plans enabled the first-tier NIC economies to modify their comparative advantages and ensured a more competitive integration into the international economy.

Second-tier NICs only focused a portion of their industrial structures on the promotion of exports towards the late 1970s, and more especially in the 1980s. Indeed, unlike Japan or the first-tier NICs, these countries possessed considerable natural resources which allowed them to maintain an import-substitution strategy and thus emphasise their internal markets. However, the drop in the price of raw materials and oil in Indonesia led these countries to review their industrial options and concentrate more on the promotion of exports. Thus, beginning in the 1980s, these countries encouraged the delocalisation of labour-intensive industries, especially from first-tier NICs.

The stability of industrial growth in Southeast Asia was linked to the ability of these economies to combine industries focusing on the internal market with industries focusing on the international market. By combining these two approaches, these economies were able to concentrate on whichever was most useful in light of the economic situation at any given time. This alternating evolution of the key forces for economic development allowed the Asian economies to 'walk on two legs'.[3] However, the Asian countries were unable to maintain this balancing act, which collapsed under the weight of the financial and industrial constraints of Asian businesses.

The second characteristic of industrial development in Southeast Asia was the ability of these economies to internalise the capital goods sector. This sector played an important role in the accumulation of capital because it constituted the interface between industry and scientific and technological research and made it possible to introduce technical innovations into the productive system. Furthermore, the mastery of this sector made rapid growth of productivity possible in all sectors of the economy.

The third characteristic of Southeast Asian industrial development was these countries' decision to build up a harmonious and dynamic industrial system. In this regard, it should be emphasised that development theories have suggested several options for developing the industrial fabric and achieving progress in the mastery of the most complex segments and sectors of industrial development. The theory of comparative advantages recommended that underdeveloped countries specialise in labour-intensive sectors in order to achieve industrial development. According to that approach, this specialisation presents a number of advantages. Firstly, it enables under-developed economies to rapidly build up their comparative advantages and integrate the international economy. Indeed, these countries can more easily compete with developed countries because the offer of labour is significantly higher than the demand, which, according to the laws of the markets, allows labour costs to be maintained at very low levels. Furthermore, labour-intensive industries have a relatively low level of technical difficulty, which makes them easier to master for underdeveloped countries. Finally, the specialisation of these countries in labour-intensive industries should make it easier for transnational firms to delocalise activities that are becoming less competitive so that developed countries also contribute to these countries' growth dynamics. Foreign direct investments (FDIs) by these firms help give these countries access to new technologies and integrate the international economy.

However, this approach has been the target of a number of criticisms. Studies of delocalisation experiences have shown that technology transfer remains very limited, since in most cases the technology involved is outdated and obsolete. Furthermore, this transfer is not accompanied by the necessary mastery and does not enable the countries concerned to develop technological adaptation and innovation skills. Delocalised industries are also very volatile and 'migrate' from country to country according to the progression of production costs and in particular higher incomes. Certain activities even return to their countries of origin when technical progress enables them to re-establish profitable conditions.

Furthermore, delocalisation experiences do not make for the close ties between local industries and delocalised sectors that would ensure real integration between the different industrial sectors and allow foreign businesses to play a real role as motors for local industry. Thus, in general, the choice of industrial development according to comparative advantage theory does not allow underdeveloped countries to initiate a genuine industrialisation strategy and does not facilitate the anchoring of industrial activities in their economies. In addition, although the delocalisation of labour-intensive activities by transnational firms allows Third World economies to experience growth and industrial development, it does not allow them to establish the necessary preconditions to make that development sustainable. Finally, the relationships between the different sectors remain relatively tenuous, a situation which does not promote consistent industrial development.

Other approaches to industrialisation have emphasised the role of the capital goods sectors in the industrialisation process. These approaches, based on Soviet industrialisation experiences, refute the ability of consumer goods and light industries to set an industrialisation process in motion and lay much greater emphasis on strategic capital goods sectors. Several arguments have been used to justify this option. Firstly, heavy industry and the capital goods sector have considerable downstream impact and can pull other industrial sectors along behind them, especially light industries and intermediary industries. This mode of industrialisation promotes the development of harmonious production systems that reduce the dependency of underdeveloped countries on developed countries.

Furthermore, developing this sector can provide the capital goods and intermediary consumption needed to modernise agriculture. Increased rural production and productivity means higher incomes, which create increased demand for light industry products. The development of capital goods industries promotes the mastery of new technologies by underdeveloped countries and their adaptation to the real conditions of their economies.

A number of Southern countries have attempted to follow this industrialisation pattern in an effort to develop consistent growth and lay the foundations of stability and sustainability. These experiences have enabled the countries concerned to build their industrial potential along with significant scientific technical capacities. However, the results have lagged far behind expectations, and these countries have been unable to forge the necessary links between different industrial sectors to develop a coherent industrial fabric and a self-sustaining growth dynamic. These experiences have demonstrated the difficulty of establishing upstream/downstream relationships between capital goods sectors and intermediary and light industries. Indeed, it is difficult to integrate the capital goods produced into the rest of the economy and the economies that have chosen this development pattern remain heavily dependent on foreign sources for their intermediary and consumer goods.

Furthermore, in most of these economies, despite the recommendations of the baseline pattern, agriculture was used to finance industrial development by maintaining low agricultural prices. Lower peasant incomes led to decreased production, which in turn led to heavy food dependency in most of these economies. These experiences also demonstrated the difficulty of mastery the technology for these complex industries. Most countries opted for turnkey contracts or operational plants as a solution to the complexity of the industrial units that needed to be set up. However, these methods of technology transfer do not allow the development of local mastery or adaptation of the technologies. Finally, it should be noted that the installation of such heavy, capital-intensive units requires considerable financial means. In this sense, internal financing capacities through bank credits have played an important role. However, the magnitude of the imported technologies required significant foreign currency resources, which only countries with considerable natural resources, such as oil, could provide.

The Asian countries followed a different pattern in their development. A study of the experience of first-tier NICs reveals that they developed an import-substitution strategy from the late 1950s to the mid-1960s. This strategy focused on local production of imported final consumption goods. Beginning in the mid-1960s, this strategy was combined with the development of export activities in order to absorb the disequilibria of the import-substitution dynamics. During that period, export promotion activities also focused on labour-intensive consumer goods. Only towards the mid-1970s did the first-tier NICs, especially Korea and Taiwan, set up heavy-industry sectors including capital goods and steel and iron industries.

In the development of their industrial fabric, the first-tier NICs followed a specific pattern. Indeed, the reasoning behind their industrialisation was to move upstream along the chain of production by successively internalising the intermediary sectors before coming to capital goods. This progression allowed them to meet the needs of the different intermediary goods sectors locally and thus reduce imports. In addition, this strategy promoted the diversification of exports and provided a response to the declining comparative advantages of Asian economies. From that perspective, this strategy combined perfectly with the coordination of sectors focusing on the external market with import-substitution sectors focusing on the domestic market. And, while a portion of the upstream production was intended for export, import substitutions of intermediary goods were essentially intended for local production industries.

This production-chain strategy differs from the strategies adopted in France in the early 1980s. Indeed, the French strategy was aimed at creating consistency in the production chain by moving downstream, starting with the mastery of the capital goods sector. In the first-tier NICs, on the contrary, the development of the chain of production started downstream and as the intermediary levels were gradually mastered, they moved to the levels further upstream (Duharcourt, 1996).

This hypothesis merits further research. But Bénabou (1982), for one, has provided information on how South Korea moved up the production chain in three different sectors. The first production chain studied by Bénabou was the textile industry. Korea set up this industry in the early 1960s with the development of businesses specialised in finished products such as hosiery, garments and apparel accessories. It began moving up the production chain in the 1970s with the incursion of Korean businesses into intermediary production such as man-made fibres and fabrics. This move upstream was planned by the businesses and supported by the state, and enabled the Korean textile industry to reduce its dependency on the international market for fibres. Indeed, the share of imported intermediate consumptions for man-made fibres and fabrics in man-made fibres respectively decreased from 62 per cent to 51.1 per cent and from 42.7 per cent to 13.2 per cent of total between 1970 and 1979.

In the late 1970s, the Korean government started a new phase in its progression upstream along the chain of production, by developing local organic chemistry and plastic fibre production capacities to meet the needs of industry. To strengthen this capacity, the state built a second chemical complex to reduce inputs for man-made fibres. This strategy of moving up the production chain enabled Korea to reduce its dependency on Japan for textiles and diversify its exports. Indeed, the Japanese trade surplus in threads and fabrics in the 1960s was reversed and became a Korean surplus in the 1970s and 1980s.

The trend in the metal production chain also followed the same pattern of moving upstream. The industry began in the 1960s in Korea. Until the early

1970s, it was limited to the production of metal furniture and metal goods for household use. In the late 1970s, Korea entered a new phase in the metal industry by extending its rangc of products to include new goods such as metal tubes and pipes, cables and wires, moulds and forgings, and other miscellaneous metal goods. Up until that period, the Korean metal industry had been heavily dependent on Japan. In fact Korean companies acted as middlemen, importing iron, steel and boilermaking products from Japan and exporting tubes, pipes and general mechanical parts to the United States.

The third phase in the movement up the production chain allowed Korea to become independent from Japan and ensured greater integration of the chain of production by developing national production capacities for heavy boilermaking, semi-finished steel goods, rolling mill products and cast iron and steel. This phase in the evolution of the industry was opposed by most money lenders and the World Bank refused to provide credit to finance the steel and iron production unit in Pohang. Indeed, based on the recommendation of comparative advantage theories, the World Bank and the American government refused to finance this project, which they viewed as capital-intensive and unsuited to the needs of the Korean economy. However, the project was financed and implemented by the Korean government with Japanese technical assistance. The implementation of this project was certainly contrary to the precepts of comparative advantage theories, but it played an important role in the move up the chain of production and the step-by-step internalisation of increasingly complex sectors by the Korean industrial system (see Bénabou, 1982).

The electronics industry also followed the same pattern. The electronic industry in Korea also started in the 1960s, with the production of mass-produced electronic equipment. Beginning in the early 1970s, Korea encouraged the production of electronic components, which were essentially made by transnational firms and re-exported abroad. However, beginning in 1974, the Korean government promoted a refocusing of electronic component production on the domestic market and the incorporation of these components into local products such as televisions, radios, tape recorders, etc. This strategy was compounded in the mid-1980s by the development of local production capacities for electronic and computer equipment in the context of joint ventures. This strategy enabled Korea to build up considerable technical and industrial capacities in a key sector of the dawning technological era.

These facts of Korean development can be used to identify the specific pattern of the development of that country's industrial fabric and integration. This pattern was based on the strategy of moving upstream in the production chain by successively internalising the production of intermediary industries. This pattern of industrial development also seems to be at the heart of the experiences of the second-tier NICs. Indeed, following an import-substitution experience with final consumer goods, these countries sought to diversify their industrial fabric in two directions. The first was the promotion of labour-intensive export activities. The second strategy was aimed at the development of intermediary industries in sectors such as textiles, steel and iron and electronics. Today, these economies are trying to enter a new phase by integrating these intermediary products into products further up the production chain such as the automobile industry, computer accessories and computers.

This approach to building up and integrating the industrial fabric enabled the Asian economies to experience strong industrial growth dynamics. It also enabled them to lay the foundations for harmonious and sustainable industrialisation. This method presents a number of advantages compared to the other two patterns of industrialisation we have described. Firstly, the role of the state in planning is a fundamental element of the progression up the chain of production. Indeed, contrary to comparative advantage theories, this approach seeks to go beyond industrial specialisation in labour-intensive products with the joint action of the state and private groups aimed at mastering new sectors of production and new technology-intensive industries to reduce imports and dependence on foreign sources and as a response to the erosion of their comparative advantages.

In addition, this pattern of industrialisation allows for a greater mastery of technologies and their adaptation. Indeed, familiarity with downstream production segments forms an important base that can facilitate the transfer of technology and learning procedures to more complex sectors of production. This pattern of industrialisation makes it possible to avoid the bottlenecks that development strategies based on capital goods sectors can run into. Indeed, the development of upstream sectors and industries always meets downstream needs which were previously satisfied by imports. Thus, the supply of intermediary goods meets a pre-existing demand, and does not face major difficulties creating demand.

The increasing internationalisation of the major Asian groups since the early 1990s weakened the regulatory and planning role of the state and the various national institutions of those countries. Through their international financing strategies, the major groups freed themselves from the control of the state and compliance with the norms of consistency within the industrial system. These businesses also developed international strategies and reached beyond the framework of the nation-state. And, while these groups experienced some success in the 1980s, by the mid-1990s they began to meet with significant difficulties and their debt load was a major factor in the destabilisation of the Asian economies and the outbreak of the crisis.

Industrial Development and New Technologies

The acquisition of new technologies constituted a fundamental objective in the industrial development strategies of Asian countries. In fact, imported technology and the development of scientific and technological capabilities were at the heart of their efforts to modernise their production systems. In other underdeveloped countries, technology transfer met with limitations, causing them to opt for turnkey technology transfers to reduce the risks of technological dependency. However, these underdeveloped countries were soon to realise that while the transfer of turnkey projects and industries reduced technological risks, it did not promote technological independence and permanently tied the businesses to their suppliers through technical maintenance and repair contracts for the assorted breakdowns that could hold up their operations. In addition to these technical problems, turnkey contracts did not promote the integration of these industries into the economic fabric of underdeveloped countries.

These limitations have led underdeveloped countries to develop new strategies for mastering imported technologies. Their experiences with the import of technologies brought underdeveloped countries to realise that the transfer of technologies does not necessarily entail that those technologies are mastered locally. The Asian countries developed active strategies to master new technologies. In this, their experiences differed from those of other developed countries. Indeed, while the industrialisation experiences of the first capitalist countries in the eighteenth century were based on invention and those of the industrial powers of the nineteenth century were based on innovation, the Southeast Asian countries sought to gain access to new technologies by importing them. However, this importation was backed up by considerable local efforts to learn, adapt and imitate the imported technologies.[4] In South Korea, licensing agreements for the purchase of capital goods were the principal sources of technology transfers. Between 1962 and 1987, royalties on imported technology represented nearly $2.3 billion, with 40 per cent of that figure for 1986 and 1987 alone. Purchases of technology by Korean firms were heavily regulated by the state, which sought to reduce systematic recourse to foreign technology and to support the negotiation capacities of local businesses in technology transfers.

In order to master imported technologies and learning dynamics, the Asian countries had to build up their scientific and technical capacities. In Korea, in the mid-1960s, the Korean government sought to establish an institutional framework capable of organising research activities. In 1966, the government founded an institute in charge of the promotion of research and technology, the KIST (Korean Institute of Science and Technology). This institute, which became the KAIST (Korean Advanced Institute of Science and Technology) in 1980, is currently the principal research organisation in Korea and employs over 4,000 engineers and technicians. In addition to the multiplication of specialised public research centres, the government encouraged businesses to set up research activities to facilitate the mastery of imported technologies.

A study of the development of the electronics industry yields an interesting example of the dynamics of the mastery and adaptation of new technologies in Southeast Asian countries. The beginnings of the electronics industry in the region date back to the late 1950s. In the 1960s, this type of industrial activity developed rapidly with the foundation of a number of national companies and the establishment of foreign export companies. The electronics industry benefited from the changes in the international environment and the delocalisation of American companies' assembly activities to reduce production costs. The Southeast Asian electronics industry also benefited from the delocalisation of Japanese industries in the region.

Until the early 1970s, the electronics industry in Southeast Asia was confined to the assembly of components for export by foreign companies established on their territory, and the production of mass-produced electronics goods by local businesses. But from this time forward, the first-tier NICs wrought tremendous changes in their electronics industries by seeking to enter into more technology-intensive sectors. Thus, Korea and Taiwan developed electronics development plans for the production of electronic components by national firms and their integration into computers and computer products by local businesses.

In order to successfully make this transition, these companies developed strategies to gain access to and adapt foreign technologies. Thus, there was a rapid increase in the import of technologies in the electronics sector under various forms such as licensing agreements and joint ventures (Bloom, 1992). Between 1962 and 1987, the percentage of licenses for electronic, electric and communication equipment rose from 12 per cent to 38 per cent of total payments for technology imports. In this regard, FDIs played a major role in the acquisition of technologies (Chaponnière, 1992).

In addition to joint ventures, FDIs and licensing agreements, local research also played a fundamental role in the development of activities assimilating imported technologies. In addition to domestic research activities, the Korean government encouraged local businesses to make investments in foreign research centres, especially in the United States.[5]

Korean businesses played an important role in training and participated in efforts to master technologies. The POSCO steel-making company is a telling example. Indeed, in 1984, nearly 10,000 of the company's 23,700 workers received various forms of training either on or off company premises. This training covered a variety of fields ranging from technical subjects to others such as learning foreign languages. This continuous training allowed the company to achieve significant gains in productivity, greater worker integration and a considerable drop in employee turnover, which fell from 4.4 per cent in the 1970s to 1.2 per cent in the 1980s, and a low absentee rate of around 0.07 per cent (Amsden, 1989).

This first part of our study compared underdeveloped countries and Asian countries with a view to identifying the principle features of a post-adjustment development strategy. The role of long-term vision was emphasised, along with the place of agriculture, industrialisation and how it can be set in place, and new technologies. However, in order for accumulation to be sustainable and stable, procedures and mechanisms capable of dealing with the tensions and contradictions which accumulation dynamics can generate need to be implemented.

Notes

1 On Japanese industrial groups, see Figuière, 1993.

2 On Tunisia, see Ben Hammouda, 1995c.

3 This expression was used by Lanzarotti to describe growth in Korea. In light of the work of Wade and Amsden, this image can also be extended to the other Southeast Asian countries.

4 On the problem of technological learning, see Amsden, 1989, 1990.

5 One of the best-known examples of this strategy was the purchase of the Amperex company by Samsung and the transfer of its equipment to Korea. Amperex was one of only three companies in the world that produced magnetrons, a necessary component of microwave ovens.

Chapter 6

Regulation and Post-Adjustment Theories

Setting growth and development dynamics in motion in underdeveloped economies can generate contradictions and problems that require external regulatory intervention. In this respect, post-adjustment development strategies can be distinguished from the theories of traditional microeconomics, which stipulate that the intrusion of any exogenous force into the economic sphere produces distortions that generate economic disequilibria and dysfunctions. From this standpoint, the objective of economic policies is to reduce these interventions so as to enable the market to ensure the coherency in the actors' choices. However, the SAP experiences in most Third World countries in the 1980s demonstrated the inability of the laws of the market to ensure that economies operate in a consistent manner and launch new growth dynamics. This failure has sparked the development of reflection on post-adjustment development strategies.

In this part of our study, we shall assume that *creative distortions* ought to be an element of post-adjustment development strategies. Creative distortions are the product of economic, political and financial mechanisms whose purpose is to absorb the contradictions of the accumulation process and lay the foundations of sustainability and stability. In the 1960s and 1970s, such interventions were carried out by the nation-state. Thus, while it appears difficult for these interventions to be reproduced by the nation-state in light of globalisation and the reduced importance of the national framework which it implies, we can, however, envisage interventions of this kind in a regional framework.

The coordination of productive structures with distribution mechanisms and methods plays an important role in the long-term stability and consistency of growth dynamics. Furthermore, state intervention is a central element in the regulation of growth dynamics in underdeveloped economies. This intervention may take several forms. Indeed, in addition to direct interventions in production and investment through government enterprises, the state can intervene through the pricing system, the regulation of competition, or funding of development. In addition to state interventions, we should also examine the place and role of international influences on growth dynamics. This part of our study does not recommend that these forms of intervention be reproduced, but rather that they be pointed out in order to understand the role they have played in the stability of growth dynamics in certain economies. This will enable us to reflect on other types of interventions that take into account the latest economic trends, particularly the processes of globalisation and regionalisation of economic structures.

In this part of our study, we shall also attempt to outline the *regulatory distortions* which have laid the foundations for stable growth dynamics in underdeveloped countries and which could serve as a starting point for a post-adjustment development strategy. From this perspective, we will focus on Southeast Asian experiences in order to analyse and understand the role of the different corrective interventions in the economy. However, it should be emphasised that these interventions are not unique to those countries. Indeed, since the 1950s, most underdeveloped countries have experienced strong state intervention, particularly in the framework of import substitution strategies. But it must be recognised that while this interventionism increased the competitiveness of Southeast Asian economies, in the rest of the Third World, it has led to rentseeking behaviours which have discouraged action to increase productivity and deteriorated the international integration of these countries. Thus, a comparative analysis of these policies is important in order to determine the conditions of successful and effective regulatory distortions.

Distribution and 'Walking on Two Legs' in Asian Economies

Asian growth dynamics were based on the coordination of a sector focused on exportation with an import substitution sector focused on satisfying internal demand. This coordination was a development option chosen by the government, especially in the first-tier NICs. The goal was to reduce the dependency of their growth dynamics on the international market, while catching the wave of innovation and technological change. This development strategy required the establishment of specially tailored distribution structures. For example, wages played an important role in the creation of the necessary demand for industries focusing on the domestic market. On the other hand, the competitiveness of exporting industries depended on the control of production costs, including the cost of manpower. From this perspective, the dynamics of accumulation depended on the ability of business and the public authorities to deal with the contradictory status of the payroll as both a production cost and a factor in internal demand.

In the late 1960s and especially in the 1970s, a number of Southern countries sought to base their growth dynamics on the coordination of internal and external markets in order to satisfy the needs of the population and import the necessary elements for accumulation. However, the coexistence of these two sectors rapidly ran into problems with the rapid rise of wages, which led to reduced competitiveness in export industries. In order to protect their comparative advantages, most underdeveloped countries sought to compress payroll costs. This choice had a negative impact on growth dynamics since it entailed a drop in local demand. Furthermore, wages were reduced without the consent of workers, through the use of force and violence by governments, thus contributing to a political instability that did not promote development.

It should also be pointed out that it is difficult to control and compress payroll costs because imports are increasingly needed for the reproduction of the labour force. Indeed, the crisis of agriculture in a great number of underdeveloped countries made the import of foodstuffs a major element in the fulfilment of national needs. Thus, the government lost control of the cost of reproducing the labour force. That is why these countries were unable to coordinate imports and exports and in most cases sought to focus their development on external markets in order to deal with macroeconomic disequilibria and the requirements of debt servicing.

However, unlike most underdeveloped economies, the Southeast Asian countries, especially the first-tier NICs, were able to coordinate their internal and external sectors for a long time. This success was due to agricultural development in their countries which allowed them to control the cost of reproducing the work force. Furthermore, the Asian countries sought to make a planned transition from labour-intensive sectors to sectors intensive in capital and new technologies. This strategy allowed their comparative advantages to evolve from those of economies with low labour costs to the mastery of new technologies. Thus, increased wages in these economies no longer posed a constraint for their international integration and did not threaten the competitiveness of their businesses. On the contrary, higher wages were necessary to maintain internal demand and foster growth.

This strategy allowed Southeast Asian countries to increase wages considerably in recent years. Indeed, in South Korea, the average wage increased annually by 9.3 per cent between 1975 and 1979. It respectively increased 7.3 per cent between 1974 and 1985 in Taiwan, 7.6 per cent between 1981 and

1986 in Hong Kong and 6.7 per cent between 1980 and 1985 in Singapore (Bouteiller and Fouquin, 1995). The increase in workers' wages was greater than the increase in managers' and technicians' salaries. Indeed, the rate of increase in workers' wages was respectively 12.8 per cent between 1965 and 1970, 7.1 per cent between 1971 and 1974, 16.8 per cent between 1975 and 1979 and 5.3 per cent between 1980 and 1984, while the rate of increase in management-level salaries was 6.6 per cent, 6.1 per cent, 15.3 per cent and 2.5 per cent during the same periods (Amsden, 1989). The structure of this increase explains the stability of the standard of consumption in Korea and the still limited development of the consumption of durable consumer goods.

This was the highest level of growth in all Third World countries. Indeed, compared to a baseline of 100 in 1970, real wages reached 276 in South Korea and 191 in Taiwan in 1984. During the same period, the index in Brazil and Mexico fell to 84 and 83 (ibid.). Argentina and Turkey were able to raise their respective indexes to 112 and 111 after a significant slide.

The gap between the Asian countries and other Third World countries widened in the early 1980s. Those Third World countries which were facing the debt crisis and external disequilibria sought to rebuild their competitiveness by compressing labour costs and reducing wages. On the contrary, the first-tier Asian countries were able to maintain high rates of wage progression, although lower than in the 1970s.

There are several reasons for the extra leeway the Asian countries had compared to the rest of the Third World, which allowed them to maintain growth. The first lay in these countries' transition from a market position based on low labour costs to one more intensive in capital and new technologies. Furthermore, in the late 1970s and the 1980s, there was a strong rise on the worker movement, which enabled them to improve their working conditions and obtain substantial wage increases. Indeed, since the early 1980s, increases in productivity have kept ahead of increases in real wages in Korea (ibid.). This trend in the 1980s contrasts with that of the 1970s, when growth in real salaries was higher than the growth of productivity.

These trends confirm the respective roles played by internal demand and exports in the growth dynamics of Asian countries. Indeed, in the 1970s, their growth dynamics were essentially driven by internal demand, which explains the rapid change in real wages. From the late 1980s onward, the first-tier NICs implemented a new form of integration into the international economy which required rapid increases in productivity, the delocalisation of labour-intensive activities to second-tier NICs, and continued wage increases to foster internal demand.

The Asian crisis strongly challenged this distribution strategy. Faced with an unprecedented crisis, the major Asian groups implemented far-reaching restructuring policies with mass dismissals which led to unprecedented development of unemployment. Furthermore, these groups distanced themselves from their employee management philosophies, particularly where job security was concerned. Finally, most Asian businesses imposed sizeable wage cuts on their employees. Thus, the Asian crisis spelled the end of the balanced distribution the major Asian groups had established more than three decades earlier, and which had laid the foundations for the stability of their growth dynamics.

The State and Price Regulation

In its analysis of Southeast Asian countries, the World Bank stressed the importance of obeying the laws of the market in resource allocation for the success of these experiences (World Bank, 1993). According to the World Bank, state intervention regarding prices was minimal in those countries, and in any case less extensive than in other underdeveloped countries. However, more recent research has shown that not only was there extensive state intervention regarding prices in Asia, but that the distortions it created were greater than those in other underdeveloped countries (Kwon, 1994).

Research on late industrialisation has focused on state intervention in pricing in Southeast Asia and the state's will to establish a *wrong pricing system* in that it does not correspond to the precepts of the market (Amsden, 1989, 1990). The state's intervention in pricing is not recent; in first-tier NICs, it dates back to the 1960s. Indeed, when they were developing their textile export industries, Korea and Taiwan rapidly realised that low wages were not enough to compete with Japanese exports. Based on this fact, the authorities in both countries granted large subsidies to textile exporters in order to narrow the productivity gap between them and Japanese business. In addition, these countries gave exporting businesses long-term credit on highly preferential terms.

These businesses also benefited from very favourable exchange rates since most Asian countries practised a multiple exchange rate system. They used high exchange rates for exports and relatively low exchange rates for the payment of the foreign debt and for imports of capital goods, intermediary goods and raw materials. In addition to these interventions, the state protected the internal market with tariffs and local businesses could count on support from diplomatic channels (Amsden, 1990).

Government intervention in pricing was also carried out in the form of action on interest rates. Indeed, beginning in the late 1960s, Southeast Asian countries systematically intervened to ensure negative real interest rates on bank loans.

State intervention in pricing had a twofold aim. The first was to try to improve the profitability of certain sectors which were considered necessary for stable accumulation, such as the agricultural sector with the double pricing system aimed at increasing agricultural production and productivity. Government intervention was also aimed at ensuring the development of new sectors in order to diversify the production system. This type of intervention was necessary because local businesses had mastered production techniques in certain labour-intensive sectors downstream in the chain of production and were not seeking to enter into new production sectors. Indeed, the relative pricing system, combined with uncertainty about the future in most underdeveloped countries, discouraged strategies to integrate upstream intermediary activities.

From this perspective, the state's action on the pricing system, and especially interest rates, was aimed at creating better conditions for profitability so as to encourage firms to diversify their activities and enter into new areas of production. This intervention stimulated the circulation of capital between different sectors of production and promoted the intensification and complexification of the production system. This circulation of capital promoted a trend towards the equalisation of profit rates in different sectors. In this regard, a study on the evolution of profits in South Korea in the 1970s and 1980s shows a convergence between the rates of profit in heavy industries and light industries (Amsden, 1989).

A number of Third World countries tried to intervene in their pricing systems in the 1960s and 1970s. However, these interventions did not achieve the expected results and did not promote greater diversification and integration of the production system, as it did in the Asian countries. Instead, these interventions, especially negative real interest rates, promoted rentseeking behaviour on the part of businesses, which sought to increase their profits by investing in light industries. This choice was a result of the undiscriminating and static nature of the state's intervention in pricing systems. Most countries applied negative real interest rates to all sectors of production indiscriminately. In that context, businesses chose light industries to increase their profit margin. However, in Asian countries, state intervention in pricing was selective in that it was only applied to sectors that were supposed to play a major role in growth dynamics. In addition, the intervention was dynamic and changed in light of the evolution of the structures of accumulation and the priorities of the development of the production system.

The second objective of state intervention in pricing systems was to help local businesses close the productivity gap between them and businesses in developed countries. Indeed, the technological head start of the latter brought them higher productivity, which provided them with competitive advantages and a more favourable relative price system. From this standpoint, the state's intervention in the pricing system was aimed at temporarily correcting the productivity differential and allowing businesses in underdeveloped countries to compete with businesses in developed countries. However, this type of intervention was not restricted to Southeast Asian countries, as most Third World countries promoted import-substitution strategies through price control.

But, while this type of intervention allowed Asian businesses to increase their competitiveness, it led to rentseeking behaviour in most other underdeveloped countries. There are a number of reasons behind these differing results. Firstly, it should be pointed out that the Asian governments demanded higher performance in return for this type of protection. Indeed, protection from foreign competition was not permanent and was gradually reduced as businesses built up their competitive advantages. However, in most Third World countries, the protection provided by the government for import-substitution industries was not dynamic, and this discouraged the investments needed to improve productivity, and encouraged rentseeking behaviour.

Furthermore, intervention in price systems to protect local industries did not mean discouraging internal competition. In most underdeveloped countries, protection from foreign competition was accompanied by domestic monopolies with considerable political support. These monopolies reinforced the rentseeking attitudes of local businesses. In Asian countries, government intervention did not eliminate competition. On the contrary, competition was encouraged, especially in mature industries (Singh, 1996).

The State as an Organiser of Competition

State intervention played a major role as a regulator of growth dynamics, particularly through its action on pricing systems. While this action led to the emergence of rentseeking behaviours in most underdeveloped countries, it allowed Southeast Asian countries to develop a dynamic of diversification of their production systems by successively internalising upstream industry segments. The fact that the state maintained and organised competition, despite concentration of production, meant Asian groups adopted dynamic investment behaviour in order to increase productivity and master new production sectors.

The development experiences of Southeast Asian countries were characterised by the emergence of major industrial and financial groups which played an organisational role in the region's development experiences. In Japan, at the end of the war, the American administration had envisaged the elimination of the Zaibatsu and the enactment of an antitrust law. However, this reform was never implemented and certain American economic advisers came to consider that these majors groups could play a fundamental role in rebuilding the Japanese economy and launching growth (Hersh, 1993). The Japanese model of combined businesses was adopted in a great many underdeveloped countries, particularly in Southeast Asia (Yasuoka, 1984). This combination enabled businesses to command the necessary financial means for their development. In addition, their large size allowed them to benefit from economies of scale.

Production was more concentrated in Asian countries than in other Southern countries. In Korea and Taiwan, businesses with over 500 workers produced respectively 52.7 per cent and 56.4 per cent of added value in the 1970s. During the same period, the share of added value of businesses of this size was only 36.6 per cent in Brazil (Cordova, 1994).

However, concentrated production was not unique to the Japanese and Korean economies. In Taiwan, contrary to its popular image as a development experience led by small and medium-sized businesses, several studies emphasise the key role played by major groups in the country's industrial development (Chou, 1988). In Korea, production was highly concentrated and the Chaebols dominated business activity. Indeed, production was more concentrated in Korea than in the other Asian countries. Between 1974 and 1984, sales by the top 10 Korean groups rose from 15 to 67.4 per cent of the GDP (Amsden, 1989).

Despite the common trend towards concentrated production in Asian countries, differences remained in the structure and organisation of the major groups. For instance, in Japan, the 'Kieretsu' did not belong to important families as in the other Asian countries, but were made up of a number of firms with shares in each other's capital so as to ensure a certain coherence in their activities. In addition, these groups had close ties to the banks, most of which were shareholders. In Korea, the major groups belonged to families, which kept control of most of the businesses. These groups did not include banks among their firms, since most of the banking sector was public. However, despite these particularities, Asian groups had close relationships with the financial system allowing them to envisage long-term investments and opt for market-share policies rather than quick-profit policies (Singh, 1996).

Alongside this concentration, Asian governments played a major role in encouraging competition between Asian firms. For instance, in Japan, the MITI and the Fair Trade Commission have spurred competition between groups. More specifically, competition was encouraged when an industry reached maturity. However, the MITI discouraged competition in new industries or when decreased competitiveness demanded a rationalisation of industrial activities. The same reasoning also guided Japanese government action in its management of international trade. Japanese businesses were not systematically protected from foreign competition. On the contrary, foreign competition is encouraged in sectors where Japanese firms have acquired a high level of technical skills and know-how.

The Korean government also encouraged competition between major groups. But this competition was not a matter of pricing, instead, it concentrated on other factors such as access to better foreign technologies in order to create a difference in the product (see Amsden 1989; Amsden and Singh, 1994). Competition between Korean groups also took place on the job market, where groups competed for the most qualified technical and administrative staff. Finally, these businesses also competed intensely in terms of their delivery time and the quality of their customer servicing.

Thus, the ability of Southeast Asian countries to combine cooperation and competition allowed them to promote the emergence of dynamic behaviour in their major industrial and financial groups. These groups sought to master new technologies and improve their competitive positions instead of confining themselves to the management of the advantages they already had, like most other underdeveloped countries. This attitude enabled their economies to accelerate investment and growth and improve their integration into the international economy. The government could also impose its development choices and guidelines through more discretionary methods such as taxation.

Cooperation between groups and the state through advisory councils composed of businessmen and government representatives was encouraged in Asian countries. These councils were either general or sectorial, concentrating on the development of a specific sector, and were used to discuss general government directions and solve information problems. These councils were established by Japan and were developed by Korea and Taiwan. In Taiwan, we can point to the Industrial Development Consultative Committee, the Overall Manufacturing Committee, the Chemical Industries Committee and the Machinery Industries Committee. In Korea, sectorial consulting boards were also formed with a view to discussing and defining sectorial development strategies between the government and businessmen (Singh, 1996). In addition, businessmen had access to labour organisations more or less independent from the state, which also enabled them to intervene and have an impact on the public authorities' development choices.

However, this equilibrium which the state was able to structure in the 1970s and 1980s was upset by the opening up of the Asian economies to globalisation. This liberalisation hurt certain groups and industries in the region. Furthermore, the groups with the best performances seized on the liberalisation movement to escape strict government control, especially with regard to access to international funding.

The Funding of Development

All observers agree on the important role played by funding in Asian growth dynamics. In this respect, Stiglitz pointed out that the Asian states intervened intensively in the workings of their financial systems (Stiglitz and Uy, 1996). The government authorities in most Asian countries helped create financial systems and institutions, regulated their operations and granted firms priority access to funding.

However, while the importance of funding is confirmed, researchers disagree as to the mechanisms and means of funding in Asian countries. For example, according to the World Bank, economic growth led to a rapid increase in savings, which meant an acceleration of credit and investment in businesses (World Bank, 1993). Other researchers emphasise the role of profits in the funding of accumulation in Asian countries (see UNCTAD, 1996; Akyüz and Gore, 1994). According to this theory, Asian governments laid the foundations for rapid growth in the profits of their businesses, thus enabling them to self-finance their investments.

Both of these theories have been subjected to a number of criticisms (see Palma, 1996; Singh, 1996). More specifically, the World Bank theories, which stress previous savings, and the UNCTAD theories, which emphasise self-financing, minimise the role of bank funding and more specifically of money creation in the economic growth dynamics of Asian countries. However, an examination of the financing structure reveals the fundamental role played by banks in these experiences. For example, between 1966 and 1970, bank credits represented nearly 50 per cent of business funding, whereas in France it was only 27 per cent, 29 per cent in Germany, 20 per cent in Great Britain and 12 per cent in the United States. The difference as compared to financing structures in developed countries was also apparent in self-financing as a percentage of total financing. Indeed, while that percentage was over 60 per cent in developed countries, except for Great Britain, where it was 51 per cent, it stood at around 40 per cent in Japan (Singh, 1996).

The percentage of bank funding in Japan did decrease to 34.5 per cent of total financing in 1989, but it remained markedly higher than in the other developed countries. Furthermore, the percentage of self-financing stood at 40 per cent of total funding, but this figure was distinctly lower than in other developed countries, where it was around 60 per cent of total in Germany and the United States (ibid.). These facts are demonstrative of the key role played by banks in the funding of Japanese businesses despite their high levels of self-financing. These differences are due to the close relationships between Japanese banks and groups, which allowed the banks to have shares in the biggest Keiretsu. Furthermore, bank credits for business funding progressed in the 1970s in other developed countries due to the emergence of inflationary tensions during that period, which led to lower interest rates.

The same trend could be observed in Korea, where the banking system played a dynamic role in growth. For example, the percentage of credit in the total funding of the economy grew from 29 per cent in 1963–64 to 38.9 per cent between 1975 and 1979 (Lanzarotti, 1992). The percentage of self-financing dropped sharply from 51.2 to 26.7 per cent of total funding during the same period. This financing structure shows the role played by the banking system in growth dynamics.

The banking sector in Korea was characterised by a strong state presence; in the 1970s, public banks accounted for nearly 87 per cent of the added value in that sector. The sector was essentially composed of specialised banks founded by the state in the 1960s to finance the development of certain priority sectors. In addition to these specialised banks, the Korean government also established development banks specialising in long-term loans. Both types of institutions were directly financed by the government. Alongside the state institutions, the financial sector also included branches of foreign banks, whose activities were restricted due to their marginal access to the local currency; financial institutions, whose role would develop with the monetary reforms of the 1980s; and other private banks. In the Korean system, a central bank directly dependent on the state ensured compliance with the funding priorities set by the government. The state banking sector played a dominant role in the funding of development, even though its share of assets has dropped from

95.5 per cent to 84.1 per cent of total assets in financial institutions. In 1979, the state sector monopolised nearly 87 per cent of credits.

But, more than bank credits, the Asian experience was characterised by the low interest rates applied by banks on credit for the economy. Indeed, most Asian governments organised 'financial repression' to maintain low interest rates and facilitate businesses' access to investments. This credit policy resulted from the close relationships maintained by banks and industrial groups in Japan. In Korea, the credit policy was due to the key role of the public sector in financing. However, although the banks granted loans at low rates, they were able to protect their profitability. The Central Bank promoted this credit policy by implementing fairly broad rediscounting policies, especially on credit for exports and commercial papers. Lanzarotti (1992, p. 233, our translation) notes that 'between 1965 and 1982, the average differential between the bank loan interest rate and the rediscounting rate was 4 percentage points, both on credit for exports and commercial papers'. Furthermore, Korean banks were subsidised to cover their negative spread, for instance, in 1965 for non-preferred credit and in 1969 for the launching of the heavy industries and mechanisation programmes.

A comparative analysis using other Third World countries reveals that they adopted similar funding strategies. Indeed, in most underdeveloped countries, banks, which were essentially state-run, applied low interest policies or even negative real interest to promote productive investments. However, it must be acknowledged today that these development funding policies did not have the same impact as in the Southeast Asian countries. In Asia, the low interest rate policy promoted productive investments and encouraged businesses to diversify their production and improve their competitiveness. But in other Third World countries, the policy did not stimulate businesses, which did not venture beyond their traditional activities despite their increased profitability.

There are several reasons behind these differences in behaviour including government intervention and control of credit. But the unique features of the credit policy in Asia and its focus on specific sectors played an important role in the attitude of Asian businesses, and in the focus of their activities. Indeed, most Third World countries did not define priorities in terms of granting credit and applied low interest rates to all economic sectors. In Asia, on the other hand, the government authorities defined a selective and preferential interest rate policy. Low interest rates were essentially aimed at strategic sectors whose development required improved profitability conditions. In the other Third World countries, an across-the-board policy of low interest rates could only increase the profitability of sectors that were already profitable and thus encourage rentseeking behaviour on the part of businesses.

In Asian countries, the public authorities practised credit policies aimed at certain priority sectors. Credit was essentially directed towards exporting sectors and basic industries such as steel and iron, heavy industry, shipbuilding, chemical industries and electronics (Stiglitz and Uy, 1996). These priority sectors benefited from preferential interest rates. The difference between normal interest rates and preferential interest rates was relatively large. For example, if we take the case of Korea, where the normal rate was respectively 19.5 in 1967, 13.4 in 1971 and 0.2 per cent in 1979, preferential rates during the same years were respectively -0.5, -2.6 and -9.8 per cent. Furthermore, the importance of preferential loans can be seen from their share of total loans, which was around 48 per cent between 1971 and 1980 and their share in bank loans, which was around 46 per cent during the same period. They included loans in foreign currencies, at 24 per cent of total, loans for exports, at 21 per cent, and loans for heavy industries and chemical industries, which dominated the structure of preferential loans between 1975 and 1980. Furthermore, a rapid increase was reported in the share of credit for exports, from 3 per cent of total credit in the late 1960s to 14 per cent in the late 1970s. The evolution in the share of credits for chemical and heavy industries was higher during the same period, increasing from 15 per cent to 28 per cent of total (Lanzarotti, 1992).

These facts allow us to seize the differences between the credit support policies in Asia and in the rest of the Third World. Indeed, while this policy indiscriminately supported all sectors in most underdeveloped countries, in Asia, it was dynamic and was aimed at supporting priority industries whose profitability was low or where foreign competition was strong. Thus, while the policy promoted rentseeking behaviours in certain underdeveloped countries, on the contrary, it played a dynamic role in Asian countries and enabled them to better diversify their industrial fabric and make it more complex.

These facts underscore the development financing practices that are now disparaged in Asian countries. Indeed, the credit policy played a fundamental role in structuring strong growth dynamics in the 1970s and 1980s. However, the liberalisation of financing mechanisms and more particularly the opportunity for major groups to avail themselves of international financing caused the destabilisation of these growth dynamics.

Internationalism and Development

The place and role of internationalism in development are very controversial issues. For the advocates of comparative advantages theories, the integration of underdeveloped economies in the globalisation movement should be promoted in order to give them access to new technologies and allow them to take part in global-scale growth dynamics. With SAPs, a number of Third World countries sought to follow this option through the reform movement and a patent desire to redirect development strategies towards the external market. But these development choices did not enable these countries to launch new growth dynamics or control their marginalisation in the international economy.

According to other economists, opening up to the international economy cannot promote development. Indeed, open trade generates problems for national production due to the productivity differential between local firms and foreign firms. Over the long term, this competition can bankrupt local industries and confine underdeveloped nations to an agro-export niche. Furthermore, the opening up of underdeveloped countries to Foreign Direct Investments (FDIs) and transnational firms can lead to an unstructured development of production sectors. For instance, according to these authors, transnational firms do not seek to integrate themselves into the local production system since they work with a broader level of consistency, which corresponds to the overall strategy of these firms on the global scale. A number of Third World economies also sought to construct development experiences inspired by these theories. However, these self-centred development theories did not enable these countries to structure coherent production systems and ensure the conditions for sustainability.

From this point of view, the experiences of the Southeast Asian countries were unusual in that they remained distinct from both of these patterns by seeking to combine a certain openness to the international economy with a high level of control and regulation. This strategy enabled them to control their opening and direct it toward their development objectives while other countries continued to suffer from the international economy due to the weakness of their internal production structures.

The opening up of Southeast Asian countries to the international economy dates back to the end of World War II. Indeed, these economies benefited from massive support and considerable aid from the United States to support the recovery effort and resist the advance of communist countries and parties in the region. Thus, after a few years of hesitation, the American administration set up a major recovery plan in Japan, called 'Economic Recovery in Occupied Areas'. In addition to massive financial, economic and military aid, the plan's objective was to:

- stop reparation payments to former Japanese colonies in the region;
- implement a stabilisation plan to reduce inflation;
- develop an industrial base tied to exports (Hersh, 1993).

For their part, Taiwan and South Korea also received considerable aid from the American administration. In Taiwan, American economic and military technical assistance totalled \$5.6 billion between 1945 and the late 1970s. Total US aid for Taiwan represented 6 per cent of the GDP and 40 per cent of investments (Wade, 1990). In Korea, aid was even higher. According to estimates, Korea received the equivalent of \$15 billion in the form of economic and military assistance, of which \$13 billion came from the United States (Lanzarotti, 1992). This aid was especially focused on the financing of the countries' imports and the implementation of stabilisation policies.[1]

To realise the magnitude of this aid, it should be compared with that received by other countries. Over the 1946–78 period, the Republic of Korea received \$6 billion from the United States in the form of loans and economic assistance. Over that same period, all African countries taken together received less than \$7 billion, and Latin America nearly \$15 billion. India was the only single country that received more than Korea. With a population 17 times bigger than Korea's, India received \$9.6 billion from the United States. United States military support for countries in the region was even more marked. During the 1955–78 period, South Korea and Taiwan received over \$9 billion in military assistance. During that same period, the United States only contributed \$3.2 billion to Africa and Latin America combined. From the 1970s onward, aid from the United States and Japan also focused on the second-tier NICs. Indeed, it is estimated that in the 1980s, Japan directed nearly 30 per cent of its foreign technical assistance to ASEAN countries.

These facts demonstrate the magnitude of the aid the Americans provided for economies in the region. This aid played an important role in the launching of growth dynamics in these countries. However, aid stopped in the 1970s and the Asian countries continued their dynamics of accumulation. Indeed, these countries had successfully established production structures that enabled them to become independent from foreign aid and assistance. Few underdeveloped countries benefited from such a massive transfer of resources for their development. These experiences have led certain economists to wonder whether international aid and a net influx of foreign resources are not indispensable for all development experiences in the Third World (Lanzarotti, 1992).

In addition to aid, input from the international community, and especially from the United States to Asian countries, lies in trade and welcoming exports from these countries. The American market was opened up in the 1950s with the early stages of Japanese recovery. Japanese businesses initially sought to develop their exports to China in order to balance their foreign trade and absorb their trade deficits with the United States. However, under American pressure, Japan respected the *de facto* embargo imposed on China by the United States in return for a more open American market for Japanese exports. At the very time they were penetrating the American market, the Korean War, which began in 1950, was a stroke of luck for Japanese businesses, with American purchases reaching nearly $3 billion in 1954.

Korea and Taiwan also benefited from the opening up of the American market to their exports. In addition, the delocalisation of labour-intensive Japanese industries in the 1960s meant the establishment of a regional division of labour. Thus, Korean and Taiwanese businesses imported capital goods and technology from Japan and exported locally made consumer goods to the American market. These businesses also benefited from American army orders and purchasing during the Vietnam War. The American army called on Korean and Taiwanese businesses to carry out its infrastructure engineering construction, thus enabling these businesses to acquire considerable experience and become major exporters of engineering construction in the 1970s. The opening up of the American market facilitated the rapid progression of exports from first-tier NICs and the transformation of their industrial structures from producing labour-intensive goods to goods intensive in capital and new technologies.

Meanwhile, the dependency of the first-tier NICs on Japan and the United States was considerably reduced in recent years. For instance, the percentage of first-tier NIC exports to the United States dropped from 40 per cent of total in 1985 to 23 per cent in 1994. The percentage of exports from these countries to Japan dropped sharply to around 10 per cent of total in 1994. The decreased weight of the United States and Japan in their commercial trade was compensated by increased trade with ASEAN countries. Their share of exports from first-tier NICs grew from 7 to 14 per cent between 1985 and 1994 (UNCTAD, 1996).

Second-tier NICs also had preferential access to the American and Japanese markets. In the 1980s, nearly 50 per cent of the total exports of these countries went to either Japan (28 per cent) or the United States (22 per cent). These countries also dominated second-tier NIC imports, with a share of 36.5 per cent of total imports (22 per cent for Japan and 14.5 per cent for the United States). Exports from second-tier NICs to Japan and the United States were essentially composed of raw materials, and the introduction of manufactured goods was relatively recent. These countries have begun diversifying their exports, especially to European countries and first-tier NICs, whose share in the total exports of those countries has grown from less than 20 per cent in 1985 to more than 26 per cent in 1994.

These facts enable us to understand the structure of commercial trade in the region. From the end of the war up until the early 1960s, trade was marked by the pre-eminent role of the United States. The bulk of the region's exports were directed towards the American market and all imports of capital goods, technology and intermediary goods came from the United States. However, the recovery of the Japanese economy brought the first change in the structure of trade in the region with the development of a trans-Atlantic triangle between Japan, the first-tier NICs and the United States (Bouteiller and Fouquin, 1995). The NICs imported capital goods and technology from Japan and exported final consumer goods to the United States.

This international division of labour characterised trade in the region until the early 1980s. Then, beginning in the early 1980s, a new trade dynamic emerged, in which the Southeast Asian countries gained independence from Japan and the United States. This restructuring of trade came about through a re-centring of trade within the region with the emergence of the second-tier NICs and the opening up of China and Vietnam and a greater diversification of trade with an outlet in Europe. Trends towards regionalisation and greater independence of the region from Japan and the United States can also be seen in the recent evolution of FDI movements.

Indeed, the Southeast Asian region was a preferred destination for FDIs. However, despite their rapid growth, FDIs have played a marginal role in Asian countries. Their share in capital formation in Hong Kong declined from 9.9 per cent of total in the 1980s to 5.7 per cent in the early 1990s. In Korea and Taiwan, their share was very small, respectively below 1 per cent and around 2.6 per cent in the 1990s. Among the first-tier NICs, only Singapore experienced a progression in the share of FDIs in the formation of local capital, more than tripling from 11.3 per cent in the 1980s to 37.4 per cent in the 1990s. On the other hand, in Korea, despite a slight increase, the share of FDIs in manufacturing added value, employment and exports was low, respectively totalling around 14.2 per cent, 9.6 per cent and 19.2 per cent of total in 1980. In second-tier NICs, despite a slight increase, the share of FDIs in local investment remained low at around 5 per cent of total in Indonesia and Thailand. In Malaysia, however, the share of FDIs rose from 11.3 per cent of total in the 1980s to 24.6 per cent in the early 1990s.

In South Korea, FDIs began in 1962 and expanded in the 1970s. From 1962 to the late 1980s, Korea took in nearly $7 billion in FDIs. The amounts began to decline from 1988 onward. This type of investment was strictly regulated by the Korean authorities. In its 1973 investment law, Korea prohibited FDIs in certain sectors, notably those that could compete with local businesses. Korea also sought to encourage forms of FDIs that would promote technology transfers. Regulation was softened in the context of the reform movement in the 1980s. At the sectorial level, FDIs were directed as a priority towards heavy industries and chemical industries, and electric and electronic industries. In 1985, the share of FDIs in these sectors represented nearly 70 per cent of the total, whereas in the textile industry, it only represented 5 per cent.

Japan's attitude differed from that of the first-tier NICs. Indeed, Japanese FDIs moved away from Asia to North America and Europe. Japanese FDIs in North America grew from 27 per cent of Japanese FDIs in the 1970s to 36 per cent in the early 1980s and reached 43.5 per cent in the early 1990s. Similarly, the share of FDIs in Europe rose from 11.6 per cent of total in the 1970s to 20 per cent in the 1990s. Meanwhile, the share of investments in Asia dropped from over 27 per cent in the 1970s to 12 per cent in the late 1980s, before bouncing back to 18 per cent of total in the 1990s (UNCTAD, 1996).

Similarly, FDIs played an important role in second-tier NICs. These FDIs essentially came from Japan and the United States and focused on raw materials. Indeed, FDIs from those two countries represented nearly 44 per cent of total FDIs in these economies (29 per cent from Japan and 15 per cent from the United States). However, that percentage has fallen in recent years with the rise of FDIs from first-tier NICs with the delocalisation of labour-intensive industries. Today, the share of FDIs from first-tier NICs represents nearly 26 per cent of total, while the shares of Japan and the United States respectively have dropped to less than 26 per cent and less than 10 per cent (UNCTAD, 1996).

Thus, while Japan increasingly seems to be pulling out of the region, Southeast Asian countries are seeking to use their international relations to develop a regional cooperation and integration zone among first-tier NICs (especially Korea and Taiwan), ASEAN countries and China. This regional division of labour can be observed in the movements of both goods and capital.

Furthermore, these economies are seeking to loosen the grip of American and Japanese domination in the region by diversifying their trade, particularly by expanding their relationships with European countries.

In addition to aid, trade and FDIs, Asian countries also benefited from significant international contributions through loans. Indeed, the East Asian debt grew from \$146.5 billion in 1986 to \$451.8 billion in 1996. However, strong growth dynamics and the accumulation of sizeable trade surpluses allowed the first-tier NICs to repay their debts without any great difficulty. Indeed, South Korea, to cite one example, was able to transfer a net amount of \$19 billion between 1986 and 1989 in repayment of its debt.

Thus, the Southeast Asian countries were able to ensure a controlled opening to the international market. This opening was necessary to gain access to new technologies and foreign markets. However, these countries integrated their internationalisation into their development needs and priorities. The development of coherent growth dynamics and controlled opening up to foreign countries were reinforced by a recentring of growth on the region and regional cooperation and integration experiments established either in a bilateral framework or in a regional framework such as ASEAN. This regionalisation formed the basis for the creation of the largest zone of economic prosperity. Furthermore, these national and regional growth dynamics were translated by a dynamic integration of the region into the economic globalisation movement. However, the Asian countries lost this control over the international context in the 1990s due to their increasing opening to the global market. On the one hand, the increased openness to capital movements led to a massive influx of short-term capital. This capital, essentially made up of American pension fund investments, was focused on immediate profitability and circulated among the different financial markets according to their performance. These capital movements played a major role in the destabilisation of the region's growth dynamics, since their lack of confidence in these economies led to the outbreak of the crisis. On the other hand, Asian groups' use of international credit meant the accumulation of a significant private international debt, which destabilised these businesses.

Thus, in the 1970s and 1980s, contrary to the other underdeveloped countries, Asian countries were able to benefit from margins of freedom created by the outbreak of the global economic crisis. Most of them managed to develop strong growth dynamics and improve their position in the international market. But, by the late 1980s, the international context was undergoing far-reaching changes and the trend to globalisation imposed greater openness to the international economy on Asian countries. And, while the state effectively controlled business activities in the 1970s and 1980s, it no longer had the means to do so in the 1990s. This openness led to the outbreak of the Asian crisis and called into question all the economic and industrial potential they had built up since the end of World War II.

In this section, we have sought to measure the impact of certain regulating mechanisms on the stability and sustainability of accumulation dynamics. Our comparative study of Asian experiences and the experiences of other underdeveloped countries has enabled us to shed light on the role of distribution, prices, competition, currency and internationalism in structuring the growth dynamics and improving the international integration of underdeveloped economies.

Conclusion

The South is currently experiencing an unusual situation characterised by a lack of development strategies and alternatives to globalisation or withdrawal. Indeed, the failure of the SAPs left a huge void in terms of development strategies. While moving away from the theoretical foundations of the Washington consensus, a great many institutions, including the World Bank, continue to advocate adjustment in practice. In this chapter, we have sought to establish a debate on the substance of a post-adjustment development strategy. And, through our comparative analysis of development experiences in Southeast Asia and in other underdeveloped countries, we were able to rough out a project to renew development practices. These experiences have demonstrated the importance of agriculture, industry and new technologies in the establishment of accumulation dynamics. In addition, the state has played a central role in the regulation and harmonisation of these dynamics.

Throughout the 1980s, the Washington Consensus sought to challenge that role, and placed the market at the heart of the coordination of actors' activities. But in many Third World countries, a weaker state has led to the breakdown of the nation. Indeed, in a great many Southern countries, the modern state is the only template for the unification and identification of populations from different ethnic, religious or regional backgrounds. From this standpoint, the reconstruction of the state and its involvement in the development and regulation of growth dynamics are urgent. However, this reconstruction needs to take account of the development and assertiveness of dynamic and diverse civil societies in most Third World countries. Thus, the state must be rebuilt, but spaces of freedom, expression and criticism need to be kept open for these civil societies, breaking with the dominating and authoritarian practices of the post-colonial state. Recent post-colonial history has shown that development is not a linear process and that the state is not an infallible source of progress. More than ever, the development of the South requires the intervention of transparent institutions to regulate growth dynamics and ensure popular participation in order to keep authoritarianism at bay. New development strategies should also consider the recent globalisation and regionalisation of economic structures whose basis extends beyond the framework of the nation-state.

Note

1 On American aid and, more generally, on the relationships between the United States and Korea, see Finan, 1992.

Conclusion

Despite their recent renewal, development theories are still having great difficulty analysing the evolutions in the South and suggesting development crisis alternatives. Of course, the renewal of the development theories have allowed us to grasp the instability and the complexity of recent evolutions in underdeveloped economies. In addition, a comparative study of development experiences in Asia and in the rest of the Third World has helped us outline a post-adjustment development strategy. However, this undertaking is still in the initial stages and needs to be taken further.

When development theory used the determinism and the linearity of the Newtonian model, it could only describe a static reality subject to mathematical laws whose workings determined the future of underdeveloped societies as in the past. However, given the emergence of complex trajectories and the instability of economic dynamics, 'traditional'[1] development theory is increasingly unable to decode reality. From this point of view, the renewal of development theory needs to break away from the precepts of traditional science, and reconstruct a theoretical framework in the wake of the current transformation of science and the development of theories of complexity, in order to reflect the dynamic instability and turbulence of the Third World.

The traditional deterministic vision is currently in crisis due to its inability to grasp fluctuations, which are becoming increasingly strong and irregular. Indeed, as Prigogine and Stengers pointed out:

> we are living in a relentlessly random world … a world in which reversibility and determinism appear as special cases, and where microscopic irreversibility and indeterminacy are the rule (1986, p. 40, our translation).

But at the same time, on the ruins of traditional science, there is a movement of reconstruction and metamorphosis that leads to the emergence of a new scientific paradigm able to grasp the complexity of natural and social phenomena. In this new paradigm, Prigogine and Stengers note that:

> we are no longer interested in stable situations and permanency, but in evolutions, crises and instability. We no longer want to study only things that remain, but also things that change, geological upheavals and changes in the standards that come into play in social behaviours (ibid., p. 36).

This metamorphosis of scientific thinking should form the framework for the renewal of development theory. Indeed, beyond the deconstruction of the concrete forms of the modernisation process, the crisis experienced by underdeveloped countries is the crisis of traditional deterministic reasoning, which dominated both theory and praxis in the post-colonial era. It challenges its metaphysics, which makes Western modernism an 'absolute' goal. This crisis is also the crisis of the economism of the modernist model, which subjects social life to economic imperatives. Finally, this crisis challenges the teleological vision of the modernist model, which considers that 'the laws of history', in the words of Amin (1994, p. 3), 'impose themselves implacably and express the progressive unfolding of progress'.

Thus, there is a need to challenge and abandon linear and traditional approaches where development is concerned. Indeed, studies of the post-colonies and of Africa in particular 'have not been notable', says Mbembe (1995, p. 92), 'for their efforts to integrate non-linear phenomena into their analyses. Similarly, they have not always been able to give an account of complex behaviours.'

This crisis requires an epistemological break with this ideal and the construction of a new scientific reasoning in the study of development problems. This new reasoning should focus on indeterminacy, randomness and the unexpected. It should be able to grasp non-equilibrium and concentrate on instability. This new theoretical perspective will enable us to perceive the contradictory movements of order and disorder, construction and destruction at work in Southern societies. In this perspective, chaos and non-linearity can be envisaged as aspects of the dynamic instability of underdeveloped societies.

By taking account of these aspects, we can also discover the complexity of historical time in the post-colonies and its diverse nature, which cannot be reduced to a peaceful, linear flow of historical laws. An irregular and a-periodical movement of time can allow us to envisage the breaks and twists and turns of the history of the post-colonies, which means that historical possibilities are still open to these societies.

Finally, the crisis of the traditional Newtonian ideal in development studies has rendered necessary the emergence of a new rationality based on a poetic attentiveness to the disturbances and the waves in the flow of post-colonial time. This new science is still in gestation, and is confined to a few analytical articles and has yet to enter into the realm of development proposals and policies. With this in mind, it is urgent that we further develop the analytical dimension of this new of development research so as to understand better the recent evolutions in Southern societies.

Note

1 We use the term 'traditional' to describe schools of development theory which, beyond their theoretical opposition, were inspired by the same traditional scientific tools.

Bibliography

Abraham-Frois, G. (1993), *Keynes et la Macroéconomie Contemporaine*, 4th edn, Paris: Economica.

Adelman, I. and Robinson, S. (1978), *Income Distribution Policy in Developing Countries: A Case Study of Korea*, London: Oxford University Press.

Akamatsu, K. (1962), 'A Historic Pattern of Economic Growth in Developing Countries', *The Developing Economies*, Vol. 1, No. 1.

Akerlof, A.G. (1970), 'The Market for "Lemons": Quality, Uncertainty and the Market Mechanism', *Quarterly Journal of Economics*, Vol. LXXXIV, No. 3, August.

Akerlof, A.G. and Yellen, J.L. (1985), 'A Near-rational of the Business Cycle, with Wage and Price Inertia', *Quarterly Journal of Economics*, supplement, 100 (5).

Akyüz, Y. (1994), 'Libéralisation Financière: Mythes et réalités', *Revue Tiers-Monde*, Vol. XXXV, No. 139, July–September.

Akyüz, Y. (1996), *New Trends in Japanese Trade and FDI: Post-industrial transformation and policy challenges*, Geneva: UNCTAD.

Akyüz, Y. and Gore, C. (1994), *The Investments-profits Nexus in East Asian Industrialization*, UNCTAD, Discussion Papers, No. 91, October.

Alchian, A.A. and Demsetz, H. (1972), 'Production, Information Costs and Economic Organisation', *American Economic Review*, Vol. 62.

Amable, B. and Guellec, D. (1992), 'Les Théories de la Croissance Endogène', *Revue d'économie politique*, No. 102, May–June.

Amin, S. (1979), *Classe et Nation dans l'Histoire et la Crise Contemporaine*, Paris: Les Editions de Minuit.

Amin, S. (1991), *L'empire du Chaos*, Paris: L'Harmattan.

Amin, S. (1994), 'L'Idéologie et la Pensée Sociale: l'Intelligentsia et la crise de la pensée du développment', *Africa Development*, Vol. XIX, No. 1.

Amin, S. (1995), 'L'Importance du Sommet Social des Nations-Unies', in S. Amin, H. Ben Hammouda and B. Founou-Tchuigoua (eds), *Afrique et Monde Arabe: Echec de l'insertion internationale*, Paris: L'Harmattan.

Amin, S. (1996), *Les Défis de la Mondialisation*, Paris: L'Harmattan.

Amsden, A. (1989), *Asia's Next Giant. South Korea and Late Industrialisation*, Oxford: Oxford University Press.

Amsden, A. (1990), 'Third World Industrialization: "Global Fordism" or a New Model?', *The New Left Review*, No. 182.

Amsden, A. (1991), 'Diffusion of Development: The late industrializing model and Greater East Asia', *American Economic Review*, Vol. 81, No. 2, May.

Amsden, A. (1994), 'Why Isn't Whole World Experimenting with the East Asian Model to Develop? Review of the East Asian Miracle', *World Development*, Vol. 22, No. 4.

Barro, R.J. (1991), 'Economic Growth in a Cross Section of Countries', *Quarterly Journal of Economics*, May.

Barro, R.J. and Lee, J.W. (1994), 'Losers and Winners in Economic Growth', *Proceedings of the World Bank Annual conference on Development Economics 1993*, Washington.

Barro, R.J. and Sala-I-Martin, X. (1992), 'Public Finance in Models of Economic Growth', *Review of Economic Studies*, No. 59.

Barsky, S. (1969), 'Economic Backwardness and the Characteristics of Development', *Journal of Economic History*, Vol. 29, No. 3.

Basu, K. (1984), *The Less Developed Economy: A Critique of Contemporary Theory*, Basil Blackwell, Oxford.

Baumol, W.J. and Lee, K.S. (1991), 'Contestable Markets, Trade and Development', *The World Bank Research Observer*, Vol. 6, No. 1.

Baumol, W.J., Panzar, J.C. and Willig, R.D. (1988), *Contestable Markets and the Theory of Industry Structure*, San Diego: H.B. Jovanovich.

Bayart, J.F. (1994), 'L'Invention Paradoxale de la Modernité Economique', in J.F. Bayart (ed.), *La Réinvention du capitalisme*, Paris: Karthala.

Bayart, J.F. (1996), *L'Illusion Identitaire*, Paris: Fayard.

Beaud, M. and Dostaler, G. (1993), *La Pensée Economique depuis Keynès*, Paris: Seuil.

Becker, G., Murphy, K.M. and Tamura, R. (1990), 'Human Capital, Fertility and Economic Growth', *Journal of Political Economy*, Vol. 98, October.

Belloc, B. (1987), 'Quelques aspects Normatifs du Problème d'Akerlof', *Revue Economique*, No. 1, January.

Bénabou, R. (1982), 'La Corée du Sud ou l'Industrialisation Planifiée', *Economie et Prospective Internationale*, No. 10.

Ben Hammouda, H. (1993), 'Développement des Rapports Marchands et Prélèvements: Une hypothèse explicative de la crise du mode d'accumulation au Burundi', *Mondes en Développement*, Vol. 21, No. 82.

Ben Hammouda, H. (1995a), *Burundi: Histoire politique et économique d'un conflit*, Paris: L'Harmattan.

Ben Hammouda, H. (1995b), 'Crise, Ajustement et Atomisation Sociale dans le Monde Arabe', in S. Amin, H. Ben Hammouda and B. Founou (eds), *Afrique et Monde Arabe, Echec de l'Insertion Internationale*, Paris: L'Harmattan.

Ben Hammouda, H. (1995c), *Tunisie: Ajustement et difficulté de l'insertion internationale*, Paris: L'Harmattan.

Ben Hammouda, H. (1997), *Les Pensées Uniques en Economie*, Paris: L'Harmattan.

Bently, M. and Oberhofer, T. (1981), 'Property Rights and Economic Development', *Review of Social Economy*, No. 39.

Berger, F. (1979), *Korea's Experience with Export-led Industrial Development*, Staff Working Paper No. 313, Washington: World Bank.

Bernis, G. de (1989), *Endettement–Ajustement–Développement – Un cercle vertueux impossible à trouver*, UNESCO, February.

Bernis, G. de (1973), ' Le Sous-développement: Analyses ou représentations', *Revue du Tiers-Monde*, No. 57.
Bernis, G. de and Jedlicki, C. (1989), 'A propos des PAS', *Analyses et Documents Economiques*, No. 37, October.
Berthélemy, J.C., Devezeaux de Lavergne, J.-G. and Gagey, F. (1991), 'L'Economie du Développement: Présentation générale', *Economie et Prévision*, No. 97.
Bhagwati, J. (1978), *Foreign Trade and Economic Development: Anatomy and consequences of exchange control regimes*, New York: National Bureau of Economic Research.
Bhagwati, J. (1988), 'Export-promoting Trade Strategy: Issues and evidence', *World Bank Research Observer*, Vol. 3, No. 1.
Binswager, H. and Rosenzweig, M. (eds) (1984), *Contractual Arrangements, Employment and Wages in Rural Labour Markets in Asia*, New Haven: Yale University Press.
Blaine, M. (1993), 'Profitability and Competitiveness: Lessons from Japanese and American firms in the 1980s', *California Management Review*, No. 36.
Blinder, A. (1979), *Economic Policy and the Great Stagflation*, New York: Academic Press.
Blomström, M. and Hettne, B. (1984), *Development Theory in Transition*, London: Zed Books.
Bloom, M. (1992), *L'Evolution Technologique et l'Industrie Coréenne*, Centre de développement, Paris: OCDE.
Boratav, K. (1994), 'Réformes de l'Etat et Développement Economique: Réflexions sur le cas de quelques pays du Moyen-Orient', *Revue Tiers-Monde*, Vol. XXXV, No. 139, July–September.
Borrelly, R. (1991), ' L'Articulation du National et de l'International, Concepts et Analyses, GRREC', *Crise et Régulation, Recueil de Textes 1983–1989*, Grenoble: Université Pierre-Mendès France.
Bourguignon, F. and Morrisson, C. (1992), *Ajustement et Equité dans les Pays en Voie de Développement*, Paris: OCDE, Centre de Développement,
Bouteiller, E. and Fouquin, M. (1995), *Le développement économique de l'Asie Orientale*, Paris: La Découverte.
Brander, J.A. and Spencer, B. (1985), 'Export Subsidies and International Market Share Rivalry', *Journal of International Economics,* No. 18.
Brander, J.A. (1981), 'Intra-industry Trade in Identical Commodities', *Journal of International Economics*, No. 11.
Brander, J. A. and Krugman, P. (1983), 'A "Reciprocal Dumping" Model of International Trade', *Journal of International Economics*, No. 13.
Brenner, R. (1977), 'The Origins of Capitalist Development, A Critique of Neo-Smithian Marxist Theory', *New Left Review.*
Brohman, J. (1995), 'Economics and Critical Silences in Development Studies: A theoritical critique of neoliberalism', *Third World Quarterly*, Vol. 16, No. 2, June.

Brousseau, E. (1993), 'Les Théories des Contrats: Une revue', *Revue d'Economie Politique*, No. 103, January–February.
Cahuc, P. (1993), *Le Marché, Loi du Monde Moderne*, Sciences Humaines, Hors-série No. 3, November–December.
Camau, M. (1990), *Le Maghreb, Collectif, Les Régimes Politiques Arabes*, Paris: PUF.
Carlton, D. (1986), 'The Rigidity of Prices', *American Economic Review*, Vol. 76.
Chang, H.J. (1993), *The Political Economy of Industrial Policy*, St Martin's Press, New York.
Chaponnière, J.-R. (1992), 'Les Nouvelles Economies Industrielles d'Asie. Investissements Internationaux et Transfert de Technologie', *Revue STI*, No. 9, April.
Cheng, T., Haggard, S. and Kang, D. (1996), *Institutions, Economic Policy and Growth in the Republic of Korea and Taiwan Province of China*, Geneva: UNCTAD, February.
Chilcote, R.H. (1981), 'Issues of Theory in Dependency and Marxism', *Latin American Perspectives*, Nos 3 and 4.
Chinchilla, N.S. and Dietz, J.L. (1981), 'Toward a New Understanding of Development and Underdevelopment', *Latin American Perspectives*, Nos 3 and 4.
Chou, T.-C. (1988), 'The Evolution of Market Structure in Taiwan', *Revista Internazionale di Scienze Economiche e Commerciali*, Vol. 35, No. 2.
Coase, R. (1987), 'The Nature of the Firm', *Economica*, Vol. NS4 (translated into French as 'La Nature de la Firme', *Revue Française d'Economie*, 1987).
Cochet, H. (1996), *Burundi: La paysannerie dans la tourmente. Eléments d'analyse sur les origines du conflit politico-ethnique*, Paris: Fondation Charles Léopold Mayer pour le progrès de l'Homme.
Coquery-Vidrovitch, C. (1985), *Afrique Noire. Permanence et Ruptures*, 2nd edn, Paris: L'Harmattan
Colclough, C. and Manor, J. (eds) (1993), *States or Markets? Neo-liberalism and the Development Policy Debates*, Oxford: Clarendon Press.
Cole, R. (1978), 'The Late-developer Hypothesis: An evaluation of its relevance for Japanese employment practices', *Journal of Japanese Studies*, Vol. 4, No. 2.
Coméliau, C. (1991), *Les Relations Nord–Sud*, Paris: La Découverte.
Cordova, D. (1994), 'Echecs et Succès de l'Industrialisation. Eléments d'Explication pour une Histoire Economique Comparée: Applications aux cas du Pérou et de la Corée du Sud', doctoral thesis, Université Pierre-Mendès France, Grenoble.
Cornia, G.A., Hoeven, R. von der and Mkandawire, T. (eds) (1992), *L'Afrique vers la Reprise Economique. De la Stagnation au Développement Humain*, Paris: Economica.
Datta-Chadhuri, M. (1990), 'Market Failure and Government Failure', *Journal of Economic Perspectives*, Vol. 4, No. 3.
Dervis, K., Melo, J. de and Robinson, S. (1989), *General Equilibrium Models for Development Policy*, Washington: The World Bank Research Publications.

Duharcourt, P. (1996), 'La Montée de la Corée du Sud et de l'Asie du Sud-Est', *Recherches Internationales*, No. 45, Summer.

Dupuy, J.P., Eymard-Duvernay, F., Favereau, O., Orléan, A., Salais, R. and Thévenot, L. (1989), 'Introduction', *Revue Economique*, Vol. 40, No. 2, March.

Dutraive, V. (1993), 'La Firme entre Transaction et Contrat: Williamson épigone ou dissident de la pensée institutionnaliste?', *Revue d'Economie Politique*, Vol. 103, No. 1, January–February.

Economie Appliquée (1990), 'Approches des Institutions Economiques', Vol. 43, No. 3.

Eswaran, M. and Kotwal, A. (1985), 'A Theory of Two-tier Labour Markets in Agrarian Economics', *American Economic Review*, March.

Fall, B. (ed.) (1997), *Ajustement Structurel et Emploi au Sénégal*, Dakar: CODESRIA.

Favereau, O. (1989), 'Marchés Internes, Marchés Externes', *Revue Economique*, No. 2, March.

Favereau, O. (1995), 'Développement et Economie des Conventions', in Ph. Hugon, G. Pourcet and S. Quiers-Valette (eds), *L'Afrique des Incertitudes*, Paris: IEDES/PUF.

Feeny, D. (1979), 'Competing Hypothesis of Underdevelopment: A Thai case study', *The Journal of Economic History*, No. 39.

Felix, D. (1994), 'Mobilité Financière Internationale: Effets déstabilisateurs et régulation', *Revue Tiers-Monde*, Vol. XXXV, No. 139, July–September.

Ferrand, D. (1993), *L'Industrialisation Tardive: Une théorie du développement?*, Mémoire de DEA, Université Pierre-Mendès France, Grenoble.

Figuière, C. (1993), 'Les Groupes Industriels Japonais: Un facteur de cohérence des structures productives nationales', doctoral thesis, Université Pierre Mendès-France, Grenoble.

Finan, A. (1992), 'Autonomie et Dépendance: Analyse historique des relations entre les USA et la Corée du Sud', doctoral thesis, Université Pierre Mendès-France, Grenoble.

Findlay, R. (1978), 'Relative Backwardness, Direct Foreign Investment and the Transfer of Technology: A simple dynamic model', *The Quarterly Journal of Economics*, Vol. 27, No. 4.

Fine, B. (1978), 'On the Origins of Capitalist Development', *New Left Review*, No. 109.

Fontaine, J.-M. (1992), 'Introduction – Enjeux du Débat et Présentation de l'Ouvrage', in J.-M. Fontaine (ed.), *Réformes du Commerce Extérieur et Politiques de Développement*, Paris: PUF/IEDES,

Fontaine, J.-M. (1993), 'Demande et Investissement dans le Processus d'Ajustement', *Tiers-Monde*, Vol. XXXIV, No. 135, July–September.

Fontaine, J.-M. (1994), 'Financement, Echanges et Investissement: Le cercle vicieux de l'Afrique sub-saharienne', *Revue Tiers-Monde*, Vol. XXXV, No. 139, July–September.

Fontaine, J.-M. and Jacmart, M.C. (1993), 'La Réhabilitation de la Demande. Points de Repères et Analyses Appliquées', *Tiers-Monde*, Vol. XXXIV, No. 135, July–September.

Frank, A.G. (1967), *Capitalisme et Sous-développement en Amérique Latine: Etudes historiques du Chili et du Brésil*, Maspéro.

Frank, A.G. (1991), 'Latin American Development Theories Revisited: A participant review essay', *The Journal of Development Research*, Vol. 3, No. 2, December.

Gillis, X. (1987), 'La Nature de la Firme et la Théorie des Coûts de Transaction', *Revue Française d'Economie*, Vol. II, No. 1.

Ginsburg, V. and Robinson, S. (1984), 'Equilibrium and Prices in Multisector Models', in M. Syrquin, L. Taylor and L.E. Westphal (eds), *Economic Structure and Performance*, New York: Academic.

Good, D.F. (1973), 'Backwardness and the Role of Banking in the Nineteenth-century European Industrialization', *Journal of Economic History*, No. 4.

Gordon, R.J. (1990), 'What is New Keynesian Economics?', *Journal of Economic Literature*, No. 28, September.

Greenaway, D. (1987), 'The New Theories of Intra-industry Trade', *Bulletin of Economic Research*, April.

Gregory, P. (1974), 'Some Empirical Comments on the Theory of Relative Backwardness: The Russian case', *Economic Development and Cultural Change*, Vol. 22, No. 4.

Grellet, G. (1994), *Les Politiques Economiques des Pays du Sud*, Paris: IEDES/PUF.

Guerrien, B. (1990), 'Quelques Réflexions sur Institutions, Organisations et Histoire', *Economie Appliquée*, Vol. XLIII, No. 3.

Guillaumont, P. (1992), 'Déclin et Renouveau de l'Economie du Développement', *Revue Française d'Economie*, Vol. X, No. 1, Winter.

Haggard, S. (1990), *Pathways from the Periphery: The politics of growth in the newly industrialising countries*, Ithaca: Cornell University Press.

Harrold, P., Jayawickrama, M. and Bhattasali, D. (1996), *Practical Lessons for Africa from East Asia in Industrial and Trade Policies*, Washington: World Bank Discussions Papers, Africa Technical Department Series.

Haubert, M. and Rey, P.Ph. (1995), 'Sociétés en Mutation entre Restructurations Mondiales et Initiatives Locales', *Revue Tiers-Monde*, No. 141, January–March.

Heller, W. (1966), *New Dimensions of Political Economy*, Cambridge, Mass.: Harvard University Press.

Hellier, J. (1993), 'La Similitude dans l'Echange International: Une revue critique des approches théoriques', *Revue Française d'Economie*, Vol. VIII, No. 1, Winter.

Helpman, E. and Razin, A. (eds) (1991), *International Trade and Trade Policy*, New York: MIT Press.

Henin, P.Y. and Ralle, P. (1994), 'Les Nouvelles Théories de la Croissance. Quelques Apports pour la Politique Economique', *Revue Economique*, Vol. 44, Hors-Série.

Hersh, J. (1993), *The USA and the Rise of East Asia Since 1945*, London: The Macmillan Press.

Hibou, B. (1996), *L'Afrique est-elle Protectionniste? Les Chemins Buissonniers de la Libéralisation Extérieure*, Paris: Karthala.
Hirschman, A. (1964), *La Stratégie du Développement Economique*, Paris: Editions Ouvrières.
Hirschmann, A.O. (1968), 'The Political Economy of Import-substituting Industrialization in Latin America', *Quarterly Journal of Economics*, Vol. 82, No. 1.
Hong, W. (1990), 'Market Distortions and Polarization of Trade Patterns: Korean Experience', in J.K. Kwon (ed.), *Korean Economic Development*, New York: Greenwood Press.
Hugon, Ph. (1989), *Economie du Développement*, Dalloz.
Hugon, Ph. (1995a), 'Robinson ou Vendredi? La Rationalité Economique en Afrique', *Sciences Humaines*, No. 47, February.
Hugon, Ph. (1995b), 'Présentation', in O. Castel (ed.), *L'Ajustement Structurel et Après?*, Paris: Editions Maisonneuve & Larose.
Hymer, S. (1976), *The International Operations of National Firms: A Study of Direct Foreign Investment*, New York: MIT Press.
Israël, A. (1996), *Le Développement Institutionnel. Les Organisations à l'Epreuve de la Spécificité et de la Concurrence*, Paris: L'Harmattan.
Janvry, A. de (1981), *The Agrarian Question and Reformism in Latin America*, Baltimore: Johns Hopkins University Press.
Johnson, C. (1981), 'Introduction – The Taiwan Model', in J. Hsiung (ed.), *Contemporary Republic of China: The Taïwan experience*, New York: Prager.
Johnson, C. (1982), *MITI and the Japanese Miracle: The growth of industrial policy, 1925–1975*, Stanford: Stanford University Press.
Johnson, C. (1984), 'The Industrial Policy Debate Re-examined', *California Management Review*, Vol. 27, No. 1.
Jomo, K.S. (1996), *Lessons from Growth and Structural Change in the Second-tier South East Asian Newly Industrializing Countries*, Geneva: UNCTAD, March.
Katz, L. (1986), 'Efficiency Wage Theories: A partial evaluation', *NBER Macroeconomics Annual*.
Kellerman, L. (1992), *La Dimension Culturelle du Développement*, Paris: L'Harmattan/UNESCO.
Kim, C.N., Hajiwara, H. and Watanabe, T. (1984), 'A Consideration on the Compressed Process of Agricultural Development in the Republic of Korea', *The Developing Economies*, June.
Kim, D.H. and Joo, Y.J. (1982), *Situations et Politiques Alimentaires en République de Corée*, Paris: OECD Development Centre, OECD.
Kim, K. and Roemer, M. (1979), *Growth and Structural Transformations: The Republic of Korea, 1945–1975*, Cambridge, Mass.: Harvard University Press.
Klamer, A. (1988), *Entretiens avec des Economistes Américains*, Paris: Editions du Seuil.

Kojima, K. (1995), *An International Perspective on Japanese Corporate Finance*, RIEB Kobe University Discussion Paper, No. 45, March.

Korhonen, P. (1994), 'The Theory of the Flying Geese Pattern of Development and its Interpretations', *Journal of Peace Research*, Vol. 31, No. 1.

Krueger, A.O. (1978), *Liberalisation Attempts and Consequences*, New York: NBER.

Krueger, A.O. (1974), 'The Political Economy of Rent-seeking Society', *American Economic Review*, No. 64.

Krueger, A.O. (1980), 'Trade Policy as an Input to Development', *American Economic Review*, May.

Krueger, A.O. (1983), *Trade and Employment in Developing Countries: Synthesis and conclusions*, New York: National Bureau of Economic Research, Vol. 3.

Krueger, A.O. (1990), 'Asian Trade and Growth Lessons', *American Economic Review*, Vol. 80, No. 2, May .

Krueger, A.O. and Summers, L.H. (1988), 'Efficiency Wages and the Inter-Industry Wage Structure', *Economica*, Vol. 56.

Krugman, P.R. (1981), 'Trade, Accumulation and Uneven Development', *Journal of Development Economics*, No. 8.

Krugman, P.R. (1990), *Rethinking International Trade*, New York: The MIT Press.

Krugman, P.R. (1993), 'The Narrow and Broad Arguments for Free Trade', *American Economic Review*, No. 2, May.

Krugman, P.R. (1993), 'Toward a Counter-counter-revolution in Development Theory', *Proceedings of the World Bank Annual Conference on Development Economics 1992*, Washington.

Krugman, P.R. (1994), 'The Myth of Asia's Miracle', *Foreign Affairs*, November/ December.

Krugman, P.R. (1995), *Development, Geography and Economic Theory*, Cambridge and London: MIT Press.

Kwon, J.K. (ed.) (1990), *Korean Economic Development*, New York: Greenwood Press.

Kwon, J.K. (1994), 'The East Asia Challenge to Neoclassical Orthodoxy', *World Development*, Vol. 22, No. 4.

Laclau, E. (1971), 'Feudalism and Capitalism in Latin America', *New Left Review*, No. 6, May–June.

Laffont, J.J. (1987), 'Le Risque Moral dans la Relation de Mandat', *Revue Economique*, No. 1, January.

Lall, S. (1994), 'The East Asian Miracle: Does the Bell Toll for Industrial Strategy?', *World Development*, Vol. 22, No. 4.

Lall, S. (1995), 'Structural Adjustment and African Industry', *World Development*, Vol. 23, No. 12.

Landsberg, M.H. (1984), 'Capitalism and Third World Economic Development: A Critical Look at the South Korean Miracle', *Review of Radical Political Economy*, Vol. 16, No. 2/3.

Lanzarotti, M. (1992), *La Corée du Sud: Une sortie du sous-développement*, Paris: PUF/IEDES.

Latouche, S. (1986), *Faut-il Refuser le Développement?*, Paris: PUF.

Latouche, S. (1989), *L'Occidentalisation du Monde*, Paris: La Découverte.

Latouche, S. (1991), *La Planète des Naufragés, Essai sur l'Après-développement*, Paris: La Découverte.

L'Hériteau, M.-F. (1986), *Le FMI et le Tiers-Monde*, Paris: PUF/IEDES.

Little, I.M.D., Scitovsky, T. and Scott, M.F.G. (1970), *Industry and Trade in Some Developing Countries*, London: Oxford University Press.

Lipietz, A. (1986), *Mirages et Miracles: Problèmes de l'industrialisation dans le Tiers-Monde*, Paris: La Découverte.

Lordon, F. (1991), 'La Redécouverte des Rendements Croissants', *Observations et Diagnostics Economiques*, No. 37, July.

Lucas, R.E. Jr (1990), 'Why Doesn't Capital Flow from Rich to Poor Countries', *American Economic Review*, Vol. 80, No. 2, May.

Lucas, R. (1988), 'On the Mechanics of Economic Development', *Journal of Monetary Economics*, No. 22.

Lundahl, M. and Ndulu, B.J. (1996), *New Directions in Development Economics. Growth, Environmental Concerns and Government in the 1990s*, London: Routledge.

Mahieu, F.R. (1990), *Les Fondements de la Crise Economique en Afrique*, Paris: L'Harmattan.

Mahieu, F.R. (1995), 'Les Stratégies Individuelles Face à la Pauvreté: Côte d'Ivoire versus Burundi', in Ph. Hugon, G. Pourcet and S. Quiers-Valette (eds), *L'Afrique des Incertitudes*, Paris: IEDES/PUF.

Majeje, A. (1994), 'Les Intellectuels Africains: Origine et options sociale', in M. Diouf and M. Mamdani (eds), *Libertés Académiques en Afrique*, Dakar: CODESRIA.

Malley, R. (1996), *The Call from Algeria – Third Worldism, Revolution and the Turn to Islam*, Berkeley: University of California Press.

Mankiw, N.G. (1985), 'Small Menu Costs and Large Business Cycle: A macroeconomic model', *Quarterly Journal of Economics*, 100 (2), May.

Mantran, R. (1990), 'Dynamique Politique: l'Evolution historique', *Collectif, Les Régimes Politiques Arabes*, Paris: PUF.

Mbembe, A. (1995), 'Le Temps qui s'Agite', *Afrique 2000*, No. 21, April–May–June.

Meir, G. and Seers. D. (eds) (1988), *Les Pionniers du Développement*, Paris: Economica.

Michaely, M. (1977), 'Exports and Growth: An empirical investigation', *Journal of Development Economics*, Vol. 4.

Mkandawire, T. and Olukoshi, A. (1995), *Between Liberalisation and Oppression: The Politics of Structural Adjustment in Africa*, Dakar: CODESRIA.

Mosley, P. (1992) 'L'Ajustement Structurel: Une vue d'ensemble: 1980–1990', in J.-M. Fontaine (ed.), *Réformes du Commerce Extérieur et Politiques de Développement*, Paris: IEDES/PUF.

Mosley, P. and Weeks, J. (1993), 'Has Recovery Begun? Africa's Adjustment in the 1980s Revisited', *World Development*, Vol. 21, No. 10.

Myrdal, G. (1957), *Rich Land and Poor*, New York: Harper.

Nabli, M.K. and Nugent, J.B. (1989), 'The New Institutional Economics and its Applicability to Development', *World Development*, Vol. 17, No. 9.

Nash, J. (1992), 'Un Examen des Réformes des Politiques Commerciales et de leurs Implications pour l'Afrique Sub-saharienne', in J.-M. Fontaine (ed.), *Réformes du Commerce Extérieur et Politiques de Développement*, Paris: IEDES/PUF.

Ndulu, B.J. (1991), 'Growth and Adjustment in Sub-Saharan Africa', in A. Chiber and S. Fischer (eds), *Economic Reform in Sub-Saharan Africa*, Washington: World Bank.

North, D.C. (1994), 'The New Institutional Economics and Development', *Forum*, No. 2, Vol. 1, May.

North, D. (1988), 'Institutions and Economic Growth: An historical introduction', *World Development*, Vol. 17, No. 9.

North, D. (1990), *Institutions, Institutional Change and Economic Performance*, Cambridge: Cambridge University Press.

North, D. and Thomas, R. (1973), *The Rise of the Western World. A New Economic History*, Cambridge: Cambridge University Press.

Ocampo, J.A. (1987), 'The Macroeconomic Effect of Import Controls. A Keynesian analysis', *Journal of Development Economics*, No. 27.

Okun, A.M. (1981), *Prices and Quantities: A macroeconomic analysis*, Washington: The Brookings Institution.

Oman, Ch.P. and Wignaraja, G. (1991), *L'Evolution de la Pensée Economique sur le Développement depuis 1945*, Paris: Centre de Développement, OCDE.

Orléan, A. (1989), 'Pour une Approche Cognitive des Conventions Economiques', *Revue Economique*, Vol. 40, No. 2, March.

Orléan, A. (1991), 'Logique Walrassienne et Incertitude Qualitative: Des travaux d'Akerlof et Stiglitz aux conventions de qualité', *Economies et Sociétés, série Economia*, PE, No. 14, January.

Orléan, A. (1994), 'Vers un Modèle Général de la Coordination Economique par les Conventions', in A. Orléan (ed.), *Analyse Economique des Conventions*, Paris: PUF.

Page, J.M. (1994), 'The East Asian Miracle: An introduction', *World Development*, Vol. 22, No. 4.

Palma, G. (1996), *Whatever Happened to Latin America's Savings? Comparing Latin American and East Asian Savings Performances*, Geneva: UNCTAD, March.

Peemans, J.P. (1996), 'L'Utopie Globalitaire', *Nouveaux Cahiers de l'IUED*, No. 5, PUF.

Perkins, D.H. (1994), 'There Are at Least Three Models of East Asian Development', *World Development*, Vol. 22, No. 4.
Polak, J.J. (1957), *Monetary Analysis on Income Formation and Payments Problems*, IMF Staff Papers, No. 6.
Polak, J.J. (1991), *The Changing Nature of IMF Conditionality*, Technical Papers No. 41, OECD Development Centre.
Prigogine, I. and Stengers, I. (1986), *La Nouvelle Alliance*, Paris: Gallimard/Folio.
Rist, G. (ed.) (1994), *La Culture Otage du Développement?*, Paris: L'Harmattan/ EADI.
Rist, G. (1996), *Le Développement, Histoire d'une Croyance Occidentale*, Paris: Presses de Sciences Politiques.
Robinson, S. (1972), 'Theories of Economic Growth and Development: Methodology and content', *Economic Development and Cultural Change*, Vol. 22, No. 1.
Robinson, S. (1989), 'Multisectorial Models', in H. Chenery and T.N. Srinivasan (eds), *Handbook of Development Economics*, Amsterdam: North Holland.
Romer, P. (1993), 'The New Keynesian Synthesis', *The Journal of Economic Perspectives*, Vol. 7, No. 1, Winter.
Romer, P. (1986), 'Increasing Returns and Long-run Growth', *Journal of Political Economy*, No. 94.
Romer, P. (1990), 'Endogenous Technological Change', *Journal of Political Economy*.
Romer, P. (1993), 'Two Strategies for Economic Development: Using ideas and producing ideas', *Proceedings of the World Bank Annual Conference on Development Economics 1992*, Washington.
Romo, H.G. (1994), 'De la Pensée de la CEPAL au Néo-libéralisme, du Néo-libéralisme au Néo-structuralisme, une Revue de la Littérature Sud-américaine', *Tiers-Monde*, No. 140, October–December.
Rosenstein-Rodan, P.N. (1943), 'Problems of Industrialization of Eastern and South-Eastern Europe', *Economic Journal*, Vol. 53.
Rosenstein-Rodan, P. (1961), 'Notes on the "Theory of the Big Push"', in H.S. Ellis and H. Wallich (eds), *Economic Development for Latin America*, New York: St Martin's Press.
Rosovsky, H. (1961), *Capital Formation in Japan, 1868–1940*, New York: The Free Press.
Rosovsky, H. (1972), 'What are the Lessons of Japanese Economic Development?', in A. Youngson (ed.), *Economic Development in the Long-Run*, London: Allen and Unwin.
Rowthorn, R. (1996), *East Asia Development: The flying geese paradigm reconsidered*, Geneva: UNCTAD, United Nations, March.
Ruttan, W. and Hayami, Y. (1984), 'Toward a Theory of Induced Institutional Innovation', *Journal of Development Studies*, No. 20.
Salais, R. (1989), 'L'Analyse Economique des Conventions du Travail', *Revue Economique*, Vol. 40, No. 2, March.

Salama, P. (1995), 'De Quelques Leçons Economiques de l'Histoire Latino-américaine Récente', *Revue Tiers-Monde*, No. 144, October-December.

Salama, P. and Valier, J. (1990), *L'Economie Gangrénée*, Paris: La Découverte.

Sargent, T.J. and Wallace, N. (1975), 'Rational Expectations, the Optimal Monetary Instrument and the Optimal Money Supply Rule', *Journal of Political Economics*, No. 2.

Sargent, T.J. and Wallace, N. (1976), 'Rational Expectations and the Theory of Economic Policy', *Journal of Monetary Economics*, No. 2.

Savvides, A. (1995), 'Economic Growth in Africa', *World Development*, Vol. 23, No. 3.

Seers, D. (ed.) (1983), *Dependency Theory – A Critical Reassessment*, 2nd edn, London: Frances Pinter.

Shayegan, D. (1996), 'Le Choc des Civilisations', *Esprit*, No. 4, April.

Sinha, R. (1995), 'Economic Reform in Developing Countries: Some conceptual issues', *World Development*, Vol. 23, No. 4.

Singer, H.W. and Roy, S. (1993), *Economic Progress and Prospects in the Third World. Lessons of Development Experience Since 1945*, London: Edward Elgar.

Singh, A. (1996), *Savings, Investment and the Corporation in the East Asian Miracle*. Geneva: UNCTAD, March.

Solow, R. (1956), 'A Contribution to the Theory of Economic Growth', *Quarterly Journal of Economics*, No. 70, February.

Stern, N. (1989), 'The Economics of Development: A survey', *The Economic Journal*, No. 99, September.

Stiglitz, J.E. (1985), 'Economics of Information and the Theory of Economic Development', *Revista de Econometrica*, No. 1.

Stiglitz, J.E. (1986), 'The New Development Economics', *World Development*, Vol. 14, No. 2.

Stiglitz, J.E. (1987), 'The Causes and Consequences of the Dependence of Quality on Price', *Journal of Economic Literature*, Vol. XXV, March.

Stiglitz, J.E. (1988), 'Economic Organisation, Information and Development', in H. Chenery and T.N. Srinivasan (eds), *Handbook of Development Economics*, Vol. 1, Amsterdam: Elsevier Science Publishers.

Stiglitz, J.E. (1994), 'The Role of the State in Financial Markets', *Proceedings of the World Bank Annual Conference on Development Economics 1993*, Washington.

Stiglitz, J.E. (1996), 'Some Lessons from the East Asian Miracle', *The World Bank Research Observer*, Vol. 11, No. 2, August.

Stiglitz, J.E. (1997), 'The Role of the Government in Economic Development', in M. Bruno and B. Pleskovic (eds), *Annual World Bank Conference on Development Economics 1996*, Washington: The World Bank.

Stiglitz, J.E. and Uy, M. (1996), 'Financial Markets, Public Policy and the East Asian Miracle', *The World Bank Research Observer*, Vol. 11, No. 2, August.

Sunoo, H.H. (1988), *Où va la Corée du Sud? Economie d'une Dictature et Enjeux démocratiques*, Paris.

Suwa, A. (1991), 'Les Modèles d'Equilibre Général Calculable', *Economie et Prévision*, No. 97.

Taylor, J.B. (1980), 'Aggregate Dynamics and Staggered Contracts', *Journal of Political Economy,* Vol. 88.

Taylor, L. (1980), *Structuralist Macroeconomics: Applicable Models for the Third World*, New York: Basic Books.

Taylor, L. (1981), 'IS/LM in the Topics: Diagrammatis of the new structuralist macro critique', in W.R. Cline and S. Weintraub (eds), *Economic Stabilisation in Developing Countries*, Washington: The Brookings Institution.

Taylor, L. (1988), *Varieties of Stabilization Experience. Towards Sensible Macroeconomics in the Third World*, Oxford: WIDER/Clarendon Press.

Taylor, L. (ed.) (1990), *Socially Relevant Policy Analysis, Structuralist Computable General Equilibrium Models for the Developing World*, Cambridge, Mass.: MIT Press.

Taylor, L. (1991), *Distribution, Inflation and Growth. Lectures on Structuralist Macroeconomic Theory*, Cambridge, Mass.: The MIT Press.

Toye, J. (1987), 'Théorie et Expérience du Développement. Questions pour le Futur', in L. Emmerji (ed.), *Les Politiques de Développement et la Crise des Années 80,* Paris: OCDE.

Trotignon, J. (1993), 'Pourquoi les Politiques d'Ajustement ont-elles Généralement mieux réussi en Asie du Sud-Est qu'en Afrique?', *Economie et Statistique*, No. 264.

Tshibaka, T. (ed.) (1998), *Structural Adjustment and Agriculture in Africa*, Dakar: CODESRIA.

UNCTAD (1996a), *Trade and Development Report 1996*, New York: United Nations.

UNCTAD (1996), *UNCTAD Secretariat Report to the Conference on East Asian Development: Lessons for a new global environment*, Geneva, February.

UNCTAD (1997), *Trade and Development Report, 1997*, New York: United Nations.

UNICEF (1987), *Adjustment with a Human Face*, Oxford: Oxford University Press.

United Nations Economic Commission for Africa (ECA) (1990), *Cadre Africain de Rechange aux Programmes d'Ajustement Structurel (CARPAS)*, Addis Ababa.

UNPD (1997), *Rapport Mondial sur le Développement Humain*, Paris: Economica.

Villé, Ph. de (1990), 'Comportements Concurrentiels et Equilibre Général: De la nécessité des institutions', *Economie Appliquée*, No. 3.

Wade, R. (1990), *Governing the Market. Economic Theory and the Role of Government in East Asian Industrialization*, Princeton: Princeton University Press.

Wade, R. (1996), 'Japan, The World Bank and the Art of Paradigm Maintenance: The East Asian miracle in political perspectives', *New Left Review*, No. 217, May/June.

Wallerstein, I. (1995), *Impenser la science sociale. Pour sortir du 19ème siècle*, Paris: PUF.

White, G. (ed.) (1988), *Development States in East Asia*, London: Macmillan.

Williamson, O.E. (1985), *The Economic Institutions of Capitalism*, New York: The Free Press.

Williamson, O.E. (1975), *Markets and Hierarchies: Analysis and antitrust implications*, New York: The Free Press

Willes, M.H. (1986), 'Les "Anticipations Rationnelles": Une contre-révolution', in D. Bell and I. Kristol (eds), *Crise et renouveau de la théorie économique*, Paris: Bonnel, Publisud.

World Bank (1987), *Rapport sur le Développement dans le Monde 1987*, Paris: World Bank/Economica,

World Bank (1989), *Rapport sur le Développement dans le Monde 1989*, Paris: World Bank/Economica.

World Bank (1991), *Rapport sur le Développement dans le Monde 1991, le défi du développement*, Washington: World Bank.

World Bank (1993), *The East Asian Miracle – Economic Growth and Public Policy*, Oxford: Oxford University Press.

World Bank (1997), *Development Report, The State in a Changing World*, Washington: World Bank.

Yaghmain, B. (1990), 'Development Theories and Development Strategies: An alternative theoretical framework', *Review of Radical Political Economies*, Vol. 22, No. 2/3.

Yanagihara, T. (1994), 'Anything New in the Miracle Report? Yes and No', *World Development*, Vol. 22, No. 4.

Yasuoka, S. (ed.) (1984), *Family Business in the Era of Industrial Growth: Its ownership and management*, Tokyo: University of Tokyo Press.

Yong, H. (1994), 'Economie Néo-institutionelle et Développement. Une analyse synthétique', *Revue d'Economie du Développement*, No. 4.

Yoshihara, K. (1986), *Japanese Economic Development: A short introduction*, 2nd edn, Oxford: Oxford University Press.

Zatman, A. (1995), 'Modèles d'équilibre général calculable et répartition des revenus dans les pays en voie de développement: quelques éléments d'évaluation', *Revue Tiers-Monde*, No. 142, April–June.

Index